Colonial Experience in the Major Fiction of V.S. Naipaul

R.S. Jhanji

ATLANTIC
PUBLISHERS & DISTRIBUTORS (P) LTD

Published by
ATLANTIC
PUBLISHERS & DISTRIBUTORS (P) LTD
7/22, Ansari Road, Darya Ganj, New Delhi-110002
Phones : +91-11-40775252, 23273880, 23275880, 23280451
Fax: +91-11-23285873
Web: www.atlanticbooks.com
E-mail: orders@atlanticbooks.com

Branch Office
5, Nallathambi Street, Wallajah Road, Chennai-600002
Phones : +91-44-64611085, 32413319
E-mail: chennai@atlanticbooks.com

Printed in India at Nice Printing Press, A-33/3A, Site-IV, Industrial Area, Sahibabad, Ghaziabad, U.P.

Dedicated to

My Parents,
Sri Ramdeo Roy
and
Smt. Godavari Devi

Preface

The present work is an attempt to project the idea and the concept of marginality in the fictional vision and world view of V.S. Naipaul. Naipaul has emerged in the twentieth century as one of the most authentic voices to create a comprehensive vision of history and experience of different places and people alike. His works show a world on the fringes of marginality and denial. He equips his observation and satirical technique with a keen political sense in order to project the idea of cultural dismissal, something which is a consequence of the destructive influences such as colonialism, imperialism, racism and cultural/economic discrimination which has disfigured the meanings of contemporary history. In most of the ex-colonial societies, communities and men that Naipaul presents, almost everything in their experience can be traced back to the deep psychic traumata that make up the identity of the colonized. He has been writing a kind of 'psycho-history' of the marginalized, derelict Third World societies which he sees as vulnerable and weak because of their historical and colonial past.

The book will be useful for the students and teachers of English Literature, particularly Postcolonial Literature and researchers in these fields.

R.S. Jhanji

Acknowledgements

I am grateful to Dr. Manjit Inder Singh, retired Professor from English Department, Punjabi University, Patiala for his valuable suggestions and keen insight. I also owe a special debt to my parents, my wife, daughter and son. I am also indebted to my friends and colleagues for their encouragement.

I also take this opportunity to express my sincere thanks to Atlantic Publishers & Distuributors (P) Ltd. for the interest evinced in publishing this book.

R.S. Jhanji

Contents

Chapter 1

An Overview of Naipaul's Bio-Literary Legacy

Sir V.S. Naipaul (1932-)—the name spells almost endless accolades and even greater number of bitter satirical attacks directed against his treatment of fictional and non-fictional material ranging from the Caribbean to India, the Islamic world, among others. Not very often does a writer in his early career receive merit and the kind of scholarly attention won by V.S. Naipaul. He has been the recipient of the Hawthornden Prize, the Phoenix Trust Award and the Booker Prize. In his acceptance speech for the Bennett Award in 1980, Naipaul expressed his particular pleasure at the recognition accorded to his writing as a whole. He felt that it is an acceptance of the relevance of his vision and his art. Naipaul has become a tradition and a precursor in his own right. The interviewers of the *Newsweek* article of August 18, 1980, call him "one of the original voices of his time". Today, Naipaul stands as the 'Master of the Novel', a creative craftsman of such surpassing talent that one of Britain's leading literary critics, V.S. Pritchett, called him "the greatest living writer in the English language." He has received most of the major awards for English fiction beginning with the first book he published, *The Mystic Masseur* (1957). William Walsh pays a rich tribute to Naipaul's genius in the following excerpt:

> Themes for him assume the forms of action and ideas appeal to him only in so far as they satisfy for him, as for Henry James, 'the appetite for the illustrational.' His vision is his own, unenervated by contemporary social cliches or political routines.... He is engaged with the stresses and

> strains we recognise as crucial in our experience now. His writing is nervous and present. This, together with the mixture in him of creeds, cultures and continents, with his expatriate career, his being able to practice an art in and of totally dissimilar worlds, all gives him a peculiarly contemporary quality. (William Walsh, 3)

He further says, "Coleridge's words about Wordsworth are peculiarly appropriate to the nature of Naipaul's sensibility. He has the telescopic sight of the unattached observer, who is not only a creative observer, even an observer of genius, but one of whom the observation of others leads to analysis of self" (William Walsh, 15).

Critics in their efforts to 'place' Naipaul fail to appreciate his 'apartness' and end up by fighting windmills. Most critics approach Naipaul with an external bias—either literary, thematic (socio-political) or biographical. The critical and racial diatribes against Naipaul have toned down a bit of late, partially due to his softening of stance with regard to India in *A Million Mutinies Now* (1990), and his becoming a degree less controversial compared to his earlier role as the prophet of "historylessness and traditionlessness" of the West Indies, apart from his rather surprising withdrawal into writing about subjects which sound more like repetitions of his earlier work, for instance, the re-examination and restructuring of almost the same historical material in *A Way in the World* (1994) that he had researched in *The Loss of EL Dorado* (1969).

Naipaul is viewed as a satirist who "makes his characters appear unnecessarily ridiculous" (Robert D. Hamner, 123), who has little sympathy with human failings, particularly those of the Third World. His literary style is examined segmentally: the value of the absence or presence of a narrator in his individual works and the uses of irony and satire as distancing devices as well as an expression of personal distaste. Besides, there is a tendency to interpret and justify such criticism in terms of Naipaul's own pronouncements over a number of years without treating them as part of a body of literary thought and criticism. The literary assessments of his work—satiric, ironic, farcical—are backed by established literary conventions applied per se to assert the richness or otherwise of his novels. This reserved response to Naipaul, contrasted with the critical success of other West Indian writers rests, ironically on the fact that he 'relates his literature to life'; he never lets either get out of hand in his novels. His fiction and non-fiction shies away from the symbolic significance of a poem. Hena Maes Jelinek writes:

> My impression, however, is that his obvious contempt for the colonial society is typical of his attitude to men in general.... If Trinidad, as part of the province of El Dorado, did not come upto men's expectations, it is because they themselves never live up to their dreams. Not all Caribbean writers look upon El Dorado as a myth which generated only disillusion and a second-rate way of life. Nor do they necessarily consider their history as something to be ashamed of.... The myth of El Dorado was given a new significance by such writers, who made it a symbol for a new quest. (Hena Maes Jelinek, 116)

Biographical criticism tends to flavour his life with his literature and vice versa. It becomes spicy, gossipy and simplistic, making no effort to grasp the imaginative expanse of Naipaul's mind and his capacity for empathy, by establishing close comparisons between incident and outlook. Keith Garebian writes:

> The plethora of direct comments on landscape in Naipaul's art indicates that the author is charting a mythology for the settings of his fiction and those of his own life. Landscapes are explored in order to provide characters with a real home, a true place of belonging so that they will not continue to be homeless wanderers unsure of themselves and their fates. But the mythology of the land is tinged with embarrassment, nervousness, hysteria, and pessimism—all products in some way of Naipaul's own history as a colonial with an ambiguous identity. (Keith Garebian, 23-24)

Many critics dismiss Naipaul in generalities. They see him as a superb writer of the comedy of manners, a man who writes about people as if they were "patients on the psychiatrist's couch" (Martin Amis). He can neither be described wholly as a historian, travel writer, journalist, novelist or a biographer. They seek to define him negatively and can be accused of applying the same techniques of questing into the unknown of which they accuse him. And so, they continue to attack and praise him for the same reasons: that his work, encompassing a single unhappy vision of the contemporary world, 'lets man down.' They fail to realize that the failures and disillusionments of his protagonists are presented as a necessary existential despair (for it is the only point at which man today touches his reality) which may become a turning-point, a cause for change, in a world that lives life as a 'comedy of manners.' The latter appraisal comes out at a first and cursory reading of his novels. Those critics who appreciate his work as a whole however agree that, "at all events, he has achieved a mature literature" (Robert D. Hamner, 125).

The only meaningful assessment of his art and vision, being without categories, can be made by divesting ourselves of literary terms and concepts and personal bias to 'sink' into the reality of the created world successively with the protagonist and the narrator and realize the differences between the two and their distance from Naipaul. That a writer's work is bound to be influenced by his life is a worn out cliche. Such a statement needs careful and discriminate handling in order that biography should serve as an entry into the fictive world.

Naipaul is a major world novelist who has successfully created prose fiction focussed on societies existing on margins. His fiction has an existential strength which redefines the established norms of the novel without destroying the latter. If he has not vanquished the fear of the "death of the novel", he has successfully kept it at bay. His most notable preoccupation as a novelist is his frustrated effort to make satisfactory contact with any of the post-colonial cultures in which he finds himself or those which 'created' him. Indian by ancestry, Trinidadian by birth, and English by education, he remains unable to singularly relate to any one culture or nation. His life has been one of constant moving about in search of identity and a "resting place for the imagination"—the phrase he uses as his title for the opening chapter in *An Area of Darkness* (1962).

Perpetual wandering was a heritage in the lives of Naipaul's father and grandfather. The grandfather, although born in India of a Brahmin family, went to Trinidad as an indentured labourer. The Caribbean was not the native environment for an East Indian transplanted there as an indentured labourer under the British colonial rule. This migration, thousands of miles away from India to a strange land, resulted in a feeling of alienation and loss of identity, in general, for the Trinidadian-Indian. The New World setting eroded Indian customs and orthodox modes of life. Yet, for the transplanted East Indian, the Caribbean could never be his home. It is in this strained and alienated setting that V.S. Naipaul was born in 1932, the son of Seepersad Naipaul, a journalist on the staff of *Trinidad Guardian*. As a young boy in Trinidad, V.S. Naipaul was never in one place long enough to form attachments because his father's assignments as a newspaper reporter kept the family on the move. In describing himself, Naipaul has always maintained: "I have nothing common with the people from Jamaica or the other islands for that matter. I don't understand them" (Ewart Rouse, 15). Even as a third-generation Indian in Trinidad, Naipaul never felt at home in the Caribbean. He is ruthlessly critical of the Indian community in Trinidad:

> A peasant minded, money-minded, community, spiritually static because cut off from its roots, its religion reduced to rites without philosophy, set in a materialist colonial society: a combination of historical accidents and a national temperament has turned the Trinidadian Indian into a complete colonial even more philistine than the white. (V.S. Naipaul, 82)

As a member of this community, he made up his mind very early in life that in order to be a writer he had to leave Trinidad.

Having already declared in 1962 that "Living in a borrowed culture", the West Indian, more than most needs writers to tell him who he is and where he stands, Naipaul has long positioned himself closer to the heart of the "borrowed culture" than at the brink of any "new" identity formations. This poses, as Fawzia Mustafa has commented, "a series of queries about his relation both to English literature and to Caribbean history, since according to him the latter is dependent on the former" (Fawzia Mustafa, 4). This has been made clear in an essay by Homi K. Bhabha where he explains some of the limits of "the exercise of colonial authority through propagating the emblematic power of the English book." To quote Bhabha:

> .... The discovery of the book installs the sign of appropriate representation: the word of God, truth, art creates the conditions for a beginning, a practice of history and narrative. (Homi K. Bhabha, 107)

Naipaul's characterization of West Indian or Caribbean culture as "borrowed" therefore merits examination. Rather than viewing the Caribbean confluence (unlike Derek Walcott) of European, African, Asian and American culture through the transforming lens of colonialism, Naipaul's assessment relies almost completely upon a belief in a system of preordained hierarchy and order. Naipaul terms his own condition as paradoxical because of the absence in the Caribbean of a tradition equivalent to the English, and he further treats the "Novel" as deeply rooted in the anxiety about the 'cultural'. rather than historical, since he believes one leads to the other. Naipaul's distrust of colonial system in that it fostered a false consciousness in turn takes him to think deeply about a culturally and intellectually peripheral state of being.

Recognition in England in the 50s was the ultimate aim of every aspiring writer from the Caribbean colonies, and Naipaul set his mind on migration to England. One way to do so was to secure a scholarship to study at an English University. With this objective in mind, Naipaul pursued a very successful academic career in Trinidad. In 1936, he was admitted to Chaguanas Govt. High School, which his father had attended some twenty years earlier. In 1938, following his father's transfer to Port of Spain, Naipaul attended Tranquility Boys' School, and in 1943 he won a scholarship to study at Queens Royal College in Port of Spain. After graduating, he returned to Queens Royal College as a student-teacher in January 1950. After six months, he achieved his coveted goal, a scholarship to read English literature at Oxford University. The scholarship to Oxford, then, gave Naipaul his opportunity to break out of a society he describes as saddled with a double inferiority because of its background of slavery and colonialism. Because he is convinced that Trinidad is no place for anyone with literary aspirations, he is impatient when charged with abandoning his native land:

> You have very nice liberal people who go out to a colony—which is deliberately created as inferior society—and wonder why people in that place are inferior, and if they wish to become writers they have to leave. They would not ask Hemingway why he left his own provincial town, they would not ask Pound why he left the Middle West, but they will ask a man from what they accept as an inferior society. (Israel Shankar, 66)

Naipaul's first eight years in England were extremely successful. He received a degree in English at Oxford, married an English woman, Patricia Hale in 1955, and, with the publication of *The Mystic Masseur* in 1957, won the John Llewelyn Memorial Prize. *The Suffrage of Elvira* (1958) was reviewed in the *Sunday Times* as a "perfect novel." *Miguel Street*, written earlier, was also ready to be published that year. In addition, Naipaul worked as an editor for the British Broadcasting Corporation (BBC), wrote reviews for the *New Statesman*, and began writing his first major novel, *A House for Mr Biswas*. Yet, at the peak of this highly creative period, Naipaul agonized over his status as an immigrant writer in England: "It isn't easy for the exotic writer to get his work accepted as being more than something exotic, something to be judged on its merit. The very originality of the material makes the work suspect" (V.S. Naipaul, 11). Joseph Conrad, also an immigrant writer in England, had expressed a similar concern many years before Naipaul, but, as he says: "Other writers have some starting point. Something to catch hold of.... They lean on dialect—or on tradition—or on history—or on the prejudice or fad of the hour; they trade upon some tie or conviction of their time—or upon the absence of those things—which they can abuse or praise. But at any rate they have something to begin with—while I don't. I have had some impressions, some sensations—in my time—. And it's all faded" (V.S. Naipaul, 21). It is the complaint of a writer who is missing a society, a complex of values and tradition. Naipaul, coming long after Conrad, found little consolation in his adopted country. England to him was intellectually and culturally bankrupt, incapable of giving him the moral support he needed. His scholarship to Oxford, an islander's dream, only isolated him further on another island. Looking back on his Oxford days, Naipaul recalls the futility of his journey to England: "It was a mistake. I shouldn't have gone to Oxford, and I remain ashamed that I did. Oxford was a very second rate provincial University" (Mel Gussow, 16). After his initial disappointment with England, Naipaul undertook two long voyages, one to Trinidad and the other to India. From the point of view of literary achievement, the two visits were extremely worthwhile for Naipaul. They not only resulted in *The Middle Passage* and *An Area of Darkness*, but also provided material for *A Flag on the Island*, *Mr. Stone and the Knight's Companion*, and *The Mimic Men*. However, the author's search for a place he could call home remained unfulfilled, abortive.

V.S. Naipaul's long, almost unending engagement with India in cultural, historical, intellectual and, importantly, in bio-psychological terms has by now become a separate subject of criticism and debate in the Naipaulian canon. One of the important issues, however, that still needs a proper projection and critical articulation is the figuration of India within his overall involvement as a writer with the Third World, together with the thin demarcation that separates his fiction from non-fictional works and travelogues, for the language, technique, and presentation of reality in the two genres has striking similarities, and it would appear at times that his travelogues might be taken as books that just fall short of being fictions. But Naipaul does create fictions; fictions of contemporary histories, people, societies, emerging cultures and competing ethnic communities, among others. Naipaul is a witness to the several 'worlds' that have made him—India, Trinidad, England—and such is the propensity and the quality of his imagination that it binds them into a new structural and imaginative unity. One could perhaps say that today, after closely looking at the immense depth of imagination and feeling, the deep resurrection of roots struck by locating other, external historico-cultural and literary developments in some of his recent works such as *Finding the*

Centre, *The Enigma of Arrival* and *A Way in the World*. One is forced to believe that Naipaul's involvement with the Third World is not 'parasitic', nor it is the outcome of 'childhood pathologies' (as charged by several Indian critics, intellectuals and sociologists), but is based on his gradually maturing insights into the making of the 'worlds', right from the New World he had written about at the length in *The Loss of El Dorado*, to the ones he had a desperate urge to know and understand. In this way, from *An Area of Darkness* where the view of India remained incomplete and purely exploratory, to *India: A Wounded Civilization* where towards the end he sees a hope, a new humanism in India's industrial development, to *India: A Million Mutinies Now*, with cross-references to his first Indian visit, the direction his physical, experiential and imaginative journey to India has taken is one of a new sustaining vision. He sees a 'new restoration' in the ongoing changes in the twentieth century, the new ideas about history and civilization, the new awareness about one's own identity, about one's community's identity in the vastness of Indian cultural, religious and ethnic pluralism. This, according to Naipaul, is the beginning of the "New awareness, a central will, a central intellect, a historical idea" (V. S. Naipaul, 517-18). It is part of India's growth through a new struggle, an intellectual life of values that the older Indian idea of itself missed. Now there are revolutions within revolution, whether these are a new promise or not would be a separate question, perhaps in the new millenium.

However, on his first visit, Naipaul could not relate the Indian experience to himself because he was looking for some personal vision which existed only within himself and which India could not provide. Therefore, India, which offered only another context for despair, finally purged Naipaul of hopes of finding his roots in any country or culture. His homelessness, exacerbated by his futile search to establish a living contact with a country or culture, intensified his sense of exile. By now, home for him had lost its meaning. Getting back to England after his long stay in India offered Naipaul little solace. He feared being confined to England, his adopted country, where his abilities would go unrecognized by an audience that did not understand him. Literary acclaim notwithstanding, he failed to reach the larger audience in England. As a typical English response to his early novels, Naipaul quotes a critic in the *Yorkshire Post* who says, "(She's) fed up with Trinidad and Trinidad dialect" (V.S. Naipaul, xxxvii). Irresponsible criticism of this nature made Naipaul conscious of his difficulty as a writer in England: "It is an odd suspicious situation; an Indian writer writing in English for an English audience about non-English characters who talk their own sort of English" (V.S. Naipaul, xxxviii). His early novels could be appreciated only by readers familiar with the people and the region Naipaul was writing about. English readers were also used to reading about non-Europeans through European eyes. Naipaul became aware, much to his dismay, that he lacked the advantage Kipling and Forster had in writing about India, or Trollope and Froude had in writing about the West Indies.

Naipaul has earned a notoriety for being an unsympathetic, negatively detached writer with an air of hopelessness and void in respect of the societies he has addressed and which have been his subject-matter. It is only recently that the seriousness and authenticity of his views has been taken notice of, notably in the West. Naipaul's own identity and his place as an 'English' writer has complicated matters, especially, since his eye is set on the dark spots of the world, and he appears to fall into the same literary line-up that contains Conrad, Forster, Lawrence, Durrell, Orwell, Graham Greene and other writers. The question that comes to the mind is the comparative sensitivity and subtle articulation of darkness, corruption, violence and the seedy side of the Third World existence and politics in Conrad and Greene. The point is that Naipaul was, for one reason or the other, felt 'not' to have a keen political sense, something which really encompasses all his writing. This has come in his work obviously because of his many-sided background and the consciousness of cultural dismissal in several of his non-fiction pieces, and in *Prologue to Autobiography*. The urge of the man and the writer to find a centre, in aesthetic and existential terms is ever-present, like the ever-sharpening discoveries of the lives of his Indian acquaintances through vignettes, flashes of comments and sudden moments of seizure. In an extensive interview with *Times Literary Supplement* on September 2, 1994, Naipaul said that he:

> Wanted to deliver the truth, to deliver a form of reality based on what I have observed, seen, experienced. Western writers come from the imperial period without considering themselves imperial writers. They inhabit a world where they do not see the other half or three quarters.... I carry many cultures in my head, and these people are much more restricted.

In a very meaningful statement in *Finding the Centre* that clarified his quest as a writer to find a centre, he states:

> A writer after a time carries his world with him, his own burden of experience, a human experience and literary experience (one deepening the other), and I do believe that I would have found equivalent connections with my past and myself wherever I had gone. (V.S. Naipaul, 10)

It is in this way that he has kept a watch on the world, and himself as a refracted theatre of the world. That it carries the reader through the hypnotic capacity of Naipaul's style, to overwhelm him is a different matter though. And to add to this, Naipaul has a technique of repeating a pattern of experience and response in stage after stage, person after person in order to establish a 'thesis'. This is particularly true of *An Area of Darkness*, and again in *India: A Million Mutinies Now*. The same kind of thesis or argument Naipaul has built about his own identity as a man with colonial background to locate his sense of rootlessness, now as a writer, now as a journalist and traveller. Writing about India, Naipaul has tried to place himself in the long line-up of British travellers, but as stated above, he also acknowledges his inability to be *that kind* of traveller, for India remained an enigma, a dark spot, a fracture in his scattered experience, so he writes in *The Enigma of Arrival*: "I was travelling to the peasant India that my Indian grandfathers had sought to re-create in Trinidad. The 'India' I had partly grown up in, the India that was like a loose end in my mind, where our past suddenly stopped" (V.S. Naipaul, 141). Hence, what is often misunderstood as an unnatural kinship that Naipaul attempts to create by linking with his past the strong diversity of

India, its languages, customs, dialects and religions—is in reality his own search for pattern, a quest for meaning that is like an anguished antenna of his poised imagination. The same is true of *The Middle Passage*, *The Return of Eva Peron*, and *A Turn in the South*. Part of the trouble with Naipaul (and his caustic views about India and the Third World that have produced so many of his furious critics and detractors), is his own situation as an outsider, emigre and rootless writer, so that when he speaks about India, its heritage, its Hinduism/brahminical thought among other things, he immediately strikes as a trespasser, ridiculing and looking down from an English/Western pedestal of ideas. No one could misjudge or even question the meaning of certain notions entertained by E.M. Forster, Graham Greene or even D.H. Lawrence because having succeeded from the long tradition of English literature, the whole exercise of the writer at that stage was more coherent and more bounded. As a contrast, Naipaul and other such writers live and write at the high noon of concepts like 'global village', the age of post-imperialism where all hegemonic and cliched concepts about the East-West, black-white divide are being interrogated. For Naipaul, as with Marquez, Milan Kundera and Rushdie, the peripheral questions for the erstwhile white writer have become central parts of his ethical and aesthetic concerns; it is a question of accountability for him. For a writer like Naipaul the urgency of writing on Africa, South America, the Islamic countries or India involves the same question of inclusion-exclusion, insider-outsider that has pre-occupied him in his fictional works such as *A House for Mr Biswas, The Mimic Men, In a Free State, Guerrillas* and *A Bend in the River.* Eugene Goodheart, in an essay pointed out, "Naipaul's emotion of resentment and outspokenness, so much a part of his identity as a writer, has crystallized around and is bound up with the history and culture of an East Indian community in Trinidad" (Eugene Goodheart, 251). Indeed, it is something so well known about Naipaul; he always connects, dates back, reminisces in a flash about his ancestry, his Indian past, the migration of his grand parents as indentured labour that it hardly needs more elaboration. To recall another comment, Naipaul is perhaps employing the mode of subjective 'psycho-history' in works as diverse as *The Loss of EL Dorado*, *The Middle Passage* and *An Area of Darkness*.

Naipaul was certainly not the first to write about the outposts of the British or European Empires. One thinks, for instance, of Joseph Conrad, E.M. Forster, Anthony Burgess, and Graham Greene, all of whom had written about places that also interest Naipaul. But the main difference between their points of view and Naipaul's resulted from the fact that they were Europeans surveying the colonial cultures from the outside. Unlike these European writers, Naipaul was not trying to analyse the psyche of the British-colonial minority cultures from the fringes. For him, the effects of colonial transplantation resulting in rootlessness were a living and central experience. Absent from Naipaul's writing, for instance, is Forster's exploration of the "good" Indians and "bad" Englishmen, the metaphysical inner struggles of Conrad's characters, who are somehow affected by opposed cultural values out of place with each other, or Burgess's anxiety over the lack of accord between British and colonial cultures. The settings in the novels of Graham Greene may take us to the Far East, and even to Africa in his novel, *The Human Factor*. His central characters are, nevertheless, Europeans involved mostly with the political rather than with the cultural confusion resulting from colonization, which is Naipaul's great theme. The non-European characters in Conrad remain shadowy. His Malaysian characters, with the sole exception of Almayer, who really was an expatriate, remain external, exotic portrayals such as Dain Waris in *Lord Jim* or Babalatchi and Aissa in *An Outcast of the Islands*. The Africans in chains whom Marlow encounters at the first trading post in *Heart of Darkness* are not developed as characters. They serve as a sombre reminder of the excesses of the colonial age, whereas Naipaul's native characters in their exotic settings are an integral part of their landscape. Salim, the central character of Naipaul's *A Bend in the River*, in spite of his Indian origin, describes himself as a man of the Indian Ocean, and the eastern coastal region of Africa, where his family has lived for four generations.

Conrad and Naipaul, no doubt, share a common interest in the remote areas of the world they write about. "Conrad's value to me", acknowledges Naipaul, "is that he is someone who sixty to seventy years ago meditated on my world, a world I recognize today. I feel this about no other writer of the century. His achievement derives from the honesty which is part of his difficulty, that 'scrupulous fidelity to the truth' of my integrity" (V.S. Naipaul, 19). But Naipaul is also aware of Conrad's limitations in writing about these places when he comments:

> The Conrad novel was like a simple film with an elaborate commentary. A film: the characters and settings could be seen very clearly. But realism often required trivial dialogue, the following of trivial action; the melodramatic flurry at the end emphasized the slowness and bad proportions of what had gone before; and the commentary emphasized the fact that the characters were actors. (V.S. Naipaul, 17)

Critical attempts at tracing influences on Naipaul's writing have always been a tenuous project. Naipaul, in his writing, has stubbornly refused to be categorized into a school or trend. A clue to this may be found in his own early disillusionment with the institutionalized practice of literary studies: "I had no taste for scholarship, for tracing the growth of schools and trends," he wrote in an article published in 1964. "I sought continuously to relate literature to life. Now I discovered that the study of literature had been made scientific, that each writer had to be approached through the booby-trap of scholarship" (V.S. Naipaul, 473). In recent years, Naipaul has become increasingly aware of the difference between himself and other contemporary writers in English. As a "Human condition" novelist, Naipaul, as early as 1964, was acutely aware of the dangers of the Novel turning inward: "Even in this period of 'internationalism' in letters we have seen literatures turning more and more inward, developing languages that are more and more private. Perhaps in the end literature will write itself out, and all its pleasures will be those of the word" (V.S. Naipaul, 474). Freshness of vision is what Naipaul looks for and does not find in contemporary writers. He himself constantly refreshes his vision by travelling to the far corners of every continent. The whole world in turmoil is Naipaul territory.

Naipaul, to date, has been a relentless critic and commentator in his keen observation of Third World societies, their histories and the human predicament therein. Indeed, Naipaul has emerged in the twentieth century as one of the most authentic voices to create a comprehensive vision of history and experience of different places and people alike. His works show a world on the fringes of marginality and denial. In most of the ex-colonial societies, communities and men that he presents, almost everything in their experience can be traced back to the deep psychic trauma that makes up the identity of the colonized. Naipaul visualizes colonialism as a system and experience which has turned nations, societies, political systems and individuals into mimic societies and mimic men of the West who exist without vision and hope. Naipaul has been writing a kind of psycho-history of these marginalized, derelict Third World societies which he sees vulnerable and weak because of their historical and colonial past. Likewise, the idea of the oppressor-oppressed, centre-periphery, inclusion-exclusion and that of the colonizer-colonized is closely related to Naipaul's presentation of history as it influences the present situation of man. Two related aspects of Naipaul's work—both relevant to his vision of marginal life in search of a 'centre'—need a final stress at this point. The first is related literally to the places where Naipaul transports his reader—Africa, the Caribbean, Asia and the Central Asia all the way to South Africa—to test his obsession what it means to become and finally be a writer. What happens when the imperial power recedes, leaving the cruelty and chaos to fill the breach. His central question, the moral centre as it were, has been the question what happens to the individual and the society after the imperial power has packed up and gone. This is what has provoked drama in the form of contestatory assessments about Naipaul. The second aspect deals with Naipaul's projected views being politically 'incorrect' because he has described the Third World as trapped and static, all presumption, grandiosity, pathetic mimicry. We may or may not like it but Naipaul projects the new man as trapped in pride and fixity, unable to get past the programmed responses to history, culture, politics and domination he hardly understands. Naipaul's idea that human beings are basically 'unequal' given their respective past, thus emerges as the result of his experience and observation.

The most important phase of the outward and dominating thrust of Europeans into the world beyond Europe was the nineteenth century (which has been most authoritatively discussed by Edward Said in *Orientalism and Culture and Imperialism*). Paradoxically, however, imperial expansion has had a radically destabilising effect on its own pre-occupation and power. In pushing the colonial world to the margins of experience, the 'centre' pushed consciousness beyond the point at which monocentrism in all spheres of thought could be accepted without question. Alternatively, one could say that the alienating process which initially served to relegate the post-colonial world to the 'margin' turned upon itself and acted to push the world through a kind of mental barrier into a position from which all experience could be viewed as decentred, splintered, pluralistic and multifarious. Marginality thus became an unprecedented source of creative energy and the quest for self-identity (ref. recent studies within post-structuralism, Marxism, Feminism and post-colonial theory). Writers as diverse as George Lamming, Dennis Lee, Wilson Harris, Robert Kroetsch, Salman Rushdie, Marquiz, Coetzee, Ngugi and Wole Soyinka have argued that not only is the notion of authentic experience as false as its validating concept of 'centre', but that the inauthentic and the marginal is in fact the 'real'.

Marginality is the condition constructed by the posited relation of one (or society, clan or class) to a privileged centre, an 'othering' directed by the imperial centre. But it does not involve the construction of an alternative focus of subjectivity—a new 'centre'. Rather, the act of appropriation in the Commonwealth or post-colonial text involves the embracing of that marginality as the fabric of social and personal experience. The 'marginal' and the 'variant' thus characterize post-colonial views of language, culture, history and society as a consequence of the process of abrogation. The syncretic is validated by the disappearance of the 'centre', and with no centre the marginal becomes the formative constituent of reality. The variations of the experience of marginality are complex and fraught with the widest possibilities in cultural, historical, sociological, philosophical, economic spheres, in gender relations and in other terms.

Naipaul does not celebrate marginality in his fiction or even in his non-fictional works unlike some of the African and West Indian novelists. On the other hand, his technique functions to project and thus lay bare the interconnections and the complex relationships of European history with the non-Western man. For Naipaul, thus, the marginal position of his characters (and his own as a writer writing from the margins or without a creative/literary tradition) is given by the peculiarity of the historical time, the geographical space, and the cultural links at a certain point of time. The vital point is to articulate the meaning of all these.

The present book attempts to explore the vast range of Naipaul's portraiture of different types/paradigms of colonial experience in the successive major works—*The Mystic Masseur* (1957), *The Suffrage of Elvira* (1958), *Miguel Street* (1959), *A House for Mr Biswas* (1961), *The Mimic Men* (1967), *In a Free State* (1971), *Guerrillas* (1975), *A Bend in the River* (1979), *The Enigma of Arrival* (1987) and *A Way in the World* (1994), which are based on the idea of dislocation, marginality and the loss of authentic modes of life as a result of the experience of colonization. These are related to the social, economic, historical, political and cultural barriers, which are now part of the emergent Third World. In his successive works, Naipaul also penetratingly explores the idea of freedom with all its complexities, ironies and imponderables. However, *The Enigma of Arrival* and *A Way in the World* are critically dealt with within the larger debate(s) on his major fictional works.

Few writers of fiction have documented marginality as well as Naipaul. His originality lies in the denial of any authentic identity to his characters, and his insistence on derivation as the essence of culture born of colonialism. In his major fiction, Naipaul portrays characters who are marginalized on the basis of race, economic and cultural subordination, class, nationality or colour, all of which are understandable in terms of intersecting dialectics of slavery and the impact of imperialism and colonization. Naipaul portrays men who cannot construct a coherent self and the reasons for this malady lie deep in the pattern of subordination and existential split suffered by them under a system that recognized no difference, humanly or culturally in its ruthless drive to hegemonize everything. As Peter Hughes has commented:

> Above all, because the writing out of the narrative of decline and fall, of disorder and lack of authority, involves, the discovery of a void at the heart of the world. Such a void lies at the heart of Naipaul's world and it has been discovered through his writings. (Peter Hughes, 11)

In a very important sense, Naipaul's work marks a turning point in English literature that concerns itself with colonialism in complex and profound ways, for in addition to depicting its effects on the imperialists and colonizers, he also portrays its devastating effects on the native civilization. For Conrad, Forster and Orwell—Naipaul's Western predecessors—the Empire consists of dark places on the earth that call into question the norms and conventions of their own civilization. Whether it is the darkness of the up country in Congo, or the echo of the Marabar caves in India, the outer reaches of the Empire touch the inner darkness, and journeys to these outposts become journeys *within*. Both Conrad and Forster are deft in portraying the compulsions of European behaviour in an alien environment. But each, in his own way, portrays the native as the 'symbolic other', whose sole function is to shake the solid foundation of Christian European-Enlightenment, in short, of Western civilization.

The one aspect that effected a total change with the emergence of Naipaul was the disappearance of the romantic edge of colonial literature. In dealing with a much later stage of colonialism and post-colonial phase, Naipaul is no longer concerned with the first traumatic encounter of the European with what he judges to be other than what he has known, the non-European. Instead, he writes about the persistence of colonialism in the era of political independence. He depicts what Frantz Fanon has termed "false decolonization", legal independence without breaking down the colonial, social and political structures. In this context, most of his major works such as *The Mimic Men*, *In a Free State*, *Guerrillas* and *A Bend in the River* are illustrations of the meaninglessness of cultural, political and economic freedom in the absence of real freedom that must come from within the depths of one's self and native consciousness. The oppressive machinery of colonization, still operating in the post-colonial era in new nations has distorted human lives and moral order in societies and nations which as a result of the former's huge presence, have failed to come to terms with their problems. It is therefore not surprising that Naipaul's characters suffer from the effects and overall decadence that surrounds their bleak and devisioned lives. Again, their self-awareness is derived entirely from culture that perceives them as 'other'. They efface the reality of their collective past or the historical break, and when it comes to the understanding of the knowledge of themselves as objects in society, it brings about a feeling of shame and self-contempt.

Naipaul has brought colonial literature to a new imaginative phase where experience is marked by being entirely derived from the culture that oppresses it (e.g. *In a Free State, Guerrillas*, and *A Bend in the River*). Indeed, the disorienting and far-reaching impacts of colonial history have surfaced in Naipaul's fictional technique and imagination as a "metaphor" in the sense that colonial experience is now no longer limited to actual slavery but has taken different forms in modern life, that it is an ineluctable part of experience in the twentieth century. For that reason, it is pertinent to state that authority, power, oppression, marginality as states of being, and alienation, exile, displacement and metaphorical subservience as states of experience are present in complex and multi-dimensional ways in Naipaul's fiction. The entire Naipaulian fictional form is related to the human encounter(s) with the changing colonial authority and setting and its wide-ranging effects. The subjects that Naipaul has dealt with have been representative and typical of the marginality of the post-colonial world and by handling these issues with a quality of feeling and conviction he has made his mark as an authentic writer. However, the areas and the issues Naipaul has traversed also come down to an idea, or a cluster of attitudes and beliefs compacted into a structure of ideas, of what we think our world was, and what we would like it to be, understanding the hostilities we have to face in the present. Ideology is tailored in a reductive way to increase its functional or political value for the present. Ideology is the politics of culture, in a culture which with pre-emptive aggressions, sees everything as political. Since Naipaul has traced the politics of culture, history, language and experience in marginal, post-colonial societies, his work has a deep relation with both intellectual and ideological configurations of different structural and experiential layers therein. In a colonial society where most of the visible and invisible structures of oppression are political and may be traced to the deep trauma of the psychological make-up of the colonized (as brilliantly espoused by Frantz Fanon, Mannoni, Memmi, Kovel), there is every reason why almost every detail of one's inheritance, environment prospects, should be subjected to a re-evaluating glance of suspicion. But ideology, its interpretations or conclusions are not always helpful. On the other hand, the left-wing or the right-wing parties' own conflicts in the West have ironically helped our understanding as to how things are in the world. Or for that matter, revolutions and ideologies help in bringing about change through cultural and literary revolutions, like the Romantic movement in the nineteenth century. A writer has therefore a lot of straitjacket material to *unlearn* through his own experience in order to see his people honestly, truthfully. But this unlearning also requires discrimination to be free from cliché's, with the exclusion of oneself from the maze of things. Naipaul had to extricate himself from these cliché's of imperialism and ideological logic to rehearse for himself the truth within the West Indian society and history, among others. In this way, the writer was able to get closer to *his* experience of Trinidad, of the squalor, poverty, dereliction, mimicry and the relationship of people with its past. Ultimately, his fiction has to do with barriers—physical, social, historical—with a sense of negation and emptiness which such a barrier-sense imposes, and this is made clear in his withdrawal from his own world and subject-matter—Trinidad. Naipaul later stepped into others' territory by shaping it into an imaginary setting of the colonial or the post-colonial 'theatre' in *The Mimic Men, In a Free State, Guerrillas, A Bend in the River* and even in *A Way in the World.* Finally, Naipaul's new associations after decades of a literary career splintered *within* the same frame of reflection—denial, deprivation, colony, blackness, with the non-rational, the de-visioned, the non-Western. Naipaul has abandoned a historical frame, a particular *type* of oppression or subjugation, and now finds the world a typological purgatory that includes a multi-geographical focus on races and nations.

Naipaul's work and the inner realities it touches upon are relevant to a study of post-colonial poetics and the way in which the colonial 'other' can be perceived from a complex of perspectives. One of the most legitimate points that has been critically examined is how a Naipaul text could be in danger of getting branded as an 'English' or a 'universal' text, especially in view of its "difference of language, historical and other underlying qualities, i.e., a novel like *A House for Mr Biswas* with its special stress on the East-Indian historico-cultural compulsions in West Indies" (Helen Tiffin, 119).

It could still be branded or commended as a 'universal' text for its underlying quest for identity and place. In much the same way, post-colonialism suffers the process of hegemonic re-incorporation by which the interior/Western centre actually draws subversive elements back into itself. One of the most insidious denials of the validity of post-colonialism is the suggestion that it demonstrates the outworking of a worldwide spread of post-modernism, and thus becomes simply another manifestation of a European cultural movement. The attitude itself is far more widespread than any organised or written expositions of the idea would suggest, but because it has the status of a prejudice, it is much more insidious.

In a study of black writers' works and the special language and experience in their texts, including Naipaul's, it is important to dig out the meanings, signs and signifiers with a *colonial resistance* in reading the texts. As Stephen Slemon observes:

> The basic maneuver in this approach is to focus on some pattern of textual echoing or repetition in post-colonial literary documents and to examine the way in which those texts 'work', the linguistic and narrative patterns of the imperial centre through a complex rhetoric of intertextual quotation. (Stephen Slemon, 35)

Further, in dealing with as sensitive and important an area as the colonial discourse and the colonized experience, it is essential for such anti-authoritarian discourses as post-colonialism to be aware of the ominous intellectual tendencies within Western theoretical practices in the last two decades. It is by a proper decolonizing of the text, language and experiences that one could read and reflect upon it without the Eurocentric intellectual hegemony. And ironically, it is again a politics of literature and knowledge that Naipaul is acknowledged as a "leading English novelist" and his works are incorporated into the existing literary canon and structure as a way of keeping them marginalized. Similarly, writing post-colonial 'place' is not writing lineaments of some geographical given but writing out of a *difference* which seeks to dismantle the binary structures in which the colonial margin is systematically negated. In fact, the notion of placelessness is a crucial feature of the discourse of *place* in post-colonial societies, and this is as much about Naipaul's understanding of placelessness as of home and rootlessness. This binary approach, i.e. European, needs to be countered by working out a text/language which affects a radical disruption of its base, as the West Indian writer Dennis Lee says:

> The colonial writer does not have words of his own. Is it not possible that he projects his own condition of voicelessness into whatever he created? That he articulates his own powerlessness, in the face of alien words by seeking out fresh tales of victims? Perhaps the colonial imagination is driven to recreate again and again; the experience of writing in colonial space. (Dennis Lee, 399)

From one angle, Naipaul has been negatively seen as part of "complicit' post-colonialism, as Bob Hodge and Vijay Mishra have pointed out in a well-known article. To read Naipaul simplistically is what in another sense Anthony Appiah has called "the Naipaul fallacy", to overlook Naipaul's favouring colonialist practices. The implication here is that the 'universalism' or 'transcendence' with which Naipaul is credited is in fact nothing other than an endorsement of so-called Western values, whether in liberal or conservative guise. Among the most sustained, thoughtful and carefully documented recent critiques of Naipaul's colonialist sympathies and colonialist referents is Rob Nixon's (Rob Nixon, 43) *London Calling: V.S. Naipaul Postcolonial Mandarin* (1992). Nixon concentrates on Naipaul's travel books to opine how deeply invested his allegiance is to the designs and desires of Victorian travel writing. Differences in political and ideological affiliations, however, cannot fully account for such divergent readings. One way of understanding the use of Naipaul's views about the non-Western world by an empirically minded, gentle audience is for purposes of self-definition. This is while acknowledging that literary theory, particularly deconstructive practice, discourse theory among others, teaches us that colonialist reflexivity—the habit of colonial representations intended to objectify others, the habit of strategic self-portioning within an objectified space—are manifestations of the ambivalence generated by colonial discourses. To break colonialist inscriptions thus requires a textual exercise to reread historical facts.

Studies such as C.L.R. James' *The Black Jacobins* (1938), Aime Cesaire's *Discourses on Colonialism* (1955), Fanon's *Black Skin, White Masks* (1952), and *The Wretched of the Earth* (1962), as well as the recent works of Said, *Orientalism* (1978) and *Culture and Imperialism* (1993), Aijaz Ahmad's *In Theory: Classes, Nations, Literatures* (1992) and inquires such as Homi K. Bhabha's and Gayatri Spivak's theoretical investigations into the constitution of the colonial subject, are among a huge body of work that has reread the history of colonialism. Along with a new generation of scholars, these studies show how the long tradition of European representations of non-European places and habits—either histories or travelogues or novels—emerged hand in hand with colonial consolidation and imperial reign. The complicity between political agendas allowed for colonial domination, and these representations in turn led to the notion that those in power could act so as to legitimize that only their accounts of 'peripheries' or colonies were authoritative. This was further strengthened through the translation of colonialist's versions of the colonized in order to dictate what the second or third worlds are, how they are to be understood or written about. The above (the colonizer dictating the terms of definition of the colonized) has been the dominating strategy of colonialist representations. The result has been that Africa, India, South-East Asia, the Pacific Islands, Caribbean, etc. have engaged in these monologic discourses for so long that contemporary literary and theoretical works must labour under the burdens of overcoming these well-established imaginary constructions, if the process of self-representation of the subjected people is to take place. Writers and critics writing about non-Western world (including writers like Naipaul) need to be vigilant against the dangers of reinscribing in their texts received colonial assumptions. Naipaul, according to some of the above-named critics, from a negative angle, has often 'failed' to exercise enough vigilance, or to acknowledge the need to rethink about the colonial past. However, Naipaul's obsession with the word and the 'book' leading to coherence and knowledge can conversely be seen as a strategy to foreground what is known about the colonialist stance; his bookishness can be read, with some justification, as Fawzia Mustafa says, as "orientalist". His writings can be charged with indictment, but, on the other hand, can also be understood in terms of the ethics of writing and reading about non-Western worlds, the way he understands the social composition of present-day ex-colonial societies.

In a related sense, the relationship of the periphery with the centre is also inscribed in one kind of diasporic writing. Rushdie's famous utterance "The Empire Writes Back to the Centre" for instance, is itself replete with the contradictions in the post-colonial writer's strategies who writes from within the centre as a critic of it, who says that the Empire could not have lasted a week without such collaborators (citing the example of Saladin, 'the chamcha' in *The Satanic Verses*) among the colonized people. And the later condemnation of Rushdie by the Islamic world raises interesting questions about the category of the post-colonial itself and whether one can ever completely remove the strains of complicity with the Empire/Centre that come with the profession of post-colonial writer. To extend the argument further, the strains of the colonizer-colonized synchronized relation are also indirectly foregrounded in the diasporic experience that comes as an extension through the experience of a migrant, a traveller or émigré, already foreshadowed by the earlier historical experiences of slavery, plantation, colonialism or indenture system. Diasporas of the nations today are a result of the complicated process of the earlier knotted relationship of the colonized societies with the colonizing nations. Frantz Fanon (Frantz Fanon see chapters I and III) had anticipated this paradox in *The Wretched of the Earth* when he wrote that the colonized is either doomed to be a mere reflection of his master, or he must fight his master through active struggle (so as "to enter into the realm of the symbolic"). According to Fanon, the withholding of legitimate consciousness, I-ness or self-hood, the impossibility on the part of the colonized even to qualify for the thingness of things produces a radical politics. But the colonizer never completely denies the "I-ness", since to do so would make the colonized worthless. There is always, in the colonial regime, a tantalizing offer of subjectivity and its withdrawal, which for the colonized momentarily confirms his entry into the colonizer's world, only to be rejected by it. The colonized never know how the colonizers consider them for what they are, humans in full possession of a self, or merely objects. Fanon's highly volatile view of his relationship is marked by a particular context and place. However, the racial question, the socio-political and even the community-based antagonism between the migrant/diasporic individual/group and the metropolitan West is one of the most incendiary issues in the process of adjustment in today's mixed, multi-racial reality of existence. The question, therefore, of living in one's "construct" is hardly simplistic because "constructs" do come from one's background, origin, religion and family, but other constructs framed by knowledge, power, history, race and professions do impinge one in the multi-cultural, multi-racial situations.

What links the experience of diasporas is marked in the aftermath of today's racial categories that speak of hybrid peoples, yoked together: Black-British, British-Asian, Kenyan-Asian, Anglo-Indian, Indo-Anglian, Indo-Caribbean, African-Caribbean, African-American, Chinese-American. The names of these diasporic 'doubles' bear more black than white identities, because in today's political terms any product of black and white must always be classified as black. It is also a truism, though that most diasporas—Jewish, Asian, Caribbean, African, Chinese—are trying to develop their own ways of living in England or Canada, a way one couldn't really call "English" or "Canadian". Elsewhere, in *The Post-Colonial Critic* Gayatri Spivak talks about the politics of migration, of speaking, of generalizing from a certain platform: Indian, feminist, gendered. Spivak avers that there is safety in "specificity" rather than in those "labels". A little later in the same interview, she relates "tokenization" with "ghettoization" like someone becoming a token for the "Third World point of view" as an Indian. Spivak says:

> Over the centuries we had histories of let's say, Indian indentured labour being taken to the Afro-Caribbean. After the change of regimes in certain African nations, Indians moved from Africa, then to Britain; then Indians in waves in the early 60s, professional Indians, went to the United States as part of the brain-drain. These Indians who are spread out over the world, for different kinds of historical reasons, they are diasporic.... (Gayatri Spivak, 60-61)

With the passage of time (a matter of less than twenty years) the writings of the immigrants of various diasporas were to become greatly privileged, classed as the most authentic documents of resistance and response in recent times. Post-modernists, post-colonialists/post-structuralists have seen these forms of literature as determined by the single factor—the colonial encounter. We learn much about Lamming, Achebe, Garcia Marquez, Naipaul, Rushdie through an inscription marked by the colonial encounter and its alarming effects. But diasporas such as the Indian have been typified by many other kinds of pre-occupations; East-West encounter, exile, immigration, tradition vs. modernity, Indian religion vs. the liberal West, rationalism vs. spirituality, India's political-colonial link with the Empire voiced by a whole range of writers from Raja Rao onwards. However, India is too large a country to have a single diaspora; there are sub-diasporas such as the Gujarati, Punjabi, Bengali, Muslim, etc., and they have their own written response in both English and regional languages of India. Writers of almost all diasporas have sought to record the manner in which they have chosen and adopted their new environment and now they have experienced both identification, nostalgia, and loss from and to their old and new homelands. This bonding of culture, religion ancestry, literature and history is especially strong in diasporic situation, but where it provides new patterns of ethnic identity (or a striving towards it), it can also place one in a situation of exclusion in the metropolitan zones of the West. Today's self-proclaimed, mobile and multiple identities may be seen "not as a marker of contemporary social fluidity and dispossession but a new stability, self-assurance and quietism" (J.C. Young, 4).

This "quietism" indicates one's coming to terms with unfixed modes of existence and professions; to opportunities the First World offers through attractive assignments, metropolitan consumerism, freedom to travel or petro-dollars sponsored in other areas of the world. The writers, and critics too, are involved in this multiplicity of global travelling, and they are part of this dislocation of peoples and cultures. Hence, Naipaul and David Dabydeen write from the West Indian diaspora, Bharati Mukherji represents the US diaspora, Rushdie and Dhondy write from the UK diaspora, Rohinton Mistry comes from the Canadian diaspora, and so forth.

That the Caribbean literary, historical and cultural imponderables against which Naipaul's situation as a 'diasporic' writer must be seen is fraught with all kinds of violent mixings, is well known. This history of the Caribbean is bloody, violent with each racial group's memories adding new dimensions to its already difficult human terrain. From the time of their discovery in the fifteenth century, the Caribbean islands were seen as objects to be exploited rather than colonies to be settled, which ultimately led to the intervention of the European powers—France, Spain, England and the fierce naval rivalry between them. This, and other such 'crossings' have affected contemporary West Indian society, that several West Indian writers such as Wilson Harris, George Lamming, Sam Selvon, Roger Mais, V.S. Naipaul and Jean Rhys, among others have fictionally portrayed. Naipaul had drawn-up the map of the Caribbean chaos and heterogeneity of races, cultures and dialects in *The Middle Passage*; the lack of educational opportunities, the picaroon society that somehow pulled on despite its astonishing lack of any cohesion. Rising unemployment, poverty, imperial restrictions created conditions for the rise of the new black middle class in almost every profession with a growing political power. A sense of pride in the history and culture of the Caribbean became fashionable, which in turn gave way to creative expression to echo this trend and the stimulus. It is to this new aspiring class to which practically most writers of this period belonged. As stated earlier, educational opportunities, tied up with the colonial languages, especially English, were something that rarely came anybody's way. Real power and status was linked with the imperial languages, till now the monopoly of the privileged class. For the West Indian blacks social or public success for their children meant winning an 'exhibition' or government scholarship. The attainment of educational, professional and academic opportunity, both for the indentured Indian as much for the African ex-slave before him, was like seizing a sudden chance to stay alive. But this chance, the decent living for their children, could only be obtained through a lifetime of self-sacrifice. This double struggle for financial security and intellectual advancement thus consisted the West Indian writers' struggles to move away to attain this coveted goal in European hibernation or exile. Eric William's *Inward Hunger*, Naipaul's *A House for Mr Biswas*, Mittelholzer's *Corentyne Thunder*, Sam Selvon's *A Brighter Sun* and *Turn Again Tiger* are variations on the theme of this struggle for attainment. However, this also meant going away, breaking off connections and a truncation of family ties. The nostalgic memories of childhood and alienation are perhaps recalled most imaginatively in Lamming's *In the Castle of My Skin*. Similarly, a vision of filth and cultural deprivation of Ghana, even more terrible and annihilating, is presented by Ayi Kwei Armah in *The Beautiful Ones are not Yet Born*. The same kind of reality is presented through the face of poverty and ugliness by Mulk Raj Anand in *The Untouchable*. Naipaul, at any rate, was successful in clothing this ugliness and decrepit state of poverty-ridden humans through the facade of fantasy and comedy. In the article "Conrad's Darkness" while commenting on what he saw through Conrad and *Nostromo*, Naipaul describes his own view of the world's 'half-made' societies as places which 'continuously made and unmade themselves' and the experience of the degradation that came with the necessities which forced them to be what they are. Naipaul's identification with Conrad is more clearly traceable in a novel like *A Bend in the River* because of its immediate locale. Naipaul's works and their ideological premise cannot perhaps be extended to explain the kind of racial protest and violence that is characterized by African novelists of the twentieth century. The colonization and its control in the previous centuries was indeed more brutal and inhuman. Foucault centres his arguments in *Discipline and Punish* on the institutionalized and subtle surveillance of the individual through knowledge in more recent times.

Writing about the relationship between power and knowledge in *Discipline and Punish*, Foucault in his famous analogy of the exercise of power details the massive but infrequent exercise of destructive force and the uninterrupted constraints imposed in practices of discipline and training, exercising on the body a subtle coercion:

> The human body was entering a machinery of power that explores it, breaks it down and rearranges it—. It defined how one may have a hold over others' bodies, not only so that they may do what one wishes, but so that they may operate as one wishes, with the techniques, the speed and the efficiency as one determines. This discipline produces subjected and 'practiced' bodies, 'docile' bodies. (Michel, 138)

Foucault's stress is on the concentration camps, hospitals, mental asylums, factories, schools and institutions. Faucault saw these techniques of power and knowledge as means of control or neutralization of dangerous social elements, and evolved into techniques for enhancing the utility and productivity of those subjected to them.

Another contention of Foucault that is significant is that power is not exercised through networks that are static; he speaks of power as 'something that circulates.' With the creation of new states and new diasporas, history and circumstance have produced more wanderers, nomads, vagrants, unassimilated in the structures of institutional power. And, because of their strange figuration between the old empire and the new state, their condition characterizes the tensions and contradictions in the cross-cultural and overlapping territories in the post-imperial scene.

The clash of Eastern and Western sensibilities has not figured only in the Commonwealth or in the West Indian literature. In Conrad's *Heart of Darkness* and *Lord Jim*, the confrontation of the white man with Africa raised complex moral issues which are equally relevant in the context of Commonwealth literature too, for it is manifested in the clash of values. The violent confrontation of the oppressors and the oppressed becomes symbolic in Naipaul's *In a Free State* where Bobby and Linda undertake a journey across a newly-independent African state, little knowing the horrible events that await them and the hatred they are to encounter at the hands of the now black masters wielding power. In the post-colonial world, still recovering from exploitation and neglect, they are humiliated, being representatives of the erstwhile white colonizers. Forster's *A Passage to India* is a statement on the sensitive moral and political problems coming in the way of East-West relations.

Jean Paul Sartre's Preface to Fanon's *The Wretched of the Earth*, based on a deep humanism, is one of the most authoritative and eloquent statements on the racial implications of colonial experience. Castigating the magical spell of the Europeans exercised over the natives, he lashes out at the European power-lust and the racial differences born of the colonial history of oppression:

> Can he not here recognize his own cruelty turned against himself? In the savagery of these oppressed peasants, does he not find his own settler's savagery, which they have absorbed through every pose and for which there is no cure? The reason is simple; this imperious being, crazed by his absolute power and by the fear of losing it, no longer remembers clearly that he was once a man; he takes himself to be a horsewhip or a gun; he has come to believe that the domestication of the inferior races will

> come about by the conditioning of their reflexes. (Jean Paul Sartre, 14)

Similarly, what the French psychologist Dr. O. Manoni terms as the 'Prospero Complex' implies the power of magic and illusion through which the white colonialists mesmerized the slaves and controlled their destinies. In Naipaul's *The Mystic Masseur, Miguel Street* and *The Mimic Men*, the awe of white cultural superiority, the mental slavery of Westernized mannerisms and etiquette, and the myopic political sense are cleverly delineated. And Lamming's *In the Castle of My Skin*, along with Jamaica Kincaid's *Annie John* (1986), analyses the lineaments of that submission and dominance using a system of literary-historical icons and measuring responses to these images. It suggests ways in which a rebellion can be fought and won, appropriating the very forces and tools which the enemy—the school system—would use to impose order, submission and obedience. Indeed, as Fanon and other existentialist writers went on to suggest, only by confrontation can the long colonial psychological attributes of dependency and inferiority be broken, to help the colonized people acquire a new status, and a new consciousness. The idea of a man getting above his bruised society, or working for his own moral reclamation has been treated earlier by R.K. Narayan in *The Guide*, though in a distinct cultural context.

Post-colonial criticism has positioned itself as a broad anti-imperialist emancipating project, thereby adding a more overtly politicized dimension to related work in the field of commonwealth studies. But it has created complications of its own, in terms of the involvement of historical and national contexts in which literature is produced and received, as well as gender, class, religion, racial and colonial experiences. It again threatens to become yet another of the First World's covert colonizing strategies over the cultural productions of the Third World. 'Post' is not only pre-mature but also has the disadvantage of embodying the ideology of linear progress that underpinned the Empire, as well as to continue orientanlyzing around the important 'centre'. Dynamics of nation, cultural resistance, history—what unites all these different, even opposite positions on the meaning of post-colonial—is a shared stake in the psycho-social analysis and colonial identity on the collective and individual levels. It foregrounds a politics of opposition and struggle, and problematizes the key relationship between centre and periphery. It has helped to destabilize the barriers around 'English literature' that protected the primacy of the canon and the self-evidence of its standards. In Fanon's version of the conditions under which the radical post-colonial might come into being, the colonial world must be strategically rendered as Manichean in its effects, since the system reduces the colonized to the status of permanent bondage. Consequently, it is in the nature of the Manichean world-order that violence should be seen as a cleansing force. This is a severe indictment of imperialist, since the withdrawal of subjectivity hits at the very core of the Enlightenment project, the civilizing values of modernity which the colonized (as V.S. Naipaul for instance) sees as imperialism's positive, reconstructive and basically humane face. The complexity of this essentially Hegelian problematic, the centrality of action in a retheorization of history as class struggle, is transformed by the authors of the well-known *Empire Writes Back* into a broader, somewhat depoliticized category, the 'counter-discourse'. Political insurgency is replaced by discursive radicalism, for which the West Indian example is offered as paradigmatic. The danger here is that the post-colonial is reduced to a purely textual phenomenon, as if power is simply a matter of discourse and it is only through discourse that counter-claims might be made. This move is clearly aimed at making the diverse forms of the post-colonial available as a single object on the curriculum of the centre.

'Post-colonial' as we define it does not mean 'post-independence' or 'after colonialism', for this would be to falsely ascribe an end to the colonial process. Post-colonialism, rather begins from the very first moment of colonial contact. It is the discourse of oppositionality which colonialism brings into being. In this sense, post-colonial writing has a very long history. But it would be true to say that the intensification of theoretical interest in the post-colonial has coincided with the rise of post-modernism in Western society/aesthetics and this has led to some confusion and overlapping between the two. The confusion is caused partly by the fact that the major project of post-modernism—the deconstruction of the centralized, logocentric, master narratives of European culture—is perhaps similar to the post-colonial project of dismantling the centre/margin binarism of imperial discourse, among other issues. The decentring of discourse, the focus on the significance of language and writing in the construction of experience, the use of subversive strategies of parody, mimicry and irony—all these concerns overlap those of postmodernism. Further, 'theory' has often emerged more in the post-colonial creative text (Atwood, Kundera, Coetzee, etc.), theoretical texts such as *Tradition, the Writer and Society* (Wilson Harris) which are of post-structuralist nature, actually precede the writings of Derrida and Foucault. The rejection of Cartesian Individual, the instability of signification, the location of subject in language or discourse, the dynamic operation of *power*; all these familiar post-structuralist concepts emerge in different guises in post-colonial thought. But post-colonialism is not simply a kind of 'postmodernism with politics'—it is a belated but sustained attention to the imperial process in colonial and neo-colonial societies, and an examination to subvert the actual material and discursive effects of that process. But there is a difference in the word *post* in post-modernism and post-colonialism. Post-colonialism takes it up as a subject—the very idea of post-colonial literary production precludes any return to the canon because the field transforms our idea of literature itself.

The 'justifying' discourse which allows this settler incorporation into post-colonialism is clearly post-modernism. In the works of someone as astute as Stephen Slemon, the strategies of modernism/post-modernism arise out of a European assimilation of the heterogeneous colonial *other* into its own social and discursive practices. It is the reading of post-colonialism as already present in European though as well as, by extension, in colonial culture, which allows Slemon to shift gear and more into Canadian settler culture forthwith. He speaks of Canada and the other white dominions as Second World societies in which the post-colonial is an anti-colonial discourse, a kind of counter-discursive energy. Through this counter-discursivity, the settler colony acquires a political agenda which demonstrates its reaction against an imperial homogenizing tendency. How this happens, in Slemon's subtle argument, is clearly based upon a 'complicity' theory of post-colonialism. Though Slemon does not make it explicit, in the complicity theory, the literature of settler colonies, which did not have to go through a prolonged independence struggle, still has post-colonial tendencies embedded within it. In the age of the post-modern, the settler colonies' counter-discursive energy can now speak with greater assurance.

Like the authors of *Empire Writes Back*, Slemon is at pains to avoid the collapse of the post-colonial and the post-modern. He must, therefore, insist upon the political strategy of post-colonialism, and argue that all post-colonial literatures demonstrate the recuperative work going on in marginalized societies. But it is salutary that the argument is developed not through, say Patrick White's *A Fringe of Leaves* but through Salman Rushdie's *Midnight's Children.* For post-modernism, Rushdie's questioning of historical certainties is exemplary of its own project; for the post-colonial what is important is the way in which another, lost master-narrative recalled through the creative power of *maya*, of illusion, is used to free the colonized. The narrative energy of Rushdie is to be found in the magical narratives of *The Mahabharata* and the *Kathasaritasagara*. Whereas a post-modern reading of *Midnight's Children* would emphasize play and deferral, a fully post-colonial reading will locate the meaning of the untranslated words and the special, culture-specific resonances of the text. It might even offer a radical reshaping or rethinking of what Habermas has called our 'communicative rationality'. The post-colonial text persuades us to think through logical categories which may be quite alien to our own. For a text to suggest even as much is to start the long overdue process of dismantling classical orientalism.

Other theories such as feminism which are also predicted upon some definition of oppression find points of contact with post-colonialism. Significant terms used by the authors of *Empire Writes Back* such as 'other', 'subversion', 'marginalized' and 'linguistic difference' are all replicated in feminist discourses. But the analogy also gives rise to a problem within post-colonial women's writing which would require a different order of theorizing since post-colonial women are like a fragment, an oppositional system, within an overall colonized framework. Women, therefore, function here as burdened by a twice-disabling discourse: the disabling master discourse of colonialism is then redirected against women in an exact duplication of the colonizer's own use of that discourse vis-à-vis the colonized in the first instance. One finds a reaction against this twice-disabling discourse even in the context of someone who writes essentially, within the *riti* ('love') and *bhakti* ('devotional') poetics of India. In Mahadevi Varma's *Chhayavad* poetry, the metaphysical domains of both *riti* and *bhakti* are replaced by a search for an ennobling humanism, the discriminatory desire of a woman herself as she seeks fulfilment in love. Into the hegemonic world of traditional Sanskrit genres and discourses, Mahadevi Varma inserts the female body, its sensations and its self-identity as woman. In the 1920s and 1930s, Mahadevi Varma, as a woman, was grasping the nettle of a poetics which had produced the great patriarchal figure of Nanak and Tulsidas.

The homogenizing drive of *Empire Writes Back* leads it to seek to establish a dominant field and not a set of heterogeneous 'moments' arising from very different historical processes. It is especially important to recognize the different histories of the white-settler colonies which, as fragments of the metropolitan centre, were treated very differently by Britain, which, in turn, for these settler colonies, was not the imperial centre but the Mother country. What an undifferentiated concept of post-colonialism overlooks are the very radical differences in response and the unbridgeable chasms that existed between white and non-white colonies. At the heart of the oppositional post-colonial are three fundamental principles—principles which are as much points of difference between white-settler colonies and the rest—which may be summarized as racism, a second language, and political struggle. For the category of the post-colonial to work in any other fashion, it must become a 'complicit post-colonialism' and therefore effectively postmodern. It is the uneasy manner in which these three principles may be discussed with reference to the settler colonies which explains the pan-textualist bias within an otherwise mutually exclusive pluralist enterprise. Thus where subversion, for instance, is emphasized, this is done in largely non-political and non-racial terms. In short, subversion becomes a kind of an anti-language (the authors call it an inter-language) which largely defines the post-colonial experience. What is worrying is that the category of subversion applies without change to literary tendencies within the canon itself (Donne, Sterne, Mary Shelley, etc.) rather than specifying those material conditions which give rise to post-colonial differences.

This is close to Naipaul's own position as a writer. Words and their usage, their alien tradition stood between him and his experience, and as Dennis Lee says: "The language was drenched with our non-belonging and words had become the enemy" (Dennis Lee, 400). In this context, it is important to see Naipaul's concentration on the viability or the lack of cultural identity and the 'centered' forces which in his works are the symbols of power, of literary, cultural or political domination. It would be apt to close with the words of Edward Said, related to the discussion in the present chapter:

> ...one cannot postpone discussions of slavery, colonialism, racism in any serious investigation of modern Indian, African, Latin and North American, Arabic, Caribbean and Commonwealth literature. Nor is it intellectually responsible to discuss them without referring to their embattled circumstances either in post-colonial societies or as marginalized and/or subjects confined to secondary spots in the curricula in metropolitan centres.... The notion of black skin in a white mask is no more serviceable and dignified in literary study than it is in politics. Emulation and mimicry do not get one very far. (Edward Said, 383-84)

Works Cited

Amis, Martin, "More Bones", *Review of The Return of Eva Peron with the Killings n Trinidad, New Statesman*, 4 July 1980.

Bhabha, Homi K. "Signs Taken for Wonders" in *The Location of Culture* (London and New York: Routledge, 1994).

Fanon, Frantz, *The Wretched of the Earth*, 1965; rpt. (Harmondsworth: Penguin, 1967).

Foucault, Michel, *Discipline and Punish*, 1975; trans. A. Sheridan (New York: Pantheon, 1977).

Garebian, Keith, "V.S. Naipaul's Negative sense of Place", *Journal of Commonwealth Literature,* 10/1.

Goodheart, Eugene, "V.S. Naipaul's Mandarin Sensibility", *Partisan Review,* 50:2, 1983.

Gussow, Mel, "The Writer Without Roots", *New York Times Magazine,* 26 December 1976.

Hamner, Robert D. (ed.), *Critical Perspectives on V.S. Naipaul* (London: Heinemann, 1979).

——— (ed.), *Critical Perspectives on V.S. Naipaul.*

Hughes, Peter, *V.S. Naipaul* (Contemporary Writers) London and New York: Routlege, 1988).

Jelinek, Hena Maes, "The Myth of El Dorado in the Caribbean Novel," *The Journal of Commonwealth Literature,* VI/1, June 1971.

Lee, Dennis, "Writing in Colonial Space" in Bill Ashcroft, Gareth Griffiths and Helen Tiffin (eds.), *The Post-colonial Studies Reader* (London and New York: Routledge, 1995).

Mustafa, Fawzia, *V.S. Naipaul* (Cambridge: Cambridge University Press, 1995).

Naipaul, V.S., *India: A Million Mutinies Now* (London: Minerva, Mandarin Paper Backs, 1990).

———, *The Enigma of Arrival* (Harmondsworth: Penguins, 1987).

———, *The Middle Passage* (New York: Macmillan, 1963).

———, "Conrad's Darkness", *New York Review of Books,* 17 October 1974.

———, *The Overcrowded Barraccoon* (London: Andre Deutsch, 1972).

———, "The Regional Barrier", *Times Literary Supplement,* 15 August 1958 (V.S. Naipaul, xxxvii).

———, "Words on Their Own", *Times Literary Supplement,* 4 June 1964.

"Naipaul: Excerpts from an Autobiography", *Gentleman Magazine,* February 1984.

Nixon, Hamner, *London Calling: V.S. Naipaul Postcolonial Mandarin* (New York: Oxford University Press, 1992).

Rouse, Ewart, "An interview with V.S. Naipaul", *Trinidad Guardian,* 28 November 1968

Said, Edward, *Culture and Imperialism,* 1993; rpt. (London: Vintage, 1994).

Sartre, Jean Paul, "Preface" to Frantz Fanon's *The Wretched of the Earth* (Harmondsworth: Penguin, 1967).

Shankar, Israel, *Words and Their Masters* (New York: Doubleday, 1974).

Slemon, Stephen, "Reading for Resistance in Post-Colonial Literature", *Critical Quarterly,* XI, Vol. 5, 1999.

Spivak, Gayatri, *The Post-colonial Critic; Interviews Strategies, Dialogues* (London and New York: Routledge, 1990).

Tiffin, Helen, "Lie Back and Think of England: Post-Colonial Literature and the Academy", in Jelinek, Peterson and Rutherford (eds.), *A Shaping of Connections* (Dangaroo Press, 1989).

Walsh, William, *V.S. Naipaul* (London: Oliver and Boyd, 1973).

Young, J.C., *Colonial Desire: Hybridity in Theory, Culture and Race* (London: Routledge, 1995).

Chapter 2

Colonial Mimicry as Subterfuge

When it comes to depicting the colonized world in English literature, the tradition that begins with Joseph Conrad, Rudyard Kipling, E.M. Forster, and George Orwell, perhaps definitely leads to another great dissector of this world—V.S. Naipaul. Though Naipaul is certainly not the first to write about the outposts of the British Empire, yet he is quite different in several ways from others. Conrad, Kipling, Forster and Orwell were Europeans surveying the colonial cultures from the outside, but Naipaul does not try to analyze the psyche of the British-colonial minority cultures from the fringes. The effects of colonial transplantation resulting in rootlessness are a living and central experience for him. He is not primarily concerned with the historical encounter with the Europeans, as he deals in his works with a much later stage of colonialism. Writing a counter-discourse of colonialism, he sees, as stated earlier, the wretchedness and persistence of colonialism in the era of political independence, and depicts what Frantz Fanon has termed "false de-colonization" which means legal independence without breaking down the colonial, political and social structures. He has brought colonial literature in English to a new phase marked by a sense of deprivation, marginality and the trauma of self-contempt. He also visualizes the colonized man living in a culture entirely derived from that of the colonizer.

Many writers from the ex-colonies (most prominently the African and Caribbean writers) have penetratingly and explicitly explored the theme of the individual's predicament in the form of rootlessness and crisis of identity, together with the colonized man's dependence on and slavery to Western and predominantly white cultural, social and other value systems. The ex-colonial peoples have had to face the problem of cross-cultural or multi-cultural adjustments. The characteristic problem facing the Western artist in modern life, is, as T.S. Eliot termed it, 'dissociation of sensibility'—the crisis of belief, the fragmentation of a culture's collective mythology. With roots in the splintering of Christianity, the rise of rational philosophy, the forced colonial system, the spread of Western imperialism, the rise of technology, this 'dissociation' of sensibility, so to speak, now extends far beyond the European continent. For the artist in the West Indies, the dislocation includes physical displacement as well as philosophical discord. Edward Brathwaite, one of the best known Barbadian poets, describes the predicament in these words:

> the most significant feature of West Indian life and imagination since Emancipation has been its sense of rootlessness, of not belonging to the landscape; dissociation, in fact, of art from the act of living. (Edward Brathwaite, 29)

Even cultures that remain rooted to their landscape are vulnerable. O.R. Dathorne notes in *The Black Mind* that "the African writer experiences the exact same predicament—the break-up of his world, the crumbling of an entire sensibility" (O.R. Dathorne, 453). Most African writers have retained the language of European colonizers but have insisted on Africanizing its rhythms and imagery, foreshadowing a need to return to the traditional collective mythologies for guidance and structure in contemporary life.

In the West Indies, however, the Middle Passage left an estranging sea and several centuries between the artist and the collective mythology of his ancestors. Yet, some West Indians believe that the link can be re-forged; for Edward Brathwaite, the solution lay in a rediscovery of original (African or Amerindian) roots. Derek Walcott, the celebrated St. Lucian poet, however, denies the possibility that African collective mythologies can fire the West Indian sensibility, for, as he feels, the relationship of West Indian artists to African mythologies is radically different.

At any rate, whatever the difference between writers and poets to resolve a historico-cultural dilemma, the root of the uncertainty of a West Indian experience collectively, lies in its disorienting phases within colonial history. Cutting short the well-known details of enslavement, decimation of Amerindians, Caribs and Arawaks, massacre and inter-continental migration of peoples, the history of the region carries the burden of a profound erasure, which haunts one's memory but with little help to think in terms of a unified cultural base. Caribbean history, which has presided over the writers' and poets' 'dissociation of sensibility', has become the prime subject in contemporary debates about its structuration; the European 'manufacture' of its populations, social structures, political organizations and its ethnic mixture. From the Spanish conquest in the seventeenth century, to the piracy of the Spanish Main by the British, French and Dutch that led to Northern European colonization of most of the region, the plantocracy of the sugar economy, the consequent Atlantic slave trade, and finally, the indenture system following Emancipation—the patterns contain the discursive Caribbean realm and the multiplicity of concerns. In a situation as diffused and complicated, the writer finds his vision obstructed, and his form uneven, given the contested accounts of history presided over by hegemonic European discourses as 'official' history on the one hand, and the new 'creolized' or the populist unofficial narratives, on the other. Fawzia Mustafa has rightly opined: "the polyglot composition of the region has given rise to the extraordinary series of taxonomic problems" (Fawzia Mustafa, 31). This refers to the problem of nomenclature, that has figured for long as to who is to be addressed as a 'West Indian'. Another minor problem is related to the use of the words 'East Indian', used for long to classify people in the Caribbean against 'West Indian', people who originated from the Indian subcontinent.

V.S. Naipaul's early experiences of the transplanted East Indian community in Trinidad, in all its historical, social and religio-cultural specificity left a deep imprint on his mind and attitude. Even today he is not comfortable with those early memories of the amorphous, mixed world in which the East Indian segment occupied an uneasy space due to its highly conservative Indian religious background, its spoken languages and cultural values due to which it remained insulated and misfit in the Caribbean mixed creole world. At best, it remained, at least till the 1950s or early 1960s, in the Trinidadian (and the larger Caribbean population) society a cross section on the fringes, unable to adjust to the growing inter-racial demands. However, at this time, the possibility of growth, maturity and awareness was nearly impossible, because of the general lack of easy opportunities in terms of education, Western knowledge and the idea of life overseas. As such, the constricted world Naipaul portrayed in his early fiction suffered a lack of real despair and disillusionment, which foreshadows the sense of failure, ennui and the imprisonment of the human spirit in his later works. Much of Naipaul's early fiction reproduces the complicity and acquiescence of characters in their colonial destiny; they rarely seek to launch a rebellion, or attempt to move away to another, better opportunity to look at the world alternately. Also absent from his early fiction in a relative sense, is the adversarial relationship between his characters and society; the grim stoicism of Mr. Biswas, or the colonial debasement confessed by Ralph Singh in *The Mimic Men*. The marginality or the peripheral, colonized, poverty-ridden, limited state of the characters' lives in *Miguel Street, The Mystic Masseur* and *The Suffrage of Elvira* is a product of their past and present, but the superficial, hallow gaiety and carnivalesque pattern of their social behaviour precludes despair or atonement. Indeed, if anything, the author provides them little room for a mature insight into anything worth value, such is the comedy of acceptance that is fictionalized through the daily routines, political fraud, or the trickster-like journey of political and social advancement of people like Ganesh. There is difference in degrees though in the three early works, of projection of marginal human status; *Miguel Street* draws together the diverse racial elements of Trinidadian society to underline the collective fate borne out of isolation, lack of initiative and poverty; *The Mystic Masseur* is 'certainly' more 'Indian' in its character, highlighting the characteristic capacity of the clever Ganesh to thrive economically and politically in the absence of any moral or ethical norm; *The Suffrage of Elvira* again exposes the mixed Trinidad world in which lack of order and discipline breed rampant corruption and moral irresponsibility.

It can thus be seen clearly that as a Third World writer, Naipaul in his aesthetic and literary moorings essentially belongs to Caribbean world, and not to London, which is a place improvised by him for work and repose. In other words, while London serves as a metaphor for retreat and flight, the Caribbean homelands serve as a metaphor for disenchantment and inverted nostalgia. London is nothing more than a neutral place which sustains and enhances his distant vision of the islands. It is impossible to come across a character or a situation in Naipaul, which is not in some way linked with the Caribbean ethos from one perspective or another. Even English characters tend to become instruments to enhance and sharpen the writer's vision of his society and its larger background.

Having the same subject matter, more or less at his disposal, Naipaul represents two polarities in literary technique and individual belief. It is now a fact acknowledged by the leading critics of Caribbean literature, including William Walsh, Kenneth Ramchand, Louis James and Paul Theroux, to mention a few. Coming from an East Indian Brahmin community of Uttar Pradesh, Naipaul has passed through many phases of personal disillusionments and doubts. Having studied in England, where he has a permanent home, Naipaul cannot shed his negative sense of belonging to a half-made post-colonial society. Though he had once declared in an article that he had achieved a "Buddhist ideal of non-attachment" living in London as a colonial, yet it is also accompanied by what he calls the "lack of representation" in today's world. In a similar way, his own alienation from London is accompanied by his failure to find a secure place in the English literary tradition. As he observed in an interview:

> It took me a long time to see that I had no society to write about. I had to write differently. I had to look at the world afresh. If you are trained by your reading and inclination to see the novel as one particular thing and if when you look at what you have, your material, and you are aware only of its shallowness and its disorder, it's very hard to know how to move on from that. (V.S. Naipaul, 42)

His awareness of belonging to an island, which is a "dot" on the world map has removed him from the mainstream of world literature in the sense that a writer cannot escape the images and symbols of his own experience. It is difficult for a writer like Naipaul to be sure about his audience in one country or the other. The problem lies in introducing heroes and settings from another society, another culture. This seems to be his dilemma as an expatriate writer, though now that he is being understood more clearly, his themes transcend one or the other country, and have become symbolic of the essential human condition.

In Naipaul's view, migration and geo-cultural transplantation emerged as the very condition of the existence of ex-colonial, mixed societies. In his works, he deals with the predicament of the twentieth-century man, torn between varied pulls, cultural, political and national compulsions on the one hand, and the huge and powerful presence of Western influence, on the other. The Western cultural, intellectual and moral standards have always posed a source of fascination for the ex-colonial man. This has been one of the dubious legacies of colonialism, which taught the marginalized and degraded ex-colonial self-hatred and native derision.

Apart from his own culturally and historically alienated and exiled status as a writer, Naipaul's works show a world on the fringes of marginality and denial. Dereliction and decadence which is a part of the total destiny of nearly all the Third World societies, is the most prevalent motif in his works. His keen political observation is a result of the destructive influences like colonialism, oppression, racism and cultural-economic discrimination, which have disfigured the meanings of contemporary history and rootedness.

Naipaul sees colonialism as a system and experience which has turned nations, societies, political systems and individuals into mimic societies and mimic men of the West, who are living a life without vision and hope. The syndrome of oppressor-oppressed, inclusion-exclusion, and that of the colonizer-colonized is something which is closely related to Naipaul's vision of history as it influences the present situation of man. He portrays the philosophical idea of marginality and under-development, and has acutely and pointedly traced the distortions and stigmas of the erstwhile colonies, left to decay and struggle with their dubious fate in the post-modern world. It is perhaps right to say that Naipaul's works constitute the colonial impact on the present-day societies, irrespective of their location and history. Colonial experience of men and societies alike, emerges as a powerful metaphor in Naipaul's rendering of the complex experience of man vis-á-vis power, authority and oppressions of all types.

At this point, it is relevant to highlight some of the contemporary critical/theoretical positions about the function of mimicry in texts dealing with colonial and post-colonial experience. One of the ideas that germinated from colonial enterprise and the formation of the Empire was the mimicry of the 'Centre' proceeding from a desire not only to be accepted but to be adopted and absorbed. It caused those from the periphery to immerse themselves in the others' culture, denying their origins in an attempt to become 'more English than English'. Edward Said has described authoritatively in *Orientalism* how the operations of colonial discourses work through institutionalized systems of power, and the asymmetrical, distorted representations of the 'other'.

On the other hand, the 'ambivalence' of colonial discourses has also been stressed, most notably by Homi K. Bhabha (Homi K. Bhabha, Ref. Ch. 4, 85-91). Basing his views on psychoanalysis, Bhabha argues that colonialism is informed by a series of assumptions which aim to legitimize its view of other lands and peoples, justifying conquest and its system of administration. Hence, the emergence of colonial stereotypes that represent colonized peoples in various derogatory ways. However, the departure that marks Bhabha's view is that *this* aim is never fully met. This is so because the discourse of colonialism is always pulling in two contrary directions at once. On the one hand, the 'colonized subject', the 'other', is thought outside Western culture and civilization; on the other, the discourse of colonialism attempts to domesticate the colonial subjects to abolish their radical 'otherness' by bringing them inside Western understanding by constructing a knowledge about them. Hence, in Bhabha's terms, colonialism itself exists in both distancing and absorbing these stereotypes its legitimacy. In his well-known essay "Of Mimicry and Man: The Ambivalence of Colonial Discourse" Bhabha explores how the ambivalence of the colonized subject becomes a threat to the authority through the effect of mimicry. Bhabha describes mimicry as "one of the most elusive and effective strategies of colonial power and knowledge" (p. 85). Citing the example of India, he argues how the colonized Indians, mimic men, required to run the British administration, threatened to become instrumental in discoloring the ambivalence of colonial operations and strategies. Bhabha goes on to say that mimicry resides between a tension, as "counter-pressure of the diachrony of history that effects, or seeks to effect change, difference: Colonial mimicry is the desire for a reformed recognizable other as a subject of a difference that is almost the same, but not quite" (p. 86). Mimicry, then, in Bhabha's thinking, is a source of anti-colonial resistance in that it presents a challenge to the entire structure of the discourse of colonialism. The colonized, by speaking English and acting out the colonizer's cultural values attempt to challenge the representations which attempt to fix and define them. Significantly, Bhabha refers to Naipaul's fictional heroes in the line of descent of the mimic man along with Kipling, Forster and Orwell. But Bhabha rejects Naipaul's (through Ralph Singh's 'parody' of history) attempts to authenticate experience through mimicry as only partial act of representation lacking the active, positive and insurgent model of mimicry. However, it must be recognized that the 'plantocracy' variety of colonialism in the Caribbean was different in character and design as compared to India. Secondly, the plurality of races and cultures helped colonial strategies to keep the colonized people apart, thus precluding a unified protest or attack. Literacy and education for the colonial Trinidadian was a way to overcome the backwardness and illiteracy, to promote himself to a 'higher culture', something that has been seen by the Afro-Caribbean writers as a sign of paralysis in its fixated portrayal by Naipaul. Naipaul's own view of the mimicry of the colonized is fairly clear; he presents mimicry as a sign of cultural and intellectual inferiority, and there is little room in it as a sign of 'spectacular resistance' Bhabha would believe as a political function of mimicry.

Naipaul inherited a legacy of multi-racialism and multi-culturalism; he was born in Trinidad with its mixed population of French, British, Portuguese, African, Chinese and Indians. Writing about the social and cultural limitations of the West Indian situation he says in *The Middle Passage* (1962) that "history is built around achievement and creation, and nothing was created in the West Indies" (V.S. Naipaul, 58). He depicts the backwardness, vulnerability, cultural powerlessness and the farcical nature of the Trinidad society and its standards. The West Indian man's predicament of living in a multi-cultural and multi-racial context has its roots in the history of colonization. Naipaul has also depicted the cultural life of the psychically imprisoned West Indian who has always lived at the margin of any success and a sense of achievement. He sums up the West Indian's condition in *The Middle Passage* thus:

> Living in a borrowed culture, the West Indian, more than most, needs writers to tell him who he is and where he stands. (V.S. Naipaul, 60)

We see the vast range of Naipaul's 'versions' of colonial experience in his novels from *The Mystic Masseur*, *The Suffrage of Elvira*, *Miguel Street*, *A House for Mr Biswas*, *The Mimic Men*, *In a Free State*, *Guerrillas*, *A Bend in the River*, *The Enigma of Arrival*, and in his later work, *A Way in the World*. All these works are primarily based on the idea of failure, marginality and loss of vision. Naipaul has a fugitive, post-Enlightenment sensibility with a keen eye to dissect the complex problems, the stunted histories, fragmented cultures, fractured societies, and existentially and spiritually meaningless lives in 'dark' places on the face of the globe. In his major fiction, he portrays individuals who are marginalized on the basis of race, economic and cultural subordination, gender, class, nationality or colour, which are understandable in terms of intersecting dialectics of slavery and the impact of colonization.

Naipaul depicts the nature of the experience of societies which were colonial outposts, used as mere tools for material gains through sugarcane estates, and then left unanchored to decay as the colonial tide turned eastwards, especially towards India in the early nineteenth century. The negro's 'Middle Passage', between

Africa and the New World sums up his predicament, where he was left to decay without a sense of place and roots. The indentured Indian labour, brought under a cheating contract and abandoned on an alien and hostile land, also faced the same destiny of neglect and ennui. Men suspended hopelessly between the act of living and the reality of dereliction in strange environs in this way, is a recurrent motif in Naipaul's fiction. In his early novels, he presents the fate and unreal existence of the characters, and the portraiture of their existence in squalor, poverty and illiteracy while they look for some source of sustenance and continuity. He also portrays the inability of the Indian community to overcome their backwardness, lack of vision inherited from a deterministic, orthodox and fatalistic view of experience generated by Hinduism, and more particularly, by Brahminical ways and beliefs because of their ignorance of history and tradition. These people hang on, blindly imitating the pseudo-Western standards like their West Indian counterparts and others (the African, the Chinese and the Portuguese). Together, they all are one in acquiring an artificial identity. Naipaul's description of the derelict world of *Miguel Street* in all its limitations and lack of self-awareness in an example of it:

> A stranger could drive through Miguel Street and just say, 'slum'! because he could see no more. But we who lived there, saw our street as a world, where everybody was quite different from everybody else. Man-man was mad; George was stupid; Big foot was a bully; Hat was an adventurer; Popo was a philosopher, and Morgan was our comedian. (V.S. Naipaul, 79)

This is the world beset with disorder, squalor and absurdity—an inheritance from the loss of natural springs of culture, identity, religion and history.

Naipaul has used fiction not only as a way chronicling life but also as an instrument of analysis and justification of the reality that human beings in a colonial situation have to confront. We also note the collision of cultures and the resultant ambiguities in human adjustments, and the colonial situation which produces a particular type of human psychosis in his fiction. David Ormerod points out that "all Naipaul's work constitutes an intense involvement with the intolerable psychological tensions created by a degrading environment" (David Ormerod, 175). The mixture of pathos and comedy in *Miguel Street* conveys the overall sense of failure in the fragmented and inorganic world of tricksters, cranks and eccentrics. The sense of deprivation, the mimicry and fakery in the lives of his characters is communicated by carefully relating them with the inseparable customs and eccentricities which make them look fully engrossed in their process of life in a society which fails to offer them any logical pattern, cultural tradition or homogeneity. An individual in a colonial set up—'mimic man'—looks down upon his community and aspires to achieve the glitter of colonial culture. In this collective habit of automatic mimicry, a number of competing sub-cultures are involved, and the colonial individual cultivates an ambivalent personality in trying to escape from his sense of dependence.

Though Naipaul left Trinidad for a life of voluntary exile in England, he returns again and again in his art to the place of his birth and his experiences there. He knew Trinidad intimately and felt an urge to escape its sterility, but he transmuted that sterility into the stuff of fiction in successive works. The first three novels—*The Miguel Street*, *The Mystic Masseur* and *The Suffrage of Elvira*—make up a trilogy based on his concrete knowledge of Trinidad, its local colour, dialect and its inhabitants.

Unlike his later fiction, which is peopled with characters from all races and set in distant places, *Miguel Street*, *The Mystic Masseur* and *The Suffrage of Elvira* depict characters and events in an island situation. The hero is not yet an outsider. He has not explored the possibilities beyond the seas. He finds his native environment listless and sterile but harbours the hope that a change in locale may make life more attractive. His insular existence leads him to believe that the quality of life overseas must be better than that provided by his own native surroundings. But his cloistered island life has also spared him the disillusionment Naipaul protagonists experience in books that follow. Despair, therefore, is less intense in these novels of the late fifties than in later ones, where the hope of a more rewarding life in a distant land disappears completely. At least on the surface, the three early novels sparkle with life and gaiety. The sense of insularity conveyed in these three novels gives them a special place in Naipaul's writing because they generate a semblance of hope and their main characters achieve some success within their island society, but they become only more diminished in the process of their blind mimicry.

In the early novels, migration is a necessary process for those who seek escape from the debilitating environs of Trinidad. The narrator in *Miguel Street* procures a scholarship to study in England; Ganesh in *The Mystic Masseur* becomes G. Ramsay Muir; and "Pat" Harbans in the *The Suffrage of Elvira* manages to extricate himself from the madness of Elviran politics by leaving with a curse on his lips: "Elvira, you is a bitch." The cultural bankruptcy which accompanies success is inevitable in a society where no real synthesis is possible. The effects of the resultant mimicry and displacement are at the heart of these three novels.

"Despite his labeling them apprentice pieces" (V.S. Naipaul, 11), Naipaul's first three books—*Miguel Street*, *The Mystic Masseur* and *The Suffrage of Elvira*—establish the dominant themes and techniques of his later fiction. One of the factors that makes *Miguel Street* and its two successors distinct in the English novelistic tradition, however, is Naipaul's variations upon the theme of role-playing, or what he calls "mimicry," a motif that attains perfection in *A House for Mr Biswas*, *The Mimic Men* and *A Bend in the River*.

Colonial Trinidad, Naipaul declares in *The Middle Passage* (1962), is as a nation "unimportant, uncreative, cynical," its inhabitants having substituted "intrigue" for "talent", their world consequently "corrupted by a fantasy which is their cross" (V.S. Naipaul, 69). Intrigues and fantasists, Naipaul's "mimic men" populate *Miguel Street*, a collection of seventeen sketches: the "romancer" poet manqué B. Wordsworth and the "pyrotechnicist" Morgan escape harsh reality through make-believe; the "badjohn" bigamist Bogart and Big Foot the boxer play their roles as petty criminals because their neighbours admire those who bring recognition, however notorious, to the street; and the confidence men or "sharp characters", Hat the gambler and Man-man the mad Messiah, pretend to be other than themselves and become folk heroes because they possess "wit and style", even to those who fall prey to their chicanery" (V.S. Naipaul, 72).

Miguel Street is in essence the young Naipaul's tribute to the Trinidad he left in 1950, its tone accepting and nostalgic. Although cognizant of the harmful effects of mimicry, Naipaul appreciates its historical inevitability and its value as a skill of survival. He views imposture and fraud as outgrowths of a picaroon society that evolved as a result of slavery and colonialism and even finds the majority of his characters who indulge in mimicry sympathetic because they have no other choice. Modern Trinidad, Naipaul suggests, is much like sixteenth-century Spain:

> ...an ugly world, a jungle, where the picaroon hero starved unless he stole, was beaten almost to death when found out, and had therefore to get his blows first whenever possible; where the weak were humiliated; where the powerful never appeared and were beyond reach; where no one was allowed any dignity and everyone had to impose himself; an uncreative society, where war was the only profession. (V.S. Naipaul, 73)

"Imposing" themselves in sundry ways, some less admirable than others, Naipaul's mimics are for the most part charming, witty, and imaginative, displaying originality amid their mimicry. The Miguel Street denizens maintain their idiosyncrasies of character and lend the savor of their inimitable selves to the plot and action of the work in which they appear. It is those idiosyncrasies, personified in a gallery of memorable characters, that make, for example, comparison to such figures in Dickens and Thackeray inevitable.

Of all the clearly identifiable tonalities that characterize Naipaul's first novel, *Miguel Street*, none are so essential to the book's total effect as closely linked ones of wretchedness, frustration, and yearning to escape. There is no story in the collection in which these tonalities are not of central importance. For example, the carefully chosen word, in the apparently simple paragraph that begins the first story, "Bogart," projects most of the major feelings throughout *Miguel Street*:

> Every morning when he got up. Hat would sit on the banister of his back verandah and shout across, "What

> happening there, Bogart?" Bogart would turn in his bed and mumble softly, so that no one heard, "what happening there, Hat?" It was something of mystery why he was called Bogart.... I don't know if you remember the year the film "Casablanca" was made. That was the year when Bogart's fame spread like fire through Port of Spain and hundreds of young men began adopting the hardboiled Bogartian attitude. Before they called him Bogart they called him Patience, because he played that game from morning till night. Yet he never liked cards. (V.S. Naipaul, 9)

The direct, colloquial, and declarative sentences suggest the dull routine of life in *Miguel Street*, where two young men spend every morning idling in bed, and one of them passes most of his time playing patience for want of anything else to do. The name Bogart, in association with the film *Casablanca*, evokes a distant world of "hard-boiled" action and romance. Yet, ironically, the namesake of Humphrey Bogart in this story plays patience from morning till night even though he does not like cards. The contrast between the exotic characters and the languid life of the street makes the reality of Miguel Street even more poignant.

The shattered dreams and destroyed lives make the narrator realize that life in *Miguel Street* is governed by defeat, ignorance, cruelty and aborted dreams. For those few who attempt to get away from the squalid life, their efforts remain in the realm of imagination, never to become a reality. The characters trapped in the street indulge in flights of fancy by identifying with people from faraway places, as we have seen with Bogart and *Casablanca*, but there is no real struggle to break away from the sterile life in *Miguel Street*. "Life is a helluva thing", says Hat, "you see trouble coming and you can't do a damn thing to prevent it coming. You just got to sit and watch and wait" (V.S. Naipaul, 116).

Naipaul, with the packaging of sardonic humour and sharp wit was able to look at the mixed, transient and unlikely world of Trinidad with a degree of compassion in *Miguel Street*. There was already enough material for fantasy and caricature for him to invent; his struggle to write himself into the remembered world of the Caribbean required more than anything else, the exile's total recall. The playing off of history, calypso and fiction, are all part of the comic fantasy of the stories in *Miguel Street*. Through them Naipaul realizes the echoes that one could hear through the carnivalesque Calypso culture. Since calypso is central to the writing of *Miguel Street*, 'Love, Love, Love alone,' 'The Maternal Instinct', 'Man-man', 'Titus Hoyt', 'Bogart' are variants on ways one lives in the wretchedness of limited, powerless life, a wry expression of paralysis. But calypso is also a form of escape, fantasy and the overcoming of the futility of all endeavour. The macho-image likewise that Naipaul talks about, is converted in *Miguel Street* to the pretence of manliness; Bogart's running away from his wives and in reverse, Popo running to his wife to become popular. But Popo's dependence on a woman and his unpopularity results in his heavy drinking and belligerence, his stealing and his imprisonment.

Throughout *Miguel Street* Naipaul is employing allusions, particularly to calypsos of the 1930s and 1940s, which, taken together, help to point the centrality of themes. In *The Middle Passage*, Naipaul comments explicitly on the importance of Calypso to the Trinidadian:

> It is only in the calypso that the Trinidadian touches reality. The calypso is a purely local form. No song composed outside Trinidad is a calypso. The calypso deals with local incidents, local attitudes, and it does so in a local language. The pure calypso, the best calypso, is incomprehensible to the outsider. (V.S. Naipaul, 70)

The same attitude is ingrained in *Miguel Street* where no less than ten calypsos are quoted. In two instances, 'Love, Love, Love Alone' and 'Until the Soldiers Came', the debt is acknowledged in titles which are drawn from the lyrics of particular calypsos. Elsewhere the allusions, sometimes the prerogative of the narrator and sometimes voiced by characters within the stories, function as incidental counterpoint to situations being described. Usually the effect of such allusions is ironic, as when Eddoes's girlfriend delivers to him the baby whose father he is supposed to be and Boyee whistles the calypso:

Chinese children calling me Daddy !
I Black like jet.
My wife like tar-baby.
And still—
Chinese children calling me Daddy!
Oh God, somebody putting milk in my coffee.

(V.S. Naipaul, 57-58)

Most of the calypsos are of this order and provide ironic comment on aspects of the society, especially the man-woman relationship. Indeed Naipaul's portrayal of the world of Miguel Street at times comes very close to the calypsonian's own often extremely ironic view of the society. Ultimately, however, he goes beyond the *macho* ethic implicit in most calypsonias' treatment of the battle of the sexes and subtly reveals what he sees as the reality underlying such attitudes. So the calypso tradition furnishes the most significant body of allusions in *Miguel Street*. Naipaul's use of such allusions has the effect of relating the work to the culture of Trinidad's urban black populace, a group he would never again depict with the same degree of sympathy. As an art form of the people calypso, then, represents an opposite pole to the metropolitan culture and, on one level, *Miguel Street* explores this cultural divide. It is most clearly reflected in the story 'B. Wordsworth' in which the protagonist sees himself as a spiritual brother of his English namesake:

What your name, mister?

B. Wordsworth.

B. for Bill?

Black. Black Wordsworth. White Wordsworth was my brother. We share one heart. I can watch a small flower like the morning glory and cry.

(V.S. Naipaul, 127)

However, B. Wordsworth's image of himself as a Trinidadian 'Wordsworth' represents only half the truth about him. He attempts to sell his poems, a practice in which, the narrator tells him, only calypsonians engage, and it transpires that he is in fact a part-time calypsonian during the season. Like the vast majority of the two to three hundred aspirants who annually compete for the title of Calypso Monarch, he finds it impossible to make a living from singing calypsoes during the rest of the year and so dispenses with this role and dons that of Romantic poet. Both roles, Naipaul implies, are variants on the same idea; both fail to bring him any real self-fulfilment.

B. Wordsworth is less a victim of his metropolitan fantasy than are certain other characters in the street. These who aspire to the chimera of a metropolitan goal are invariably disappointed. In 'His Chosen Calling' Elias sits the Cambridge School Certificate exam on three occasions with scant success and the narrator comments: "We felt it wasn't fair making a boy like Elias do litritcher and poultry" (Landeg White, 41). The attempt of Titus Hoyt, 'I.A.', a kind of adult equivalent of Elias, to bring 'litritcher and poultry' to the boys of the street by forming the 'Miguel Street Literary and Social Youth Club' proves equally abortive. His Latin lessons give the boys the feeling that one man sit down one day and make all this up and have everybody else learning it. They can see little more sense in the historical outing to Fort George which he organizes, an episode which serves to dramatize one of the central themes of Naipaul's work: the colonial's alienation from involvement in history, which leads him to feel that his actions are of no real importance.

The most extreme metropolitan fantasy is, however, acted out by Man-man, who assumes the role of hell-fire preacher and shows himself to have a Christ complex when he 'stages' his own crucifixion. The ingenuous boy narrator introduces Man-man by saying:

> Everybody in *Miguel Street* said that Man-man was mad, and so they left him alone. But I am not sure now that he was mad, and I can think of many people much madder than Man-man ever was.

What follows leaves the reader in little doubt that there is method in Man-man's madness. After his well-trained dog 'sullies' clothes left out on lines overnight, their owners have no further use for the sheets and shirts thus dirtied; they give them to Man-man and he sells them. It is the dog's death which leads to his turning over a new leaf and becoming a preacher. In this role, he claims to be in direct contact with God and to have been granted an apocalyptic vision of the reality inherent in the politicians' promise of self-sufficiency for the island:

> .... You know what God tell me last night? Last night self, just after I finish eating? God say, "Man-man, come and have a look at these people." He show me husband eating wife and wife eating husband. He show me father eating son and mother eating daughter. He show me brother eating sister and sister eating brother.

For Naipaul this is not simply an expression of fanaticism: it is also a veiled statement of the situation in the dog-eat-dog society, a society which is lacking in moral norms, with the resultant effect that the trickster comes to usurp the place of the hero. Man-man's trickery reaches a logical extreme when he dons the mantle of spiritual guide. However, he oversteps himself in staging his own crucifixion and inviting onlookers to stone him. Bits of sand and gravel quickly give way to longer stones and he protests loudly before being taken away and, eventually, committed to a lunatic asylum. Like B. Wordsworth, Elias and Titus Hoyt, Man-man is a casualty of the society in which, as Naipaul sees it, success is a virtual impossibility. The narrator is the only person in the end who is saved by being sent abroad for a metropolitan education; ultimately, this is the only way to success for those born in a climate of failure and in an insensitive society.

The characters of *Miguel Street* typify the vacancy and waste in the years when the middle class was vying for importance in the newly emerging social circumstances. The peripheral figures in this work are those without education and power, whose predicament and wilderness is shaped by the colonial situation and its psychological consequences. With a language barrier and illiteracy, they are cut off from the Creole-speaking majority, without a hope of promotion into the ranks of the elite. The seediness of life contrasted with metropolitan fantasy is itself a clue to their colonial mimicry in the absence of any other outlet. The imposture and fraud, the skill of surviving, which are central to *The Mystic Masseur* and *The Suffrage of Elvira*, nevertheless have their germ in *Miguel Street*, these being the inevitable outgrowths of a stunted, colonized society.

Towards the end of the book, the narrator refuses to sit and watch and wait. His ability to see through the surface sparkles in *Miguel Street* makes his disillusionment absolute. He is the first one of Naipaul protagonists to question life and feel that one can do something to avoid becoming a victim of one's surroundings. This is what really sets him apart from the other characters who embark on their imaginary flights only to return to the "safety" of Miguel Street. He alone finds the escape which every other person in the street dreams of. In this the narrator joins the Ohio village boy, George Willard, in *Winesburg, Ohio*. In the last story, "Sophistication", the author comments on Willard:

> If he be an imaginative boy, a door is turn open and for the first time he looks out upon the world, seeing, as though they marched in procession before him, the countless figures of men who before his time have come out of nothingness into the world, lived their lives and again disappeared into nothingness. (Anderson Sherwood, 295)

But the narrator in *Miguel Street* and George Willard extricate themselves from the "nothingness" that surrounds them.

On the surface, the protagonist in *Miguel Street* achieves his goal. Still, the freedom he gains remains only physical. He merely leaves one island to set off for another. In this he differs vastly from George Willard, who, as he prepares to leave Winesburg, also achieves the maturity to accept loneliness as the essential human condition. Naipaul stresses the point that freedom at the expense of spiritual integrity is ultimately limiting and confusing. According to Alfred Kazin, "Naipaul's great subject is the old imperialism, the leftovers that that make up his world. The past is never dead, said Faulkner; it is not even past" (Alfred Kazin, 22).

The narrator's disillusionment with life in *Miguel Street*, though it comes late, nevertheless completes the process of his 'education' and his ability to see through the vacuity of superficial gaiety. After Hat disappears from the street in the story with the same title and is punished for his trickery and his false exhibition of manliness, the narrator is able to sustain the older view about the street. However, after Hat emerges from prison three years later, the narrator is eighteen, 'a big man'. During this period, the narrator has matured to a point where he is able to see through the presence of men of *Miguel Street*; he no longer wants to be like any of those men. Ironically enough, the narrator, as a result of frustration that he inherits, takes to heavy drinking and womanizing, largely because the destitute, marginal society fails to offer any real alternatives. By saying that no one can do anything here except drink, he sums up the inner emptiness and despair of people in general behind the veneer of calypsonian gaiety and moral irresponsibility. Naipaul's portrayal of the confusion of values as a product of colonial situation is quite different from literary parallels attributed to it. John Thieme is right to comment that *Miguel Street* comes closest to Joyce's *Dubliners* in its social context:

> Like Joyce's *Dubliners*, the residents of Miguel Street are victims of their own psychological make-up, conditioned as a result of living in a colonial society which offers them virtually no opportunities for self-fulfilment. (John Thieme, 31)

The feeling of despair is nevertheless less intense in the first three novels set in Trinidad. Although despair and desolation exist within the confines of the island, the hero, an island character who has not yet explored the opportunities beyond the seas, has thus far been spared disillusionment. There is even a small sense of achievement, though at a price.

Almost all Naipaul heroes are margianlized, exploited and corrupted colonials. Their desires, whether of power, literacy, success, home, emigration or riches are generated by their status of being rootless exiles and cultural orphans. The atmosphere of caprice, trickery, opportunism, imposture, coupled with cultural dependence accounts not only for Trinidad's charm but also for its frequent sense of suffocating enclosure in the early novels. Here Naipaul seems to have fully grasped and creatively realized the deepest hurts of a backward, wayward society. Whether it is Mr. Biswas's predicament of finding security, Ralph Singh's quest for order or Mr. Stone's will to fight the oncoming emptiness, in each case the impulse is to seek refuge, a removal from the constricting, suffocating air of imprisonment and non-fulfilment.

A.C. Derrick in his essay, "Naipaul's Technique as a Novelist" points out:

> Repeatedly he shows the frustration of energy and ambition. Success is the reward of trickery, vulgar materialism, self-delusion, or the values of the 'colonial', 'monkey-game', for the individual rebellion or non-acquiescence proves a largely futile exercise. (A.C. Derrick, 194)

It is mostly the irony of this futility in which all the Naipaulian heroes are trapped.

In most of Naipaul's novels, the common thematic strand is the satiric demonstrations of individuals and their social limitations. Mimicry or role-playing is an important theme and he handles it with unusual complexity, to delineate three sides of it—human, cultural and socio-political. In *The Mystic Masseur* and *The Suffrage of Elvira*, he views imposture and fraud as outgrowths of a picaroon, nomadic society that evolved as a result of cultural transplantation, slavery and colonialism.

In *The Mystic Masseur*, Naipaul depicts a society in which the individual is forced to use subterfuge if he is to survive. The novel enlarges the world of crookedness, role-playing and mimicry, and Ganesh, the mystic masseur-turned colonial statesman, the petty trickster transformed into a corrupt politician, has become the supreme mimic man. He takes the meaningless appendage (M.B.E.) so seriously, suggesting a naive delight in cheap glamour. Thus, his whole career and fame are the result of highly laboured and well thought-out exercise in mimicry, sycophancy and clever role-playing. Ganesh's life and career serve as a gloss on the con-manship and imitativeness characteristic of ex-colonial countries, and the whole novel serves to allegorize the 'history of our times'. The whole setting in *The Mystic Masseur* emphasizes the alienation of Trinidadians from their surroundings. The images of decay, decrepitude and dereliction suggest a breakdown of their identities and the consequent tendency for artificial behaviour and mimicry.

The effects of the resultant mimicry and displacement which are at the heart of *The Mystic Masseur*, *The Suffrage of Elvira* and *Miguel Street* are summed up comically as also pathetically in the scene of the dinner party at the government house in *The Mystic Masseur*. Guests arrive wearing dinner jackets, jodhpuries, a khaki suit, and a sun helmet, and Ganesh himself is arrayed in 'dhoti', 'koortah' and turban. Mr. Primrose, the blackest M.L.C., turns up in a blue shirt and yellow gloves. He gets aggressive racially when during dinner his monocle falls into his soup. This scene stresses, above all, the conditions and surroundings responsible for the lack of harmony in a colonial society. The culturally bastardized society described in the government house is only another aspect of the mimic colonial world that absorbs the interest of the author. The colonial man has little choice but to follow his society and the standards it has set for him.

The strictly stratified colonial society permits little intermingling between the classes. The achievers, even if they come from the masses, are forced to sever their ties with the people in order to maintain their newly acquired status. They cannot afford to look back. Naipaul states:

> The chaotic social divisions also help. Each of the island's many cliques believes that it is the true elite; the expatriates believe they are the elite; so do the local whites, the businessmen, the professional men, the higher civil servants, the politicians, the sportsmen. This arrangement, whereby most people don't even know when they are being excluded, leaves every one reasonably happy. (V.S. Naipaul, 78-79)

Ganesh, "Pat" Harbans and the narrator in *Miguel Street* are very much a part of this clamorous grab for social status and respectability. As soon as they achieve their goals, they completely disregard the people at whose expense they had achieved the position. The colonial value system that gives these men their new identity also forces them to sever links with their culture and community. But as their newly acquired identity provides only a facade of change, even the very successful end up as victims of their own success. Naipaul's first three novels are in a way a prelude to a cultural isolation, a subject he gets involved with much more deeply in successive works.

Ganesh Ramsumair, the hero of *The Mystic Masseur* embodies all the contraries of a colonial village society. His rise from masseur to mystic masseur, to radical politician, to colonial "yes man" epitomizes the slavish colonial mentality that produces the compulsive mimic men that Naipaul so abhors. Hence, the 'spirit' of Ganesh dominates Naipaul's early works where he sets out to expose the follies and the limits of life in a remote colonial culture. He appears twice in *Miguel Street*, once in the story "Man-man" when he sets the trend for "seeing God", and in the final story where the narrator's mother bribes him into giving her son a scholarship to study in England. He is also mentioned in *The Suffrage of Elvira* as Trinidad's 'greatest' mystic. Trinidad is the perfect setting for Ganesh to emerge from a fraudulent mystic to the hero of his people. Ganesh's questionable rise to the echelons of power and political importance pre-empts the post-colonial facet of nationalism in the Caribbean, an instrument through which the author satirizes the national political process. Following Fanon's warning in *The Wretched of the Earth* on the pitfalls of national consciousness, it has become a subject of deep disillusionment, the way Third World societies have mismanaged their national affairs following independence of nation states. What *The Mystic Masseur*, and *The Suffrage of Elvira* make evident is that these participants in politics and electioneering are already schooled in a long tradition of 'brokering' for personal gains. The careful documentation of the personal gain that the major figures of both novels enjoy is a measure of the corrupt practices they engage in while participating in public, civil services. Naipaul's use of satire to look at the characteristic class and ethnic divisions of Trinidad, even while the process of 'decolonization' was under way, explains some of the contentious issues raised in relation to his irresponsible irony and 'castrated satire'. In *The Middle Passage*, Naipaul remarks:

> Corruption, not unexpected, aroused only amusement and even mild approval: Trinidad has always admired the 'sharp character' who, like the sixteenth century picaroon of Spanish literature, survives and triumphs by his wits in a place where it is felt that all eminence is arrived at by crookedness. (V.S. Naipaul, 72)

The place where Ganesh operates, therefore, has a lot to do with the way he operates. He is both affected and revealed by the setting in which he finds himself. The remote village of Fuente Grove is the stage on which the advancement of Ganesh's career takes place. In order to point out how meticulously Naipaul maps out the setting, a couple of detailed passages describing Fuente Grove and its inhabitants deserve mention here:

> Fuente Grove—Fountain Grove—seemed a curious name. There was no hint of fountain anywhere, no hint even of water. For miles around the land was flat, treeless, and hot. You drove through miles of sugar-cane; then the sugar-cane stopped abruptly to make room for Fuente Grove. It was a sad little village, just a dozen or so thatched huts strung out on the edge of the narrow, bumpy road. (V.S. Naipaul, 9)

The very name Fuente Grove for such a place suggests a euphemism, a deception, a conglomeration of cultures and a haphazard mix of colonial past and its present. As deception is the main ingredient for success in Trinidad society, and particularly in Ganesh's own career, Fuente Grove provides a perfect background for Ganesh's activities. It obviously does not take Ganesh long to establish himself as a leader among these poor and ignorant East-Indian villagers. From this base Ganesh eventually turns to the colonial masters for recognition of his 'talents' as a leader of his people.

The author's disapproval of Ganesh's mimicry of colonial values is voiced subtly by the narrator in *The Mystic Masseur*. The narrator in this book is a mature young man and a student at an English university, much like the author himself. His voice is that of a reminiscing adult, as we can see from his observation of the ceremony related to the death of Ganesh's father:

> Ganesh had remembered applying the caste marks on the old man's forehead, and doing many more things until it seemed that ritual had replaced grief. (V.S. Naipaul, 26)

This personal reminiscence by the narrator reveals his keen awareness of a mimetic world where the religion and philosophy of India have been replaced by a series of empty, meaningless rites. Though Ganesh is never portrayed directly as an imposter, the narrator's ironic tone clearly makes him out to be one. The narrator's last meeting with Ganesh in the Epilogue highlights his desertion of all principles and his identity for a minor imperial title. The Epilogue makes Ganesh's transformation to a colonial puppet, his surrender to cultural bastardization, complete. Dressed in a khaki topee and a khaki suit, he might have been a little "Sahib" in his native village, but in Port of Spain he was the object of constant derision among his fellow students. As he grows more respectable, he is embarrassed to use the Trinidadian dialect. He tells his wife:

> Leela is high time we realise that we living in British country and I think we should not be shame to talk the people language good. (V.S. Naipaul, 71)

Linked with this aspect of Ganesh's desperate attempts to communicate in the 'Master's' language, is also the question of literacy in colonial Trinidad. In post-colonial theorizing, the textual control of metropolitan language is related to indegenize and appropriate the contested 'site' of the textual meaning. In other words, the wresting of meaning and power through language becomes an important strategy for cultural representation. It must be admitted that *The Mystic Masseur* is not a serious work that seeks to destabilize the Western colonial authority by subverting or wresting power and control through appropriating the linguistic authority and superior cultural values. On the other hand, the novel ironically presents the hero's amusing drive to transcend his limited and backward community which is hopelessly trapped in a disadvantageous situation, being peripheral or marginalized in the context of the more progressive world outside. In a way, Ganesh gains 'authority' and a 'textual' significance through his publications to enhance his political career. Fawzia Mustafa states in this context:

> The inflation of the significance of Ganesh's writings, therefore, is the first gesture of the novel's pleasure in playing with the idea of "literacy" and the conflations and subterfuges that characterize the multilingual aspect of Trinidadian cultural polygenesis. (Fawzia Mustafa, 46)

What is both interesting and significant is the way Naipaul allots a 'role' to Ganesh, the namesake of the Hindu God of learning, to emulate his own heritage, but also the need to attain success by elbowing one's way through the place's competing cultural legacies—of Hinduism, colonial education, English commerce—that conflate and exchange themselves in the course of Ganesh's successful creolization of his politics. The glossings and cross-references of linguistic turns, between Hindu texts and standard English allow Naipaul to equip Ganesh with the art of misleading the populace to misread the significance of his 'books', confusing quantity with quality. Ganesh, with his library and learning creates an awe by referring to them (as Leela does) as "big books, six or seven inches altogether" (p. 15). Thus, Ganesh's trickster—like success is almost wholly founded on a confused notion of his progressive self and 'modernity'. In effect, the chronicle of his success as a flawed and a misguided achievement within a political and social milieu centrestages itself because of the society's lack of reading into Ganesh's 'manufactured scholarship' and intellectual prowess—both products of his unscrupulous drive to capitalize on the vacuum that so overwhelms his environment. What, however, must also be remembered (as many authors and critics such as George Lamming, Derek Walcott, Caryl Phillips, Gordon Rohlehr, Amon Saba Saakana and others have noted) that the process of Naipaul's own anglicization through his migration, education and writing, is dialogically related to the figures he creates. Ganesh Ramsumair's transmutation into G. Ramsay Muir does suggest that his career marks the character's voyage to 'whiteness', as a sign of colonialism's power as the predetermined end of all its cultural identity formations for which there is hardly an alternative way except mimicry.

Ganesh continues his efforts to master the language that he feels might bring him status in a colonial society but on the other hand, these changes in his personality and appearance bring his loss of stature among his own people. In the final analysis he is more in bondage at the end of the novel than he was at the beginning as a poor masseur in a small village. "The history of Ganesh", the narrator tells us, "is in a way the history of our times", hinting at the hyperbolic intention behind the otherwise pathetic story of a hollow man. The cultural and human poverty of Ganesh is transferred into a collective one affecting a whole society and its standards of judgement.

Ganesh, Behary, Chander Shekhar and Narayan anglicize their names as a concession and gratitude to their English rulers. The names of places too, reveal the fictionalizing tendency of Trinidadians. Queen's Royal College in Port of Spain is a mere secondary school that imports a Victorian educational system ill-suited to the needs of an emergent nation that succeeds only in fostering in the students a need to mimic the English values. The whole setting in *The Mystic Masseur* emphasizes the alienation of Trinidadians from their surroundings.

Apart from the several categorizations into which Ganesh can be fitted or absorbed—the role of the picaroon, rogue and the hero in search of material success—he can be more fruitfully understood in terms of the island's cultural milieu, bequeathed to it by the damaging colonial situation. For one, Naipaul effectively explores the complex contours of the Caribbean mixed world in general where politics were gaining recognition around the 1950s, whatever their nature and level. More specifically, the East-Indian placement in this world (Trinidad) has been problematic in terms of its failure to enter the competitive mixed, and black society in a state of transition. It is interesting to conjecture how Mr. Biswas, modelled on Naipaul's late father, is only partially and tragically able to make some mark on this world. The reason for this is not far to seek: colonial-mimic society, a product of the vagaries of change and damages of history, is unable to recover from its dubious limitations and legacies, and hence, can scarcely see the difference between genuine talent and struggle, and the falsity and trickery practiced by the likes of Ganesh. Hence, the mock-heroic dimension of Ganesh's ladder-success story fits into Naipaul's observation of a tattered, amorphous Trinidad world whose 'heroes' would emerge from cricket, or through political intrigues meant to mimic metropolitan authority. Significantly, the only difference between Ganesh, and Ralph Singh, whom he anticipates, lies in Singh's coming to a state of realization of the taint, the deep disorder one carries as a psychic burden *en route* the road to metropolitan mimicry.

The Suffrage of Elvira dramatizes the period of transition from colonial rule to self-government. The turbulence of this period is the consequence of the loss of colonial order with nothing to replace it except borrowed forms and concepts which are manipulated by personalities motivated by the historical fear of non-existence. Trinidadians have retained a confused racial and cultural memory but no political memory whatsoever. The novel is set in rural Trinidad with Port of Spain providing the stepping stone to the metropolis which is London. London, as the capital of material and cultural success, provides the distinct signals which guide the subconscious and conscious thinking of Naipaul's characters. The chaos of multi-ethnic society is presented through the conglomeration of religions and festivals in the novel:

> Things were crazily mixed-up in Elvira. Everybody, Hindus, Muslims and Christians, owned a Bible; the Hindus and Muslims looking on it, if anything, with great awe. Hindus and Muslims celebrated Christmas and Easter. The Spaniards and some of the Negroes celebrated the Hindu festival of lights. Someone had told them that Lakshmi, the goddess of property, was being honoured, they placed small earthen lamps on their money boxes and waited, as they said, for money to breed. Everybody celebrated the Muslim festival of Hosein.

Naipaul in *The Suffrage of Elvira* also presents a queer world, one that is the dubious recipient of 'democracy', but it knows nothing about it except the picaroon delight in festivities. It is a place where things, ancient and modern, intellectual and illiterate, scientific and superstitious, religion and immorality are mixed up to unleash all the elements of entertainment, slapstick comedy and farce. In the words of William Walsh:

> Religion, rum, family jealousies, Obeah, the care of the sick and the spotting of the morbund, together with a generous sprinkling of modern devices, loudspeaker vans, car cavalcades, the sugar of dollars, when brewed together

> transform the bleakness of democracy into 'the election bacchanal'. (William Walsh, 9)

A newly born concept, democracy, alien to people riven by considerations of race and class, then, provides Naipaul with a subject that aptly demonstrates the Trinidadian penchant for imitation. Eric Williams underlines the very concept of mimicry that Naipaul conceptualizes, in describing the West Indian 'dependence' upon other countries as models of democratic action:

> Political forms and social institutions were imitated rather than created, borrowed rather than relevant, reflecting the forms existing in the particular metropolitan country from which they were derived. (Eric Wiliams, 501)

The Surface of Elvira is a dramatic account of the political 'awakening' of the village of Elvira—remote and unconnected. Its knowledge of the outside world is limited to the comings and goings of the two American girls, Jehovah's witnesses, or the frankly money-making activities of Mr. Surajpat Harbans, P.W.D. contractor as well as proprietor of the transport company which transports the road-building materials. It is during the election compaign that it realizes the value of printing press as a medium of communication and coercion. The literal personality of this village is established and summed up by the narrator in the Prologue and the Epilogue: Elvira is "the smallest, most isolated and most neglected of the nine counties of Trinidad" (V.S. Naipaul, 9). It has not changed significantly as a consequence of the elections:

> So, Harbans won the election and the insurance company lost a Jaguar. Chittranjan lost a son-in-law and Dhaniram lost a daughter-in-law. Elvira lost Lorkhoor and Lorkhoor won a reputation. Elvira lost Mr. Cuffy. And Preacher lost his deposit. (V.S. Naipaul, 207)

The Suffrage of Elvira delineates a place that has lived out its days of glory. On the surface Elvira seems a charming place, where everything is unpredictable, where moral lapses are harmless, and where the different cultures merge to form a special community. But beneath the apparent show of harmony amidst complexities, Elvira recognizes only the value of money and power. Elvira, like Miguel Street, has a public personality. Its striking feature is the cohesiveness of its inhabitants despite the conflicts of race, religion and personal interests. They live very much in the present propelled by immediate needs. They can put aside their differences to unite in the demand for cases of whiskey for the whole community or for a religious thanksgiving ceremony for the victory of Harbans. They can recognize justice when they see it and can speak as one voice in their claim for fair play. Those who want to get away are few—Lorkhoor, Dulahin, Teacher Francis, Nelly—but they have no goals, just a feeling of being deprived by staying on in Elvira. Harbans and Chittranjan are the truly trapped. Harbans has invested so much money to win this election that he cannot escape Elvira even though he privately disowns it. He feels less welcome than Tiger, the mongrel pup, among those who courted him before the elections. The fact of his mobility and residence in Port of Spain, providing an immediate escape from Elvira, diminishes his existential despair at his heavy losses:

> Harbans was talking to the back of his hands: "New symbol, eh? New slogan. New posters. What sin I do to get myself in this big big mess in my old old age?" (V.S. Naipaul, 146)

With the Prologue we are back in the picaroon society where the "smart-man" triumphs, yet not quite back in the world of *The Mystic Masseur*. Most of the "possibilities" centre on the local people's financial exploitation of Surajpat Harbans, the candidate from Port of Spain, who comes to Elvira to buy himself a seat. The price, as Harbans discovers, is high; for despite the banner of election and democracy, what really matters in Elvira is money. Not only do Baksh and Chittranjan, the leaders of the Muslim and Hindu communities, have to be bribed into a temporary alliance against the Negro candidate, Harbans discovers that he has to pay for every vote in Elvira. The formula of *The Mystic Masseur* has been reversed: Ganesh is the trickster, whereas Harbans, though no more exemplary a character than Ganesh, is tricked. Unlike Ganesh, who was aided in his rise to fame by a generous dose of good luck, Harbans meets his match in the likes of Baksh and Chittranjan in Elvira. But as soon as he wins his seat, Harbans reneges on every promise he made, specially to Baksh and Chittranjan. In *The Mystic Masseur*, Ganesh exchanges his constituency for the title of *Member of British Empire* and anglicizes his name to G. Ramsay Muir. In *The Suffrage of Elvira*, as Robert Morris observes:

> Surajpat Harbans' shakey course to the legislative council carcems through the comic intrigue, boon doggling and logrolling attending democracy's rise in Trinidad and its first general election. "Pat" totally sells and in order to win the seat, in winning, disowns all those factions that helped him—Hindu, Moslam, black—surrendering honesty, innocence, and wander to the fascination for the power that transports him from Trinidad's backward counties to Port of Spain. (Robert K. Morris, 14)

For Harbans and Ganesh politics has meant success of a kind which had absorbed their sense of failure. Ganesh as M.B.E. can forget his political defeat by Indar Singh. Harbans is only temporarily non-plussed. He can still look forward to financial gains which will banish the pain of his losses.

What sets Harbans apart from the group with whom he is working closely and whose interests he seeks to represent in the government is his greater imaginative self-involvement so that the external contexts of politics and money became indexes to individuality. He has more money than he knows what to do with, yet money is his motive for entering politics. Money being a concrete reality, unable to expand like a metaphor, Harbans is the loser of what he prizes most and for which he is courted by the villagers.

The ironic/satiric tone of the narrator makes him an indirect participant, an observer in the drama of Elvira. He speaks like an insider become an outsider. He dramatizes the chronological sequence of events of the period preceding the elections and reserves his comments for the epilogue and prologue. He shows the development of democracy in a vacuum which makes a mimicry of the whole concept of community and individual responsibility. The minimum terms of survival are economic-material self-interest rather than any platform of political action which activates the various alliances. These alliances change partners as rapidly as in a country dance, guided by the desire of extracting as much benefit from Harbans as is possible: medical welfare, burial expenses, free drinks at Cuffy's Wake and to celebrate victory, vans, loudspeakers, marriage alliances and business deals. The other factor which stresses their literal existence and guides their votes is their preconceived notions: the fear of magic and Obeah in the shape of the unsuspecting Tiger as the sign of evil things to come. The presence of Tiger releases similar older memories of dreams and signs in other residents of the village and altogether helps to build up the prevailing sinister atmosphere intensified by the sudden death of Cuffy and the disappearance of Dulahin, so that, for the older generation, democracy and the gift of the vote becomes a symptom of bad times.

The younger generation is as entrapped as their elders but they are aware of it and hate it and wish to get away from it. As individuals they might escape their physical and economic deprivation, but the lack of educational opportunities or the mimic nature of those available has entrapped them in repetitive patterns of behaviour, though the elections have brought the promise of a wider world. Foam summarizes the younger generation's greater awareness of political reality as a process of maturation:

> "You shy, Mr. Harbans", Foam said, "I know how it is. But you going to get use to this waving. Ten to one, before this election over, we going to see you waving and shouting to everybody, even to people who ain't going to vote for you". Harbans shook his head sadly. Foam settled into the angle of the seat and the door. "Way I see it is this. In Trinidad this democracy is a brand new thing. We is still creeping. We is a creeping nation", Foam dropped his voice solemnly: "I respect people like you, you know, Mr. Harbans, doing this thing for the first time."
>
> (V.S. Naipaul, 25)

The thrust of the theme of colonial mimicry in *The Mystic Masseur* and *The Suffrage of Elvira* has to do with an instinct for survival and a false identity while remaining within the system. The phenomena of European literacy and its colonial extensions have provided Naipaul a vast ground to explore the fractures in the colonized man's experience. The operations of mimicry in these first few novels have to be seen in relation to 'exploitative' colonization. Ganesh and the politicians of his ilk make the best of the damned and the amorphous little world in which an honest reciprocity is an impossibility; the only way for them with their inner knowledge of the society and its powerlessness is to put to use their duplicity in order to succeed. But, bereft of conscience or guilt and lacking vision, Naipaul's early protagonists fail to see through their colonized state. Their complicity and material ambitions make them a part of the dereliction that colonialism and its exploitative machinery has situated them in.

The Suffrage of Elvira is perhaps a sharp and unsparing indictment of the roguery, cheating and mimicry which is an inseparable part of the Trinidadian character. Harbans's 'political journey' suggests that the newly acquired role or identity is only a facade, and even the most successful end up as victims of their own success. Like the characters of *The Mystic Masseur*, several characters in *The Suffrage of Elvira* too Westernize their names, revealing an obvious propensity for mimicry. Democracy marks the obvious display of the Trinidadian mimicry and the novel symbolically portrays the losses and gains of the Trinidadians in their early flirtations with democracy. Harbans and Ganesh being colonial politicians, automatically take on a role assigned by the colonial legacy or system. Their personal loss, measured against the mimicked concepts of success explains Trinidad's continuing dependence and unimportance—the results of the pervasive Euro-colonial hangover.

Works Cited

Bhabha, Homi K., *The Location of Culture* (London: Routledge, 1994).

Brathwaite, Edward, "Timehri" in *Is Massa Dead?* (ed.), Irde Coombs (Garden City, New York: Anchor Press, 1974).

Dathorne, O.R., *The Black Mind* (Minneapolis: University of Minnesota Press, 1974).

Derrick, A.C., "Naipaul's Technique as a Novelist", in *Critical Perspectives on V.S. Naipaul* (ed.), Robert D. Hamner.

Ian Hamilton in Interview with V.S. Naipaul, *Critical Perspectives on V.S. Naipaul*, ed. Robert, D. Hamner (Washington: Three Continents Press, 1977).

Kazin, A.C., "V.S. Naipaul: Novelist as Thinker", *New York Times Book Review*, 1 May 1977.

Morris, Robert K., *Paradoxes of Order: Some Perspectives on the Fiction of V.S. Naipaul* (Columbia: University of Missouri Press, 1975).

Mustafa, Fawzia, *V.S. Naipaul* (Cambridge: Cambridge University Press, 1955).

Naipaul, V.S., *Miguel Street* (London: Andre Deutsch, 1959).

———, "Speaking of Writing", *The Times* (London), 2 January 1964.

———, *The Middle Passage* (1962; rpt. Harmondsworth: Penguin Books Ltd., 1969).

———, *The Mystic Masseur* (London: Andre Deutsch, 1957).

———, *The Suffrage of Elvira* (London: Andre Deutsch, 1958).

Ormerod, David, "In a Derelict Land: The Novels of V.S. Naipaul," in *Critical Perspectives on V.S. Naipaul*, ed. Robert D. Hamner.

Sherwood, Anderson, *Winesburg, Ohio: A Group of Tales of Ohio Small-Town Life* (New York: Modern Library, 1947).

Thieme, John, *The Web of Tradition: Uses of Allusion in V.S. Naipaul's Fiction* (Hansib Dangaroo, 1987).

Walsh, William, *V.S. Naipaul* (Edinburgh: Oliver and Boyd, 1973).

White, Landeg, *V.S. Naipaul: A Critical Introduction* (London: Macmillan, 1975).

Wiliams, Eric, *From Columbus to Castro: The History of the Caribbean 1492-1969* (New York: Harper and Row, 1970).

Chapter 3

Marginal Man's Quest for Order

In the foregoing chapter, what becomes clear is that Naipaul was basically using the satiric-comic device in his early work to expose the inadequacies and the malaise that afflict the colonial society. The materiality of colonial social institutions in the economic, political, commercial sense has been geared to maintain a dependent system. The conditions of human existence within such a society are tied to the confines of predetermined and limited opportunities, offering little release from such restrictions and a set of stratifications. *Miguel Street*, for instance, fictionally renders of these less-privileged strata in Trinidad, but it is the characters' domestic lives that illustrate the issue of colonial dependency, or the impossibility of breaking away from its confines. Likewise, the moral decay, the degrading marital and sexual relations, trickery, buffoonery and escape are offshoots of the characters' colonial dependency. Their peripheral existence amidst the otherwise ramshackle lives helps to dig out the roots of dependency through a daily cycle of life. On the other hand, Naipaul expands the domestic scene brilliantly, to project a multi-dimensional view of the colonial scene in all its variety in *A House for Mr Biswas*, perhaps his most politically significant work.

Naipaul's fourth novel, easily one of the finest to be written by a West Indian author and considered by many to be among the best novels in English literature, is *A House for Mr Biswas*. The story of Mohun Biswas captures authentic West Indian life, but beyond that, it transcends provincial boundaries and evokes concepts that are universal in their human implications. The novel has been called an epic and its protagonist an everyman. Biswas's desperate fight to attain his own house, his own piece of earth, is symbolic of man's need to develop an authentic identity.

A House for Mr Biswas culminates the early phase of Naipaul's artistic development. Combined with his use of vivid colour and action is an increased depth of character exposition which anticipates the dark seriousness of his recent work. The mixed nature of Biswas's desire for self-reliance echoes existential absurdity. Stifled by communal pressures, yet afraid of the chaos of an unstructured society, Biswas is in constant state of suspension. His marriage into the Tulsi household provides greater security than he has known before, but in return the family demands strict conformity, and anonymity. More than any of the characters in the previous novels, he strikes out with desperation and foolishness, utilizing his imagination to impose his own sense of personal order on a meaningless, often malevolent surrounding reality. On one level, Biswas shows a courageous, individual struggle; on another his story is allegorical, dramatizing the legacy of colonial paternalism in a post-colonial world. The conclusion is ambivalent. At the time of his death of a heart attack at the age of forty-six, Mr. Biswas is living in his 'own' home, but he is unemployed, his house is a structural disaster, and the mortgage is well beyond any possible means of payment. Dubious as his victory seems, it is still better than an unknown life, and death in the house of the Tulsis. However, the details in the prologue: Mr. Biswas's struggles, his illness, his children's growth, the mortgage of the house, seem to underscore the nature of this claim to inform about the limitations of his sense of achievement. The determinist nature of the plot, that stretches far backwards than Biswas's own life, indicates that his life is already doomed to curtailment. Mohun Biswas's birth rings prophecies of doom for his parents, and so many other ill-omens, including the oedipal allusion to him, which inaugurates, through the funereal image, the macabre impulse behind the theory. Without the father, Biswas is born an orphan, who will turn into the fate of the worst subaltern.

Mr. Biswas's house, which is not acquired until near the end of the book, after three other unsuccessful attempts at building, is the primary symbol of the novel, and represents the hero's furthest success in turning the traditional passivity of his religion and society into some purposive activity. As an almost archetypal symbol, the house would have connotations of stability and permanence, something solid as an achievement in life, and in the context of this novel, it certainly carries these ideas—and others. It represents, also, Mr. Biswas's partially successful attempt to escape the ancient, matriarchal order of his family—here represented by his wife's relations, the Tulsis, and all their dependents into a more Western, private and, frankly bearable state of life. The Tulsis, after all, do themselves have a house; but as it belongs to them, not to him, and is inhabited by a large number of families, it offers no refuge to Mr. Biswas. It is his own house, occupied by his family alone, that is his aim.

While he is struggling to assert his independence, we also see the decline of the Tulsi family, the break-down of their self-sufficiency and family ties, and their absorption into a larger multi-racial community. The novel thus continues Naipaul's interest in the social change of the West Indian society.

Early in his life, Mr. Biswas begins to associate his feeling of personal unreality with the large number of houses, none belonging to him, that he has lived in:

> Suppose, Mr. Biswas thought in the long room, suppose that at one word I could just disappear from this room, what would remain to speak of me? A few clothes, a few books. The shouts and thumps in the hall would continue; the puja would be done; in the morning the Tulsi store would open its doors. He had lived in many houses. And how easy it was to think of those houses without him.... In none of these places was he being missed because in none of these places had he ever been more than a visitor, an upsetter of routine. Was Bipti (his mother) thinking of him in the back trace? But she herself was a derelict. And, even more remote, that house of mud and grass in the swamplands: probably pulled down now and ploughed

> up. Beyond that, a void. There was nothing to speak of him. (V.S. Naipaul, 462)

He lives his whole life, until he buys his own house, in this state of semi-permanency. He is never really at home anywhere, and has no stable relation with anyone until late in his life. He wears himself out finally to death in a grim struggle to find his personal identity.

Here we should understand the basic 'placement' of a man like Mr. Biswas; ordinary, poverty-ridden, resourceless, and caught in a conventional, obscurantist East Indian community in Trinidad. As he grows up amidst some of the most unenviable credentials he is part of, Mr. Biswas becomes a victim of circumstances, private and public, of community and those beyond it which from the beginning produce a feeling of being trapped and dependent. It is against these given odds that he sets out to declare his freedom and individual rebellion. Paradoxically, Mr. Biswas's sense of loneliness and helplessness compounds from one situation to the next, till he enters the Tulsi household and its meshes which completely seem to smother the individual's spirit and inner self. A critic has rightly termed that the Tulsi family presents a large scale of fictional exploration, which among other things explores "the profound consequences attendant upon the community's transition from a quasi-feudal to a capitalist mode of operation" (Fawzia Mustafa, 61). In the same way, Selwyn Cudjoe places this shift (as above) as one of the central tension informing Biswas's role. Cudjoe reads Biswas as an emblem of the "newly emerging social order", signifying Mr. Biswas's assertion of manhood and independence as a passage from the patriarchal order into another" (Selwyn Cudjoe, 54). While on the one hand Mr. Biswas is an outsider, marginalized in the Tulsi household and its shifting neo-colonial operations, he is, on the other, a part of the growing class of individuals in Trinidad (a well-known sociological fact of the Trinidad and the West Indian populace in the pre-fifties) who aspire to education, enterprise, freedom and Western exposure in material terms. Thus, this 'double' alienation of Biswas from the older semi-feudal structure of colonial Trinidad, and the worn out Hindu/Brahminical rites and restraints, contains in itself some central doctrines of capitalism:

the material gain through enterprise and advancement, equality of men and women, and the freedom of choice. But also worth noting is the fact that the colonized mind of Trinidad has hardly struck any balance between democracy and capitalist aspirations; at best the emergent economic and social order (if at all viable) is a form of neo-colonial capitalism in which it is further an appendage of the Western 'paradigm', or more appropriately, a mimicry. There are other simple paradigms too; the movement from the country to the city, from pre-industrial to industrial modes, illiteracy to literacy, innocence to experience, etc.

The tenacious hold on life and the infinite creativity of man and nature underlie the whole story, and in this sphere, Naipaul has full scope for the creation of character and incident with which the book over-flows. The incredible Tulsi family, a whole array of eccentric pundits, settings extending all over Trinidad, a member of the family known as W.C. Tuttle because of the books he reads; they leap from every page, all obviously delighting the author. Yet, the main aim is not lost sight of: the minor tragedy of Mr. Biswas proceeds realistically, and not without humour, amid the luxuriant growth of environment, character and incident. Rob Nixon in his study of Naipaul states that *A House for Mr Biswas* "remains (Naipaul's) most remarkable work. Nothing has equalled the inventiveness and emotional generosity of that homage to his father's misfortunes in the strained circumstances of colonial Trinidad" (Rob Nixon, 3).

It is a tragedy of a man who wears himself out trying to adjust himself to a profound change in his society, and in his personal outlook, who, before he is forty, considers his career closed, and rests his ambition on his children. Mr. Biswas himself achieves little (even the house is jerry-built and only fractionally paid for when he dies), but he leaves his children in a better position to go on into a changing society. He himself is a first-generation casualty of that change. He begins with nothing, and achieves only a little early in the book, he had been taught to recite his multiplication tables beginning 'ought oughts are ought', and this idea (nothing will come of nothing) haunts his life. It is his achievement to make a little (a house), come of nothing. There are two great obstacles Mr. Biswas has to overcome in order to achieve more than 'ought'. The first is to conquer the fatalistic, passive attitude bequeathed from his ancestors; the second is to break away from an oppressively traditional society, itself in the process of decay. The hostility, or, at best, indifference of fate is an idea handed down in Mr. Biswas's family, his maternal grandfather having greeted Mr. Biswas's own birth as another manifestation of it:

> Bipti's father, futile with asthma, propped himself up on his string bed, and said, as he always did on unhappy occasions, 'Fate'. There is nothing we can do about it. (13)

Mr. Biswas's father inherits the idea:

> Though he saved and made himself and his family go without many things, he never ceased to feel that destruction was very nearly upon him. The more he hoarded, the more he felt he had to waste and to lose, and the more careful he became. (18)

A point that assumes significance is the shift from the socio-cultural milieu in which Biswas has grown up, and his entry symbolically to into the urban Port of Spain setting, where he discovers new openings professionally and materially, but which also implies new challenges in the multi-racial, competitive world that the protagonist has to face. However, Mr. Biswas's longings to be free and to find a 'centre' for his creative urges entail some obvious compromises and pitfalls that will ultimately complicate his already none too happy state. Along with some of the changes mentioned above, *A House for Mr Biswas* has to be seen in terms of the hero's fighting the pervasive "chaos around him", finally to move "beyond the chaos and to a new setting" (Nondita Mason, 40), in short, a triumph over his hostile environment. Biswas's state, to say in so many words, has itself been a 'confined' one, first at the hands of his cursed destiny going back to transportation of his ancestors, and indenture, to the ultimate loss of all native geography and contact. On the other hand, the shift occurs in a parallel way in terms of the appropriation of the colonial state into the dependencies of the neo-colonial situation, as he marries and enters into the extended, matriarchally hegemonized world of the Tulsis. Biswas's subordination, his role as a decentered spirit, therefore, carries the double burden of being illustrative of the general historico-social process, as well as of a specific and local situation. Mr. Biswas's early life lived on the edges of the extended family and an insulated East Indian life pattern of rituals and conventions prepares the reader to see the analogy between one stage of colonial administration. On the other hand, Biswas's experience ('Green Vale', 'Chase' episodes) illustrates, beyond the domestic hierarchization and psuedo-colonial 'order', the co-dependency that conditioned the debilitating circumstances of the authoritarian colonial state. Mr. Biswas's so-called 'freedom' acquired through his journalistic career, and the house, also mock the much trumpeted 'postcolonial freedom' with all its dependent facets and self-delusions. Mr. Biswas's life, as such, runs like the tragi-comedy of the modern man, albeit in the Third World, who having tasted the fruits of Western modernity only indirectly, in the end finds himself exhausted by the endless demands of that existence.

Much later in his career, Naipaul returns to the Caribbean setting, framing it through several tropes and motifs in *A Way in the World* (1994). What is interesting is the way Naipaul blends together the autobiographical, historical, socio-cultural, political and literary materials into a unity. And this is done to convey a continuous pattern of experience, personal and impersonal, that has shaped Caribbean society and its discursive cultural forms, along with the writer's own set of responses he has developed *en route* a long 'journey' of meditating over issues. From colonial conquest to personal recollection-history and incident interact with older forms in terms of a collective background. It is the first small section, "An Inheritance" in *A Way in the World* that connects itself with Naipaul's early memories of Trinidad/Port of Spain; how each time he returned, he found that its topography acquired for him a dream—like quality. The immediate context of recalling the significance of these autobiographical pieces (as those in *Finding the Centre*) is that Naipaul had possibly used the same observed memories of his early ancestors in *A House for Mr Biswas* and other early works. Another section, "History: A Smell of Glue Fish" recalls the time when the young man (Naipaul) in-between leaving school and leaving Trinidad, was waiting for a scholarship, a most hopeful time of his life. The striking aspect here is the shifting emphasis given to historical/biographical details of Naipaul's life. On the one hand, there are the English street names, the buildings housing the offices of *Port of Spain Gazette*, *Guardian* and *The Trinidad Guardian*; connecting them with his father Seeparsad's own precarious career as a journalist. Amidst details of the Registrar General's office—another reminder of the colonial phase—it is further surrounded by the famous Woodford Square named after the nineteenth-century English Governor. This coincides with the narrator's earliest visit to the town before the War, when he observed poor, homeless Indians living in open squares, without a home or security. This poignant recollection links it with the fate of figures like Bipti and her father in *A House for Mr Biswas*, who inherit the collective fate of East Indians; the slow dereliction of the unwanted men, betrayed and cheated into a contract of indenture, and further disowned by their immediate communities. This vision, essential to the understanding of their predicament, of which Mr. Biswas is a later recipient, reiterates the destitution of poor East Indians in the black-dominated society, in which they had no place. They could, of course, only lament their 'fate', as Bipti's father does, carrying the burden of Indian religious principle of *Karma*. However, for Naipaul these were memories that hurt, remained enmeshed in his psyche for delineating the idea of 'cruelty' that he saw all around:

> It must have been that I carried in my blood and brain very old Indian ideas about the indifference and arbitrariness of rulers and governments.... Or it might have been that—without any words being spoken—I had grown up thinking of cruelty as something always in the background.... There was the cruelty of the extended-family life; the cruelty of the elementary school; the cruelty of the Indian countryside and the African town. The simplest things around us held memories of cruelty.
>
> .... They were people who had been, as in a fairy story, lifted up from the peasantry of India and set down thousands of miles away—weeks and weeks of sailing—in Trinidad. In the colonial setting of Trinidad, where rights were limited, you could have done anything with these

> people.... We all lived easily with this kind of cruelty. We saw it, but we seldom thought about it. (V.S. Naipaul, 18-19)

Mr. Biswas spends most of his life struggling against these forces, and only holding his own. His struggle with society in the form of the Tulsi family, continues simultaneously, and is never really resolved. The closed, communal life of the traditional Hindu family is remarkably conveyed, and Mr. Biswas's struggle against it, which lapses occasionally into grateful acceptance of its warmth and protection, is shown to us in a combination of incident and symbol. Fights, arguments and reconciliation abound in all the details, as the Tulsi family life is intricately analysed. It is a life based on accepted ritual and feeling:

> ...there was no doubt that this was what Shama (Mr. Biswas's wife) expected from life; to be taken through every stage, to fulfil every function, to have her share of the established emotions: Joy of a birth or marriage, distress during illness and hardship, grief at a death. Life, to be full, had to have this established pattern of sensation. Grief and joy, both equally awaited, were one. For Shama and her sisters and woman like them, ambition, if the word could be used, was a series of negatives: not to be unmarried, not to be childless, not to be an undutiful daughter, sister, wife, mother, widow. (139-40)

This established pattern is decaying, and the disastrous interlude where the family moves to the villa at Shorthills, gradually lets it decay and fall, unproductive as it is, it can no longer support them, and their move back to town symbolises the gradual decay and fall of the family itself. It is not coincidental that the Shorthills interlude ends with the deaths of several of the oldest and most respected members of the family. Death is in the air.

As the Tulsi family decays, Biswas's escape is made easier—though the fact that he and other members of his generation are trying to escape is one cause of its decay. As the larger family ties disappear, so those of Mr. Biswas's own immediate family increase in importance, both to him, and in the structure of the book. His relations with Shama, Anand and Savi are distinctively 'modern' by the end of the book. They treat each other as different, equal human beings, rather than father, husband, wife, children, their traditional relation to each other. By the time of his final illness, even Shama has deserted the old pattern:

> (Mr. Biswas) didn't now care to do anything against his wife's wishes. He had grown to accept her judgement and respect his optimism. He trusted her. Since they had moved to the house, Shama had learned a new loyalty, to him and to their children; away from her mother and sisters she was able to express this without shame,...and to Mr. Biswas this was a triumph almost as big as the acquiring of his own house. (7-8)

Rebellion in Biswas is defined by his state as a cultural, psychological and social orphan. So often his revolt contains a child-like rage and grief at violated innocence, and a child-like need to prove that his suffering is always the fault of someone else. Indeed, he assumes that because he is oppressed, he is therefore innocent. This assumption enables him to justify some of the less pleasant aspects of his revolt; like kicking pregnant Shama in the belly, because he sees each—new child as another Tulsitrap. Biswas is living to an extreme degree anxieties of the uprooted man. His elaborate poses, daydreams, assertion of self and evasion of responsibility, are a result of the cultural, social and psychological nowhereness produced by his position as an untalented second generation Hindu in poverty-stricken colonial Trinidad. He is appropriately an orphan. As an Indian in the Trinidad of the 1930s Biswas is insecure and perhaps needs support of the family or the clan. At no time in the book is he, or any of the Tulsis, able to come to any meaningful compromise with the outside creole world, though he absorbs some of its spirit in his love for repartee and caricature. When he marries into the Tulsi family, he is offered protection, the sort of job which he could scarcely get anywhere else, given his limited talents and lack of drive. Yet he rebels and makes the Tulsis the target of his revolt.

To understand Biswas's rebellion one must understand the social structure of Hanuman House. On closer examination, Hanuman House reveals itself not as a coherent reconstruction of the clan, but as a slave society, erected by Mrs. Tulsi and Seth who need workers to help rebuild their tottering 'empire'. They therefore exploit the homelessness and poverty of their fellow-Hindus, and reconstruct a mockery of the clan which functions only because they have so completely grasped the psychology of a slave system. Like the West Indies, at the micro level, Hanuman House is constructed of a vast number of disparate families, gratuitously brought together by the economic need of a "high-caste" minority. Men are necessary here only as husbands for the Tulsi daughters and labourers on the Tulsi estates. To accept Hanuman House is to acquiesce in one's slavery.

The Tulsi daughters have no choice since they have known no other world. It is only late in the book that education becomes a means of emancipation from Hanuman House, since it places the Indians on par with the creoles as competitors in the wider, aspiring society of Trinidad. But the Tulsi daughters are inalienably bound to the rhythms and rituals of life in Hanuman House—the daily *puja*, the seasonal wedding, the occasional funeral. It gives them relief from the tedium and submissiveness of their daily lives. They vie for crumbs of authority which Mrs. Tulsi allows to filter down to them from time to time. Mrs. Tulsi knows that she must remain at the centre of her daughters' consciousness; they must see her as their sole reason for existence. There is something archetypal in the organization of Hanuman House. Mrs. Tulsi is a powerful Mother-figure, and rules through an understanding of the psychology of both power and slavery. She is constantly demanding to be loved and worshipped, and is very good at staging strategic 'illnesses' in order to inspire feelings of guilt in those who have failed in their worship. She has instituted an elaborate system of rules which make devotion easy for the would-be believer. Biswas, an inveterate enemy of ritual, assents. His deep scepticism preserves him from the necessity of paying the emotional blackmail which Mrs. Tulsi constantly demands. A bad slave, he cannot be brought to feel grateful for his conditions or feel sorry for the trouble he causes.

One notices that Mrs. Tulsi and her daughters only mention the fact that Biswas came to them. They never speak of their efforts to get him to join the system; of the original pressures which they applied to get him to marry Shama. It is important for the smooth running of the system that the impression be maintained that everyone joins Hanuman House of his own free will. What Mrs. Tulsi grasped is the fundamental idea that a slave system must be able to prove and contain all the apparent evidence of its own legitimacy. As Albert Memmi observes, in *The Colonizer and the Colonized*:

> In order for the colonizer to be complete master, it is not enough for him to be so in actual fact, but he must believe in its legitimacy. In order for that legitimacy to be complete it is not enough for the colonized to be a slave, he must also accept this role. (Albert Memmi, p. 65)

Hence, Mrs. Tulsi, good colonizer as she is, justifies her exploitation with the explanation that she is really doing her subjects good. Her argument is the one which ex-colonial peoples most bitterly resent, and also the one which gives them a cause to fight. Biswas "could not reply at once" partly because he suspects that part of what Mrs. Tulsi says is true, and he cannot afford to admit that any good at all can proceed from so iniquitous a system. "Virtues are forced upon us by our impudent crimes", as T.S. Eliot's 'Gerontion' conveys. It is this irony of the colonial process which paralyses Conrad's Marlowe in *Heart of Darkness*, and humiliates Mr. Biswas. He knows at last that he has to forget all arguments of right and wrong, and leave the system once and for all; that too much energy has already been lost in debate and in working out the paradox of the master-slave relationship. The children in Hanuman House are taught to ridicule the non-conformist in much the same way as creolized Negro slaves were used to mock new arrivals from Africa into submission.

The society of Hanuman House differs from this pattern of slavery in degree, but certainly not in kind. It also is pre-individualistic, and that is why Biswas's greatest crime is to have tried to be an individual. When he tries to make a sharp and complete break with Tulsidom, Biswas does go mad. Trinidad laws do not permit the Tulsis to lynch, but they do know how to commit symbolic murder. When Biswas, ignoring the pressures which the Tulsis bring to bear on the aspiring individual, gives his daughter a doll's house, he upsets the entire equilibrium of Hanuman House, and their rejoinder is to tear the doll's house apart:

> None of its parts was whole. Its delicate joints were exposed and useless. Below the torn skin of paint...the hacked and splintered wood was white and raw.... The edge of a wall scrapped against his shoulder, tearing his shirt and tearing the skin below.... (197)

It is Biswas who is being 'torn apart', and this encounter with the full malice of the pre-individualistic world leaves him tired beyond irony, and beyond speech:

> And suddenly his rage had gone. His shouts rang in his head, leaving him startled, ashamed and tired. He could think of nothing to say. (198)

This inner weariness too is a dimension of rebellion, this sudden apprehension of a silence that mocks the rhetoric of protest, and of a malice at the heart of things which paralyses both speech and pre-meditated action. The next stage is a retreat from complexity, a simplification of the issues, and a blind commitment to action. Biswas lacks the strength to take this final step, and gains it only at the end of the book, when after another paralysed silence he decides to leave Hanuman House for good.

Chandra Jayawardena in his *Conflict and Solidarity on a Guianese Plantation* shows how the plantation system by requiring a large unskilled and uneducated labour force leads to an egalitarianism of under-privilege. The result of this is continual social conflict, which is most pronounced whenever anyone through industry, craft or thrift lifts himself a little above the rest of the community. Then complex feuds arise and almost ritual quarrelling in which the slighted party is really appealing to the solidarity of the group to join him in censure of the social climber. Biswas's experience of Hanuman House, then, is a more extreme version of what was still happening in those large segments of West Indian society, where the patterns imposed by a plantation system still retained their strength and form. It is therefore, possible to see his rebellion—grotesque and strange as it is—as a paradigm of the perennial West Indian struggle for a more truly democratic society.

No one can deny the danger of regarding Biswas as a figure representative of the Caribbean predicament. He is so strongly individual, and his limitations so grave. Moreover, if he resembles some of the grotesques of Dickens, he has been created by a writer who has a more contemporary sense of the themes of void, loneliness, meaninglessness and absurdity, so prevalent in modern European literature. Biswas's nowhereness may be something much more universal. Yet, as we have seen, he is representative enough of a local predicament. A man without a past, an orphan wavering between equally dubious cultural alternatives; winning a sort of independence and returning in humiliation to the people he is still forced to fight; turning anxiety into absurdity by using humour as a weapon and an escape; trying to create an identity from the void, and sometimes unknown to himself, exercising and expressing identity in the very act of searching for it.

The book can be interpreted on a metaphysical level, since it questions the basic meaning of personality. An interesting ambivalence emerges from *A House of Mr Biswas*. Firstly, there is the dependence of the individual upon society for his sense of being; whereby society one means not only other people, but a whole concrete world with which the consciousness establishes some deep intimacy, and claims as its own. As soon as Biswas "stepped out of the yard, he returned to nonentity" (p. 195). Outside Tulsi society he is lost. Secondly, there is the necessary rebellion which the individual must make against society and the void which must be confronted. In the void are meaninglessness, nonentity, fear, lunacy and chaos, the storm within and the storm without. It is out of this confrontation that the new personality grows.

In many ways, Biswas is an archetypal figure. He is described as stranger, visitor and wanderer. Weak and frequently absurd, he is recognized in Hanuman House as a buffoon, and the role of fool is one which he at times accepts in humiliation and at others rejects with bitterness. But Biswas the clown is also Biswas the rebel. He is also the artist, and his art is the only aspect that the Tulsis really admire, not realizing that it is an expression of the very personality they detest. Whenever Biswas is attacked by the sense of life as meaningless void, he immediately turns to his paint brushes and tries to create something against the emptiness. Perhaps he himself gives the best definition of his significance. To his bewildered son who asks him, "Who are You?" he replies, "I am just somebody. Nobody at all. I am just a man you know." Biswas is everyman, wavering between identity and non-entity, and claiming his acquaintance with the rest of men.

The book is powerfully symbolic, but it is never crudely or obtrusively so. If Biswas represents all the things he does, it is because he is fully presented as a person whose every quirk and idiosyncrasy we know, in a world whose every sight, sound and smell is recorded with fidelity and precision. Whatever is suggested of the numinous and universal, is conveyed through a fidelity to the concrete and particular. Landscape and life are not treated as isolated, but both conform to the artist's unity of purpose. Description is organically employed to reinforce theme. In the end, nature which, when associated with the Tulsis, takes the form of jungle, nettle and weed surrounding 'The Chase', or "decaying leaves on half-dead trees" surrounding Green Vale, or the landslide at Shorthills manifests itself in the coolness of the laburnum, and the scent of the lily in Mr. Biswas's yard. His house may be dangerously cracked in places, but because it is his own, there is grace in its grotesqueness. In his attempts to build a house we can see his desire to assert his own significance and to establish a small centre of order in a society "that had no rules and patterns" (459).

There were many like Mr. Biswas who may have wanted to build houses, to establish themselves as necessary parts of their world. But the houses that they build reflect the incompleteness of the lives of Mr. Biswas and his generation:

> His way lay along the Country Road and the Eastern Main Road. Both were lined for stretches with houses that were ambitious, incomplete, unpainted, often skeletal, with wooden frames that had grown grey and mildewed while their owners lived in one or two imperfectly enclosed rooms. Though unfinished partitions, patched up with box-boards tin and canvas, the family clothing could be seen hanging on string.... (83)

Mr. Biswas had moved into the incomplete house in Green Vale because "there was his hope that living, in a new house in the new year might bring about a new state of mind" (253). Earlier he had dreamt of what his new house would be, had bought a doll's house as a symbol of his dream, had seen the house destroyed to appease the Tulsi children, and then had watched his vision of his own house degenerate, until, like Anand, he too "didn't care what the house looked like now" (p. 233). The act of moving into the new house in the new year, instead of bringing a new state of mind brought a further awareness of isolation, fear, incompleteness, and futility.

The search for a house is the symbolic expression of a search for order. The house itself reflects Mr. Biswas's mental state at the time of building it. For the mind or life which is incomplete, in Green Vale, there is suggestively an incomplete house. In Shorthills Mr. Biswas's house is built in the forest to reflect his isolation of personality. When he reaches the end of his career he has a house which is made of odd scraps picked up wherever they could be found, in the same way that he has accumulated things and relationships unthinkingly as he has proceeded through life. Finally, when the family moved into the house on Sikkim street, in spite of its eclectic structure they were assured that "their memories [would be] coherent" (p. 523) from this point on. In a society that can offer no unity of religion or culture, the house takes on a function of ritual which the individual needs in order to give significance to his actions.

In *A House for Mr Biswas*, the act of planting or destroying vegetation is symbolic of the acceptance or exploitation of the land. Vegetation also reflects a mental or spiritual state as much as the different types of houses do. Mr. Biswas's feeling of temporariness is reflected in his attitude to plants: "Never ceasing to believe that their stay at 'The Chase' was only temporary, he made no improvement...he had not thought it worthwhile to plant trees that would bear flowers or fruit..." (pp. 167-68). When he is in Green Vale, in a state of mind which verges on madness, he is surrounded by grotesque trees:

> They were tall and straight, and so hung with long, drooping leaves that their trunks were hidden and

> appeared to be branchless. Half the leaves were dead; the others, at the top, were a dead green. It was as if all the trees had, at the same moment, been blighted in luxuriance, and death was spreading at the same pace from all the roots. But death was forever held in check. (185)

Mr. Biswas does not plant anything in Green Vale because he does not wish to claim this nightmare existence, but when he does plant a garden, the act symbolizes his claim of ownership, or at least of acceptance. He was happy living in Port of Spain in Mrs. Tulsi's house: "so used to thinking of the house as his own, and in his new confidence, he made a garden" (312). When the Tulsis came to prepare for Owad's departure they destroyed the garden, and when they left he knew the land was not his:

> Mr. Biswas set about restoring his rose-beds and the lily-pond.... He worked without heart, feeling the emptiness of the house and not knowing how much longer he would be allowed to stay there. (p. 328)

Following his loss of interest in the garden:

> Untended, the rose trees grew straggly and hard. A blight made their stems white and gave them sickly, ill-formed leaves. The buds opened slowly to reveal blanched, tattered blooms covered with minute insects; other insects built bright brown domes on the stems. (340)

And when his stay in the house was nearing an end, Seth drove his trucks over the garden and completely destroyed it, thus destroying Mr. Biswas's claim to the land and his will to live there.

When Mr. Biswas finally settles in his house in Sikkim street, he plants flowers and trees everywhere, and on realizing that he has been cheated out of some land he extends his fence and plants a tree in the extra strip. He has found his home after a life of searching, and by planting flowers and trees he finally lays claim to his portion of the earth. The Tulsis never claim land in this way. They see their home always as temporary, which is reflected in their attitude to vegetation. They destroyed Mr. Biswas's garden in Port of Spain, and at the lush plantation in Shorthills they indulged in an orgy of destruction:

> Waiting, the children stripped the saman tree of its lianas.... Hari cut down the Juli mango tree on the raised bed at the end of the garden and built a small, kennel-like boxboard hut, this was the temple. (362-63)

In short, Tulsis realized that they are not returning to India, and that they must grasp what they can of the wealth of the island before there is none left.

In the widely different setting of his novels, Naipaul is able to suggest a fluid social reality beyond the level at which societies function, which is the ground for human agreement. The obviously different narrators are affected by a similar mood and probe for its causes beyond their apparent sources in the respective contemporary situation to a more fundamental understanding of human responses to existence and non-existence. It is possible for Naipaul and the narrator to realize this relationship between the individual and society, society and social reality, the particular and the universal, past and present, at different levels of consciousness because of their respective understanding of man's relationship to his environment.

The boundary that separates an individual's consciousness from the consciousness of the society in which he lives, unlike political reality, is relatively fluid. The distinction between subjective and objective cannot be as clearly defined for the interaction between the two is not always visible or known. The narrator can depend on the concreteness of political action to reveal the individual and social pre-occupations of the protagonist. It represents, in the context of the novels projecting the political reality of Trinidad, the conjunction and conflation of the subjective and the objective. Society is more apt to become a part of the individual's mental landscape and vice versa and is by its nature, restrictive. The values generated by this relationship are subject to fluctuation and are not supportive, giving way under the pressure of a crisis. Biswas's emotional comprehension of the Tulsi house alters rapidly depending on whether he feels the need for security or desires freedom from restraint. The knowledge of Tulsi security is also his experience of existential suffocation. A promise as well as a threat, its ambivalent nature is insufficient to combat the existential fear of extinction which leads to his nervous breakdown. Biswas's alienation is the consequence of his vivid imaginative life created and sustained by the alien influences of his education and his reading which channelize his ambitions unrealistically. Though sensitive, imaginative and, to a degree, rational, he is not a thinker and planner who exercises control over the direction of his life. He is unable to transcend the limitations of which he is conscious.

Naipaul operates the dialectical pattern of the novel through the differing consciousness of the protagonist and the narrator, both responding to the same narrow external reality and so, indirectly, to each other. He thus suggests the complexity of the relationship between man and his historical imponderables and his inability to escape it. He can rise above it momentarily, like Biswas, he can realize that one's portion of the earth is all a lucky man can hope to possess after a lifetime of endeavour. He acquires a new humility by a ready and gracious acceptance of actual life—which is an urgent awareness of the perishable nature of one's body as the only source of the self. The narrator's transcendence through his dual vision of distance and identification does not suggest a release from his society. Narration for him is a more coherent form of the life of fantasy that Biswas indulges in to escape material restraints. He is unable to suggest a new direction or alternative to his present society. Alienation becomes a condition of survival and is projected in the novel as the fantasy of free movement that the protagonist indulges in to relieve depression and boredom. His movement away from his immediate environment becomes the condition for a breakthrough into the larger world and also "his subsequent self-imprisonment" (William Walsh, 45). The reader sees this journey as a marginal movement away from an original position which is subjectively fulfilling but does not manifest sufficient opposition to alter the direction of society.

This novel thus describes a closed world. It reflects on the relationship between the homeless individual (only in a critical situation realizing the need for home), his society and the larger social reality. It develops the frightening paradox of a shrinking world progressively developing sophisticated techniques of 'functional' communication, and so trying to come closer to its material reality, by widening the gap between subjective and objective life, indirectly creating the conditions which make 'human communication increasingly difficult' (Cf. Herbert Marcuse, xvi). Social reality, as an achieved personal vision, emphasizes the greater distance the modern man has to travel between subjective and objective reality to arrive at a sense of wholeness. It is also with the greatest difficulty that a man, once alienated, can hope to re-enter society.

In this novel, one sees both society and individual alienated from the larger social reality whose presence, as stated earlier, is experienced as fantasy and the urge for a personal vision of life, because of a static relationship to the past. Biswas mockingly caricatures his past society. The situations which highlight human need of the other—alienation, isolation and deprivation—are all present as concurrent causes in the personality of Biswas. These conditions are inherent in a society which is atomized and destructured, inducing a similar personality trait in its members.

A House for Mr Biswas and *Mr. Stone and the Knight's Companion*, novels written between a brief period frame, are interesting studies of protagonists whose immediate societies have smothered their natural sense of the larger social reality instead of providing a passage to it. Biswas identifies his highest achievement with owning a house; Stone's vision is a desire to penetrate to the truth of relationship between the corruptible, finite body and the infinite, pure world of ideas. According to a critic, both can be taken as "Prufrockian men", granting the difference in their existential struggles. In each case, the uncongenial society around exhausts them by their early middle age:

> And this final peace is as much a consequence of a personal triumph as of exhaustion, sickness and failure rationalized and accepted.
>
> .... The opposition in these novels is not only between the marginal man and his society, but also between society and the larger social reality. Man is the victim of society rather than its guide and beneficiary. Social reality keeps man in step with his times. But any society which encourages and engenders dependency—a desire for security rather than

> creativity and equality—and is coercive, necessarily utilizes the past as a weapon to control, hampering its members from moving into the present: it is an inadequate society. (Shashi Kamra, 83-84)

Both Mr. Biswas and Mr. Stone acquire a new humility by a ready and a gracious acceptance of actual life—to develop an awareness for going beyond the transience of the body and the material reality around. Journeys undertaken in both cases enable the two heroes to transcend the restricted geographical space, depression and boredom; it serves as a condition for a breakthrough into the larger world. Biswas's movement from one to the next Tulsi houses surrounding Arawacas prepares him for the final move to Port of Spain, after his recovery from the Greenville disaster becomes a fresh start to a more successful life. He will not allow fear of failure, fear of Tulsi mockery to immobilize him. His aesthetic development, long held up due to his economic and social handicaps, will ultimately find release, however small or unenviable it may be. Mr. Biswas, like Mr. Stone starts life outside a context of meaningful human relationships which would involve them in the life of a community; instead they take up the role to modify and create a new 'tradition' of their own. The reader is made to see the reality as the outsider-hero sees it—for instance, the Tulsis, who are agents of containing the hapless East Indian members of a community that is static and powerless, are seen by Biswas far more meaningfully than one would see them dispassionately:

> We see the Tulsis as Biswas sees them: the destructive impregnability of Hanuman House dominating the novel to the end. (Shashi Kamra, 89)

Mr. Biswas (along with Mr. Stone) can thus be understood as marginal men from whom society as a sustaining positive experience was snatched away at an early age, almost fatalistically, leaving him (and Stone) an orphan. Life for him is part of the hostile fate with which he engages himself. But they are not rebels against a social ideology, nor do they break rules, being law abiding citizens. However, as is the case with Biswas, initial inner freedom makes them unfit to absorb themselves in social institutions which demand compromise and consent. Yet he is also obsessed by his own insecurity, which only the outer social world can grant through any agency. Paradoxically, then, self-imprisonment conditions their subjective freedom as the instrument for attaining a personal vision. Naipaul, unlike a Lamming, Wilson Harris, Selvon (or for that matter, Walcott), never celebrates or writes *into* the community, does not identify its native assets as warming or idealistic. Biswas is denied the honour to absorb himself into the Hindu world or to represent it from outside. He remains an outsider, a victim of denial, betrayal and tyranny. As Naipaul says in terms of his own aspiration to be a writer at an early stage, and one which fits into Biswas's wish to sustain the oppressive reality: 'Fear could only be combated by exercise of vocation'.

Naipaul presents the personality with a literary potential entrapped in his societal reality which is seen as "the most vicious single cause of alienation" (Herbert Marcuse, 230-43). An irresponsible society, as a reductive agent, is a farce for its more sensitive, inquiring members. They can remain alive only when "they cease to live in tune with themselves" (Herbert Marcuse, 9). (It is a society in which material success and aesthetic development are opposed, not integrated possibilities), for the assumptions underlying its self-perpetuation are the colonial attitudes of power and possession. It is a society which is unable to either provide sustenance for a creative existence or succour in times of crisis. Each society is a different configuration of social reality and both are seen to betray the possibilities of its individual members.

Another and a notable distinction that sets Mr. Biswas apart is his urban, cosmopolitan and literary sensibility through which he seeks to carve a new, untainted identity. The urban, individualistic and idiosyncratic tendencies stand out glaringly against the rural, communal and collective Hindu pattern of life that discourages freedom and identity. Naipaul does not set Mr. Biswas apart to attain any great heights of wealth or achievement in his exhausting fight against the Tulsis, and the amorphous Trinidad society. Ultimately, the 'house' turns out to be the image of fulfilment, a release from years of slavery and tyranny of the extended family. Laying claim to "one's portion of the earth", these oft-quoted lines in fact contain a pathetic lower-middle-class dream within them; the wish to realize a lifetime's struggles, anxieties and humiliations with the assets and the merchandise of industrial capitalism. In the colonized, pre-independence and derivative Trinidad society where a white-collar job and self-respect were rare things to achieve, Mr. Biswas's possessions—the Ford Prefect, the slumberking bed, and most of all the literary gifts—are the fulfilments that he will be allowed.

Right from his early adolescent years, Biswas has a passion for reading, and a flair for writing and journalistic reportage. Biswas's rather haphazard collection of reading material from Samuel Smiles to Epictetus and Marcus Aurelius, later turns out to be his life-line in carving out a niche for himself in the semi-literate world of provincial Trinidad, a way of looking down upon the backward, noisy and philistine world that he has been trapped in. Naipaul's privileging of the word and the book is amply illustrated throughout the novel. However, the books and writers mentioned above, are 'alien' to the novel's setting, but they provide comfort and security to Biswas. The idea behind it is perhaps indicative of the colonial and post-colonial situation in its relation to the English language and Western education: the responses of the borrowed, half-made cultures and societies that receive them, are often absurd, misplaced and impractical. This is further made significant in terms of Biswas's anglicized, semi-Western attitudes through which he seeks to parallel a future life along with other races in their drive to emulate the colonial institutions and values. However, Anand and Savi moving abroad on scholarships, symbolize and characterize the last option open for the new generation of colonial subjects. The Biswas children are exempt from the trials he endured because of the single agency of education: "From now onwards their lives would be ordered, their memories coherent" (p. 581).

A House for Mr Biswas presents an experience of colonization on a different plane in both tone and intention, theme and breadth, compared with the early and other works of Naipaul. What is of central significance in *A House for Mr Biswas* is the state of one's being colonized by system, society, institution, power, authority and economic forces. Secondly, the hero is not an accomplice or a passive participant in his own colonization. In contrast to Ganesh, Harbans and Ralph Singh, who accept or see through their entrapment and inscription of being colonized or 'mimic men', Mr. Biswas finds himself caught in the webs of colonial control and manipulation. He is as much a victim and a recipient of the manipulation and machinations of others who seek to keep violence or rebellion away, but unlike the above-mentioned figures, Biswas's sensitivity to his existential and human desires, his longings to be a happy man, to own a small home, separate him from Ganesh or Ralph Singh who have entered into a pact with their marginalized state. Biswas may be colonized in the physical, economic and 'political' sense, but his emotional urge for freedom, his sensitivity to humiliation and slavery are signs of a temperament that bristles with rebellion and subversion. Naipaul's aim in *A House of Mr Biswas* was as much to recall a world of imaginative fullness, on the lines of Dickens, George Eliot and Hardy, even Lawrence, as to connect it with the void of unidentified and an 'unqualified' (in the literary sense) Caribbean experience. The discontentment and inner violence that characterize a 'little man's' disgruntled quest for independence is a far cry from the parody and self-exhibitionism of a Ralph Singh, or the cheap and lumpen rhetoric of the comparatively uneducated Ganesh. *A House for Mr Biswas* is made up of interrelated but complex literary, autobiographical and historico-social experiences that symbolize the confinement of the hero in many ways in the novel.

Writing about the relationship between power and knowledge in *Discipline and Punish,* Michel Foucault details the massive but infrequent exercise of destructive force and the uninterrupted constraints imposed in practices of discipline and training, exercising on the body a subtle coercion:

> The human body was entering a machinery of power that explores it, breaks it down and rearranges it.... It defined how one may have a hold over others' bodies, not only so that they may do what one wishes, but so that they may operate as one wishes, with the techniques, the speed and the efficiency as one determines. This discipline produces

subjected and 'practiced bodies, 'docile' bodies. (Michel Foucault, 138)

Foucault saw concentration camps, hospitals, factories, schools and institutions, etc. as means of control or neutralization of dangerous social elements, and evolved into techniques for enhancing the utility and productivity of those subjected to them. Foucault called the broadening of these techniques as 'swarming of disciplinary mechanisms.' Foucault quite often discussed normalization as a technique of power (extendable to the use of slave labour in colonialist control) to reduce difference and subjectivity. The connection that he proposes between power and knowledge is not just a particular institutional use of knowledge as a means to domination. He objects to the very idea of knowledge or a truth outside of the networks of power relations. Another contention of Foucault that is significant is that power is not exercised through networks that are static; he speaks of power as 'something that circulates'. The classic form in which power relations have been thought to be rule-governed is that of the contract, but Foucault, against this static exchange of something for something, pictures a society shaped by militant conflicts.

Naipaul's works and their ideological premise cannot perhaps be extended to explain, for example, the kind of racial protest and violence that is characterized by African novelists of the twentieth century. The colonization and its control in the previous centuries was indeed more brutal and inhuman. Foucault centres his arguments on the institutionalized and subtle surveillance of the individual through knowledge in more recent times. The plantation economy that called for a larger labour force from Asia to the Caribbean is in any case concerned with European Imperialism, so that this transportation in the nineteenth century became more a matter of forced migration from one to the other colony. The idea of discipline and control even in this indenture contract was imperative, till a time after which the British left the islands. These migrations inscribe the truth on the political map of the contemporary world. For surely, the twentieth century has produced more refugees, displaced persons and exiles than ever before in history, most of them as an accompaniment to the great post-colonial and imperial conflicts. And, because of their strange figuration between the old empire and the new state, their condition characterizes the tensions and contradictions in the cross-cultural and overlapping territories in the post-imperial scene. Edward Said says in an illuminating statement that also includes the creative production of writers like Naipaul and Rushdie:

> ...yet it is no exaggeration to say that liberation as an intellectual mission, born in resistance and opposition to the confinements and ravages of imperialism has now shifted from the settled, established, and domesticated dynamics of culture to the unhoused, decentred and exilic energies, energies whose incarnation today is the migrant, and whose consciousness is that of the intellectual and artist in exile, the political figure between the domains, between forms, between homes and between languages. (Edward Said, 403)

A House for Mr Biswas as a novel voices some of these imponderables of the dislocations of history and journeying, as some other characters of Naipaul (Salim in *A Bend in the River*, Santosh and Dayo in *In a Free State*) also reflect. At the same time, the cultural and historical experience of colonialism and post-colonialism could not be arbitrarily stacked into one type. In the Caribbean itself, for instance, such forms were widely different in Jamaica, Guyana and Trinidad, let alone the French-dominated islands. Mr. Biswas, a fictional transmutation of a variety of dominance under imperial arrangement, though, is not directly a 'slave' or in servitude. As a critic observes:

> ...his oppression and stultification of personality come from another, borrowed form of colonization. But people like him—wasted, decentered, unwanted—fill the fictional gallery of Naipaul as late as *A Way in the World*. With Naipaul this decentering and loss is part of the geography and experience that runs through like a streak of anguished concern. (Manjit Inder Singh, 118)

The autobiographical concerns that heavily influence the story and the structure of *A House for Mr Biswas* are well taken by critics such as Landeg White, Anthony Boxhill and John Thieme, among others. Naipaul's acknowledgement of the debt he owes to his father's stories and other pieces is quite evident in the 'Foreword' to *The Adventures of Gurudeva*. John Thieme has provided an excellent background of these details in *The Web of Tradition: Uses of Allusion in V.S. Naipaul's Fiction*. Thieme states at one place:

> This pattern lends itself, to interpretation as an allegory of the predicament of colonial/determinist man, with a fairly thorough portrait of Hindu life in pre-independence Trinidad being realised through the description of Biswas's experiences. (John Thieme, 66)

Thieme's view is correct in that he locates the circumstances, socio-cultural and historical in character, that go into the making of Biswas's experience of a community caught somewhere in the larger process of acculturation. One has to acknowledge the fact that *A House for Mr Biswas* remains Naipaul's most sensitively written novel, the treatment or the context notwithstanding, and the one in which the East-Indian diaspora in the Caribbean is extensively represented.

The novel also voices indirectly the restless drive for accommodation in the erstwhile and present-day racial/cultural diasporas, the cross-cultural and overlapping territories between the old and post-imperial regimes, of migration, dislocation and displacement. At the same time, there are dangers of stacking all colonial and post-colonial experiences into one type. In the Caribbean itself, for instance, such forms were different in Guyana, Jamaica and Trinidad, let alone other islands.

Following John Thieme's excellent study, wherein he locates Mr. Biswas's experiential journey through "the Hindu life in pre-independence Trinidad as the description of Biswas's experiences" (John Thieme, 66). It is imperative to underline the hero's 'experience meshed' in the life of a community in the process of racial adjustment. One has to agree with Thieme and other critics that Mr. Biswas is 'colonized' under conditions which are specific to his setting and background. In too much of critical acclaim of *A House for Mr Biswas*, the hero is taken to be representing a 'universalist' and a trans-cultural vision of man's rootlessness and the search for identity and place. This 'extension' of Biswas's personality as an unlikely man, a new kind of hero whose experience is born out of uprooting and migration perpetrated by impersonal forces, though, is viable and workable. However, it does assimilate Biswas into the exiled everyman across world literary portrayal, which is distinct in Western, and other non-Western contexts. Much of this analogy, a critic writes:

> ...is carried out in a generalized terminology of New literatures or under the comparative methodology of Commonwealth literature, which sees Naipaul as a crusader of lost histories and identities, if also patently, anti-colonial. (Manjit Inder Singh, 119)

Naipaul has been well known to have extended his diatribe against mixed, second-rate post-colonial societies in his later career to other areas, though the initial impulse did germinate from his observation of the Caribbean, more specifically, the East Indian destitution. Also, Naipaul has never been racially aggressive as a writer for launching an attack on colonial system on the lines of Lamming, Brathwaite or the African writers, which is in fact a grave charge against him for handling colonial subjects un-empathetically. Hence, in the absence of a vigorous, healthy resistance to colonialism, Naipaul's approach and literary aesthetic is conditioned more by limitation, cultural and historical specificity, and *A House for Mr Biswas* makes sensible reading when placed in the above said context.

Works Cited

Cf. Herbert Marcuse, *One Dimensional Man: Studies in the Ideology of Advanced Industrial Society* (London: Routledge and Kegan Paul, 1964), Preface.

Cudjoe, Selwyn, *V.S. Naipaul: A Materialist Reading* (Amherst: University of Massachussets Press, 1988).

Foucault, Michel, *Discipline and Punish*, trans. A Sheridan (New York: Pantheon, 1977).

Kamra, Shashi, *The Novels of V.S. Naipaul* (New Delhi: Prestige Books, 1990).

Marcuse, Herbert, *One Dimensional Man: Studies in the Ideology of Advanced Industrial Society.*

Mason, Nondita, *The Fiction of V.S. Naipaul* (Calcutta: The World Press Pvt. Ltd., 1986).

Memmi, Albert, *The Colonizer and the Colonized* (New York: Orion Press, 1965).

Mustafa, Fawzia, *V.S. Naipaul* (Cambridge: Cambridge University Press, 1995).

Naipaul, V.S. *A House for Mr Biswas*, 1962; rpt. (Harmondsworth: Penguin, 1969) (All subsequent references are from this edition and are given in parenthesis with page nos.).

———, *A Way in the World* (London: Heinemann, 1994).

Nixon, Rob, *London Calling: V.S. Naipaul, Post-colonial Mandarin* (New York: Oxford University Press, 1992).

Said, Edward, *Culture and Imperialism*, 1993; rpt. (London: Vintage, 1994).

Singh, Manjit Inder, *V.S. Naipaul* (Diasporic Writers Series) (Jaipur: Rawat Publications, 1998).

Thieme, John, *The Web of Tradition: Uses of Allusion in V.S. Naipaul's Fiction* (Hansib Dangaroo Press, 1987).

Walsh, William, *V.S. Naipaul* (Edinburgh: Oliver and Boyd, 1973).

Chapter 4

Of 'Shipwreck' and Post-colonial Disorders

> Above all, we lack power, and we do not understand that we lack power.... Our transitional or make shift societies do not cushion us...for those who lose, and nearly everyone in the end loses, there is only one course: flight. Flight to the greater disorder, the final emptiness: London and the home counties. (V.S. Naipaul, p. 8)

The above passage from *The Mimic Men* presents Naipaul's caustic and unchanging meditations on the fate of men and societies. The novels themselves, which deal with this early preoccupation with the Caribbean society's lack or order and authenticity—*Miguel Street*, *The Mystic Masseur*, *A House for Mr Biswas* and *The Mimic Men*—stand testimony to the writer's original stance which produced them. The difference between these works is of degree, technique and tone to expose an experience that runs through them and connects the Caribbean society's abysmal 'lack' of values and order, as Naipaul would believe. The endeavour here is to deal with critical areas of contemporary response to colonialism and colonial mimicry, as also, Naipaul's attempts to find an elusive 'subject' for writing in the early years in London.

Contemporary critical theorizing of colonial discourse, while it is highly complex and technical, has little to elaborate the way Naipaul approaches colonial uprooting, dereliction and illiteracy, besides the post-colonial political hollowness and corruption as a theme in *The Mimic Men*. Colonial mimicry and illiteracy, the existential trauma, and finally, the colonized politics in the phase of de-colonization constitute a longish journey in Naipaul's own career from 1957 to 1967. His works constitute a sub-corpus of pure Caribbean fictional setting that includes Naipaul's close and intensified observation of its multi-racial and multi-lingual manifestation. Naipaul being a writer from a remote island geography and history, and his views on the Caribbean in the socio-cultural and historical sense are, and can be taken up as separate, but related issues. This could perhaps clarify some of his pre-occupations for being a writer of a mixed world. Naipaul's personal frustrations and the 'inadequacies' in his subject-matter could be directly transferred to his intellectual views on societies, though one can see a close relationship or a correlative between the two. The origins of Naipaul's dissent or derision of the place of his birth are literary as well as political:

> To us without a mythology, all literatures were foreign. Trinidad was small, remote and unimportant, and we knew we could not hope to read in books of the life we saw about us. Books came from afar; they could only offer fantasy.... (V.S. Naipaul, pp. 24-25)

It is possible to locate the literary and the non-literary connection in the above excerpt, the distinction between the loss to the man and the writer, the link between the actual and the artistic world of the writer. Naipaul describes the lack in a history without systematic origins, human subjects and collective sites of production. Nevertheless, it is a history born out of power relations and the way these Imperial-Third World relations both restricted and defined the boundaries of life itself, let alone literature or myth. Ultimately, the colonial cringe, the mimicry and fraud became the central target of Naipaul's attack when he did re-form that society through his work. Indeed, Naipaul with the packaging of sardonic humour and sharp wit was able to look at the mixed, transient and unlikely world of Trinidad with a degree of compassion in *Miguel Street* and *The Mystic Masseur*. The characters of *Miguel Street* typify the vacancy and waste in the years when the middle-class was vying for importance in the newly emerging social circumstances. The peripheral figures in this work are those without education and power, whose predicament and wilderness is shaped by the colonial situation and its psychological consequences. With a language barrier and illiteracy, they are cut off from the creole-speaking majority, without a hope of promotion into the ranks of the elite. The seediness of life contrasted with metropolitan fantasy is itself a clue to their colonial mimicry in the absence of any other outlet. The imposture and fraud, the skill of surviving, which are central to *The Mystic Masseur* and *The Suffrage of Elvira*, nevertheless have their germ in *Miguel Street*, these being the inevitable outgrowths of a stunted, colonized society. The political gimmickry and fraud perpetrated by the politicians on the people in *The Suffrage of Elvira* is an offshoot of the same syndrome mentioned above. The trickery and opportunism represented by Harbans or a Baksh in this novel essentially foregrounds its limited aim to expose through comedy and irony the 'democratic institutions' which were taking 'root in Trinidad' in the 1940s and the 1950s. This has its relation to Naipaul's later and bleaker vision of politics and politicians in *The Mimic Men*. However, the statement of Dr. Eric Williams, the Prime Minister of Trinidad and Tobago, underlines the very concept of mimicry that Naipaul conceptualizes:

> Political forms and social institutions were imitated rather than created, borrowed rather than relevant, reflecting the forms in the particular metropolitan country from which they were derived. (Eric Williams, p. 501)

The chaos resulting from blind imitation of the West is anticipated here in its relation to Naipaul's bitter and harsh attacks on other Third World societies in *Guerillas* and *A Bend in the River*. The inflated rhetoric of the contestants likewise, echoes their total lack of concern for any morals or conscience, and the flirtations with democracy. However, in Naipaul's later works the idea of colonial mimicry acquires dangerous and nihilistic overtones, for the innocent farce of politics in *The Suffrage of Elvira* will turn into racial antagonism, leading to murder and outrage in the post-imperial world. On the other hand, the gaiety and celebration of the politician's clout and importance will ironically give way to the damaged and corrupted visage of Ralph Singh, the ex-politician belonging to the Caribbean.

Naipaul's interest in the real-life politics is peripheral in *The Suffrage of Elvira*, as he has acknowledged that he was simply 'recording' his reactions to the world', without having come to any conclusions. The relation, nevertheless, between colonial mimicry and the psychic effects of being 'colonized' is significant.

The political fraud and metropolitan mimicry is a simpler theme, compared with the life and times of the master-trickster Ganesh Ramsumair in *The Mystic Masseur*. Yet, Naipaul traces another facet of the destitution and derivativeness of Trinidad society to survive, for Ganesh, the successful mystic turned politician is an illustration of the scandalous ways to ascend the ladder in the colonized outposts. Ganesh, a rank outsider to politics and an East-Indian post-indenture survivor, but unlike Mr. Biswas, symbolizes the Indians' art of aggrandizing the colonial powers, at whatever price. The result is unbelievable: form Ganesh Ramsumair to G. Ramsay Muir; from Fuente Grove to London, the journey of mimicry is also a journey from the peasant anonymity to metropolitan 'recognition'. The colonial mimicry in the comparatively unproblematic imperial-colonial stage that Ganesh is living in, requires no qualms of conscience or the guilt of being an accomplice in the public corruptions that invariably corrode the fabric of politics. As though this is not enough, Ganesh, the confidence man, the imperial insider, is flaunted as a fit material for being a 'hero', in effect a demonstration by Naipaul that 'you get the politicians you deserve' in axiomatic terms. From 'hero' to the anti-hero, this constitutes the mimic man's journey in Naipaulian sense from *The Mystic Masseur* to *The Mimic Man*.

The trickster is a folklore figure in Caribbean literature, symbolized through Anansi, whose trickery involves deceit and greed, who survives by his wits. His transformation took place during the period of slavery, and in the West Indian stories he is clearly an allegorical representation of the erstwhile slave who used his wits to survive in the hostile colonizer's world. The slave's descent into subterfuge and resource is also linked with his cultural and folk experience, through which he indulged in night fantasy. However, Naipaul sees the trickster figure as part of the picaroon society, bereft of national pride and the closed colonial system. The Anansi trickster figure and its use is largely a fictional celebration in the works of Afro-Caribbean writes, and poets such as Wilson Harris and Brathwaite among others. The trickster figure is portrayed as compulsive to the oppressed Caribbean world of the native, where survival and a zest for life is necessary. Naipaul's attitude, quite characteristic of his views, is wry and detached, so that the trickster is essentially the wily human being, hardly sympathetic or liberating, rather closed and meanly narcissistic.

The beginning of the 'journey' of colonial mimicry through setting, symbols, books, the desperate attempts at modernization is in fact the result of confused origins, loyalties, customs and beliefs in the colonial society. Ganesh's house and his store are a queer amalgam of tradition and modernity, Indian and Western, cosmopolitan and local, just as he cleverly alternates between superstition and rationality, vernacular and English, native religion and emancipation, the conservative and the revolutionary. Ganesh raises his mimicry to art, he establishes the most compelling category of role-playing in Naipaul's cannon —the mimic man as artist. Colonial mimicry for Naipaul's protagonists and other figures in *Miguel Street, The Mystic Masseur* and *The Suffrage of Elvira* is a precondition for retaining a borrowed way of life, an odd mixture of floating experiences. They have hardly any desire to ponder into a revolt against the system that reduces them to the general flotsam of history. Indeed, the absence that reduces them to the general flotsam of history. Indeed, the absence of any sense of history whatsoever is largely responsible for their derivative and adulterated response to life and its complex undertones. *The Mimic Men* in this sense is the novel that sets the tone of the Naipaulian malaise of the New World conditions and their deep impact on one's psyche. Ralph Ranjit Kripal Singh, the exiled expolitician hero of *The Mimic Men* is an 'insider', one who has practiced the most dubious forms of colonial mimicry as a politician and dandy, as husband and businessman, and sees through the charade of politics, the deep humiliation and self-contempt that results from defeat and failure. The first-person narrative of Ralph Singh tells the story of a middle-class West Indian of the author's own generation, who, after a colonial education including at a British university, returns with an English wife to the fictional island of Isabella. While there, he helps orchestrate an election, but after he has been deserted by his wife. The party he has 'floated' with others—nationalist multi-ethic, quasi socialist—soon ousts him following its ideological split. His subsequent exile back in England at the age of forty sees him writing the memoirs of his active life from a room in a suburban London hotel, avoiding contact with any one. The memoir takes up a ruminative, if also, analytical tone that probes the nature of his own fall as well as that of the general quality of the island life.

Ralph Singh is the example of a thoroughly, psychologically colonized man, one who knows both the hurts and the excitements of short-lived euphoria of inconsequential 'empires of our times.' The burden of guilt and betrayal, the consciousness of a collective 'shipwreck' which all imitative and third-rate mimic societies suffer, makes Ralph Singh the voice of a quiet acceptance of colonial complicity. Ralph Singh is the mimic man raised through a through-bred colonial education in England and Isabella and belongs to a class that abuses power and has to own its equally destructive fall out.

History teaches us clearly that the battle against colonialism does not run straightaway along the lines of nationalism. For a very long time the native devotes his energies to ending certain definite abuses: forced labour-corporal punishment, inequality against the oppression of mankind will slowly leave the confusion of neo-liberal universalism to emerge, sometimes laboriously, as a claim to nationhood. It so happens that the "un-preparedness of the educated classes, the lack of practical links between them and the mass of the people, their laziness, and, let it be said, their cowardice at the decisive moment of the struggle will give rise to tragic mishaps" (Frantz Fanon, rpt. 197). These are the cracks in the edifice which show the process of retrogression that is so harmful and prejudicial to national effort and national unity. This is all due to the historical result of the incapacity of the national middle-class to the national consciousness of under-developed countries, is not solely the result of the mutilation of the colonized people by the colonial regime. It is also the result of the intellectual laziness of the national middle-class, of its spiritual penury, and of the profoundly cosmopolitan mould that its mind is set in.

The national middle-class which takes over power at the end of the colonial regime is an under-developed middle-class. It has practically no economic power and it is in no way commensurate with the bourgeoisie of the mother country which it hopes to replace. In its wilful narcissism, the national middle-class is easily convinced that it can advantageously replace the middle-class of the mother country. But that same independence which literally drives it into a corner will give rise within its ranks to catastrophic reactions, and will oblige it to send out frenzied appeals for help to the former Colonial Mother country. The university and merchant classes which make up the most enlightened section of the new state are in fact characterized by the smallness of their number and their being concentrated in the capital, and the type of activities in which they are engaged: 'business, agriculture and the liberal professions.' The national bourgeoisie of under-developed countries is not engaged in production, nor in invention, nor building, nor labour; it is completely canalized into activities of the intermediary type. Its innermost vocation seems to be to keep in the running and to be part of the racket (Frantz Fanon, p. 120). The greed of the settlers and the system of embargoes set-up by colonialism has hardly left them any other choice. Under the colonial system, a middle-class which accumulates capital is an impossible phenomenon. After independence this under-developed middle-class reduced the significant point that Fanon make in this statement is that in numbers and without capital, which refuses to follow the path of revolution, will fall into deplorable stagnation. The precariousness of its resources and the paucity of its managerial class forces it back for years into a borrowed economy model. The native bourgeoisie which comes to power uses its class aggressiveness to corner the positions formerly kept for foreigners. It is from this viewpoint that we must interpret the fact, that in young, independent countries, here and there federalism triumphs. The colony's economy is not integrated into that of the nation as a whole. It is still organized in order to complete the economy of the different mother countries, thereby, certain sectors of the colony relatively rich but the rest of the colony follows its path of under-development and poverty, or at all events sink into it more deeply. *The Mimic Men,* both symbolically and fictionally, is the novel about such post-colonial realities and effectively deconstructs the fall out of imperial legacies in the psychological social, personal and political sense.

Ralph Singh himself, quite unlike the diminished and flattened or deflated figures in *Miguel Street, The Mystic Masseur* and *The Suffrage of Elvira,* is not always the victim of the oppressive colonial conditions which play out and render the individual drive ineffective. Ralph Singh has in his 'English' past already practiced a self-willed 'deracination' into cosmopolitanism in terms of his sexual adventures with Sandra, neighbours, and prostitutes, and these are interracial and even incestuous (with his aunt Sally). Having had a brush with this kind of false liberation, he and his ilk, seem to enjoy this deracination linked with Western 'liberalism' on their return to Isabella. This way, he and his companions reinvent a new identity as a class in opposition to an old world which they feel they have escaped. Having schemed to grab power by design in the destitute, backward and illiteracy-ridden post-colonial setting, Singh's first success is as a property speculator through which he achieves financial independence. Despite the fortune, the fame and the Roman House, security is short-lived in his political career, obviously the central thesis about the ephemeral nature of post-colonial 'stability'. Political system needs a solid foundation in terms of values, ideas and principles; but Naipaul would not grant to the fictionalized version his former birthplace.

Ralph Singh and his weather-friendly, opportunistic friends and political co-partners abysmally lack a sense of history. Hence, Singh is portrayed as the new mimic man, incomplete and atrophied on both political and historical sense. The feared hazards of de-colonization in *The Mimic Men* are reduced to a charade of 'play-acting', but as Naipaul can wryly think, they are quite expected and dramatically revolve in a repetitive stasis rather than as a fruitful realization of dialectics of race, culture and hybridity. Ralph Singh is not marginal in the sense in which

Naipaul's earlier peripheral figures are; he moves from a centre-stage of politics and life to periphery, both as an initiator of post-colonial appropriation of authority and as a result of the contaminated sense of himself that he later sees.

The following two comments by a critic sum up the complex ramifications of the post-colonial condition of which it is a product, and Naipaul, by subtly piecing together the components of mimicry and ambivalence, marginality and the 'writing' about it, paradigmatically fictionalizes his observations:

> ...presented in a realist mode, Ralph Singh's embodiment of what can be termed a post-colonial dyslexia, is played out as though an historical determinism forecloses any possibility of its cure, despite the fact that his voice is the one to articulate it. (Fawzia Mustafa, pp. 102-03)

The 'knowledge' that is supposed to stem from 'self-knowledge' through the agency of writing is, for Ralph Singh, only an existential epiphany of marginality through choice. Or, his reclusiveness at the end of the novel stems from choosing to be embarrassed. Mimicry and repetition, therefore, are the two narrative forms that Naipaul locks the colonial and post-colonial characters he creates and their respective situations into (Fawzia Mustafa, p. 106).

Mimicry, through its camouflage, splits the element of colonial culture it seeks to expose. Naipaul's attitude and his structuration of *The Mimic Men* preclude a celebration of that initiated culture, rather, the split that is effected through separating life and politics is significant. For, the novel shows how antithetical and damaging the latter can be to the former. One can withdraw from politics and careerism, but from life? *The Mimic Men* includes a whole gamut of history and its complex variants, the process by which civilization travels and touches societies. The sieve of memory which is the distilling power of Singh to deconstruct experience, also enables him to mentally absorb the contradictions in one's involvement in public affairs, the remnants of the legacy of another culture and civilization, never one's own. The troubled knot of race, ancestry, origin and education becomes a way of dissecting a whole array of inauthentic representation, the impact of uprootings, the brutalization, the shifts of power relations, to the final inability of the colonial politician to absorb and assimilate power.

In the article "Conrad's Darkness" while commenting on what he saw through Conrad and *Nostromo*, Naipaul describes his own view of the world's 'half-made' societies as places which 'continuously made and unmade themselves' and the experience of degradation that came with the necessities which forced them to be what they are. Naipaul's identification with Conrad is more clearly traceable in a novel like *A Bend in the River* because of its immediate locale. However, Ralph Singh appears to echo a similar vision of colonial and post-colonial society. Singh echoes and parodies a settled, deserved view of history because of his premature and forced reflection on 'our times'. Writing about the Caribbean colonial history and cross-migrations that made it, Singh says:

> ...give expression to the restlessness, the deep disorder, which the great explorations, the overthrow in three continents of established social organizations, the unnatural bringing together of peoples could achieve fulfilment only within the security of their own societies and the landscapes hymned by their ancestors. (V.S. Naipaul, p. 38)

It indicates Singh's design of the project, much in an identical way in which Naipaul writes a sort of psycho-history of his ancestry, his father, his community and its relation with the larger drift of the Caribbean society under the impact of imperialism. The New World setting of Ralph Singh's memoir, the half-made societies that form the central focus of his quest for order, however abortive, are reflected in the mimesis motif in the title of *The Mimic Men*. Ultimately, the scattered fragments of his life—studentship, dandyism, marriage, his Aryan ancestry and his short but charged political career—betray a nexus or centre, indeed that is something he is trying to locate and reorder through a rational linkage between the personal and the impersonal.

One of the differences in the structuration of *The Mimic Men* from Naipaul's previous works, is the detailed stress on the protagonist's subjectivity in terms of his narrative voice that recoils on his multiple background. Ralph Singh's memoir, so to speak, becomes paradigmatic of the social organization in Caribbean colonies such as Isabella, an act of writing that emanates from an empirically determined state of mind. The post-colonial in Singh, therefore, presents a realist self-portrait that reflects the hidden flaws and blemishes, underneath which lies a sick soul. Singh's self-consciousness is also a form of his self-knowledge, as he dissects the origins of failure and disenchantment both in personal and politico-social terms. What is more, in the course of his writing himself out of a nagging, dyspeptic state of mind, Singh allows his self-reflexivity to become a kind of trope through which, time and again, he reverts to the cycles of experience stretching across biography, education, habits, political opportunism, sex, race among other things. This private act of exorcism that Singh settles down to, in fact acquires the overtones of a 'fiction' that he creates out of apparently unpalatable moments of defeat, deceit and humiliation. Behind it lie his earliest ambitions while he was a student, connected with his colonial education and racial consciousness the way he reacts to 'elements' like snow. Right from the beginning, then, the contradictory, ambivalent responses to experience and future are ingrained in Singh's panicky decisions, quite understandable of the colonial condition of a Caribbean expatriate/traveller in the Western metropolis. Later, the misdirected ambitions to achieve through imagination are centered in Singh's racial origins (Aryan, in his case), as they are 'Chinese' in the case of Hok. This aspect is also part of Singh's disability and shame about his ancestral origins. Race and class, which are important attributes in the problem of colonial dependency, and which carry an unusual dimension in Naipaul's later fiction, are perhaps first indicated here as a proscription of the post-colonial condition.

The order-disorder theme itself, which is crucial to the understanding of Naipaul's fictional portrayal, is central to Ralph Singh's negative stance towards societies such as Isabella. Singh's deflation of the overall poverty of tradition and order in such post-colonial territories results from his own defeat and withdrawal from the scene of political activity after having failed to get close to public reality at any time in his political career. The futile attempts to escape the consequences of Western cultural imperialism in the face of a pattern of growth and indigenous development is Singh's confession as a public man who is smeared with guilt of having betrayed the cause, if ever there was one. At the back of Singh's polished and extended self-meditations is the nostalgia of Asiatic Indian myth and religion that accounts for his racial maladjustment in a rootless West Indian island. Mentally colonized and trapped in the history of geographical uprooting, he is more subtly aware of his Indian roots and is also a more glaring victim of the attenuation of his ancestral culture. Singh is one of those who have been thrown up into the conundrum of island politics, as he says, ironically because of his 'superior' education, his complicity to mistake the colonial models of authority, his rich background provided by his mother's family's Coca-Cola bottling plant. Singh's assets of education, dandyism and political masquerading turn out to be mere hypocritical attempts leading to self-deception and inner trauma. Driven by a misguided dream of public-good and selflessness, he perpetuates a fraud on them because of the inherent streak of betrayal and falsity in the colonial politician, as *The Suffrage of Elvira* suggests in a more comic and superficial way. But even Harbans is the one who is tricked by others. The "commonest desire", as Singh says, is "eviction and succession". But already, it is another 'order' that the colonial politician succeeds; destruction comes with his emergence—indeed, it is the very condition of his power. The fate of the colonized man and politician, as *The Mimic Men* conveys, shall remain tied to its peculiar features conditioned by a psycho-pathology of one's being unwanted and unimportant.

Singh is clear about the imitative language of politics, now liberal, now socialist, now democratic. And yet, this borrowed political rhetoric is 'a way of escape from thought.' The colonial politician is amusingly caught in the double trap: while he wants people to 'see' the reality, his own cowardice and mimicry scarcely allow him to face fact. The 'enthroning' of dignity and distress are the short-sighted and fabricated slogans to cheat and befool. The loneliness and the unease of the mimic, almost tailored politician in the colony with all kinds of reactionary and racial outfits, is natural. The lack of organized capital, the absence of any cohesive nationalism, the racist policies, the heavy dependence for resources, these are pointers to the unstable West Indian national governments in the 1960s after the collapse of the Federation in 1962. Further, power and the consolidation of power for self-interest dominated the national political structures. Singh, who sees through the poverty of intellect and resource, finds it hard to face the truth:

> ...that in a society like ours, fragmented inorganic, no link between man and landscape, a society not held together by common interests, there was no true source of internal power, and that no power was real which did not come from the outside. (V.S. Naipaul, p. 246)

Having corrupted themselves with this borrowed idea of power, Singh and his friend Browne find it difficult to go on in the immoral game of politics where every truth contains a hundred lies. In the end, a kind of neurosis sets in to carry Singh to the limits of self-derision. The mimic man's emancipation is an impossibility, knowing the degree to which he has betrayed and violated himself, killing all truth and native purities. As Naipaul wrote in *The Overcrowded Barracoon*, the blacks "see themselves as British, made in the image of their former owners, with British institutions," he further states that the Caribbean territories are "not like those in Africa or Asia, with their own internal reverences that have been returned to themselves after a period of colonial rule" (V.S. Naipaul, rpt., p. 274).

The precariousness of colonial or post-colonial leader, highlighted in *The Mimic Men*, is his slavery to the West on the one hand and his unease with his 'portion of the world.' The 'imported' culture, economy, industry, institutions and education are the mark of societies that Singh or Browne hoped to retrieve from disorder. Ralph Singh, the mover between cultures and geographies, politics and exile, finally turns a complete colonial, waiting 'perhaps' to work on 'a history of the British empire.' He is a contrived figure who dramatizes through the image of 'shipwreck' the psychosis of a colonized man, washed up and vacuumed by inner emptiness. Singh's vision of the writing of 'a history' is informed by, as has been noted by John Thieme (John Thieme, pp. 120-21) and James R. Lindroth (James R. Lindroth,

p. 528), 'a Gibbonesque history of Empire', while striking a notable inversion to the former's view. Far from being sheltered and fortunate unlike Gibbon, Singh feels castaway, prematurely finished, by those very consequences of colonial history. Ralph Singh's exhaustion, ennui and his conviction of having 'played' all kinds of roles in 'play-acting', that all experience is tainted and all political activity is ultimately futile, expose him to many critical viewpoints. The problem seems to lie in the highly orchestrated and condensed structure of ideas through which Singh mediates, and often dove tails one into the other. Significantly, he often communicates in a terse, aphoristic language, giving a final verdict to things.

The Mimic Men returns to the subject of West Indian politics and, as its title suggests, the story undertakes the theme of colonial mimicry, the charade of purpose and meaning. The structure of the novel is complex, with the narrator-protagonist "Ralph" Kripal Singh breaking up chronology to piece together and bring a sense of order to his 'autobiography'. He spends his childhood on the island of Isabella, goes abroad to attend school in England, marries an English girl, and returns to his newly independent homeland where he makes money and rides the swell of nationalistic fervor to political power. His eventual exile from Isabella is even more final than the spiritual downfall of Ganesh Ramsumair in *The Mystic Masseur*. He retires to lick his wounds, perhaps to begin again, but in his fate Ralph detects a pattern that is all too familiar in the West Indies: a pattern leading from "isolation and frenzy to irrelevance, failure and inevitable disorder" (V.S. Naipaul, p. 220).

In spite of the varied content of Naipaul's work, the socio-political aspect stands out so prominently that sooner or later nearly every critic feels it necessary to address himself to the theme. R.M. Lacovia seizes upon the manner in which Naipaul portrays the impact of the media on an *audile-tactile* society (R.M. Lacovia, pp. 3-6). R.H. Lee argues that it is the "documentation of sociological transition in individuals and groups that provides the basic material of the novels, and the main critical interest as well" (R.H. Lee, pp. 68-69). Karl Miller expresses concern that readers in the Caribbean will find it difficult to get beyond interpreting *The Mimic Men* as anything other than "Naipaul's political testament" (Karl Miller, p. 111). Miller's point is well taken, but it is interesting to note that Peter Nazareth sees *The Mimic Men* as almost purely political—it "is not about corruption of the human being in any metaphysical sense. It is a political novel" (Peter Nazareth, p. 76). Victor J. Ramraj takes an almost opposite view. He observes that politics actually enters directly into only the third section of this three-part novel. He finds that Naipaul is "more interested in a study of the unanchored, estranged individual than with the issues of politics" (Victor J. Ramraj, p. 132).

Wherever such divergent conclusions lead, there is general agreement that Naipaul's treatment of his material is basically satirical. Much of the controversy surrounding his work, in fact, results from the way in which his incisive satire, irony and humor is received. Speaking of the early novels, George Lamming, decries their satire, seeing it as an inadequate refuge from hard experience—laughter as a cowardly defence machanism (George Lamming, p. 225). In turn, Gordon Rohlehr reiterates the offensive power of satire, its usefulness in confronting the very problems Naipaul is sometimes accused of avoiding (Gordon Rohlehr, pp. 125-26). It is more probable—and this is argued by Rohlehr and David Ormerod—that Naipaul's humor, irony, and satire provide indispensable means for keeping his personal involvement as a man from eroding the detachment which is essential to him as an artist. In Ormerod's opinion, Naipaul chooses deliberately to avoid short-sighted propaganda in order to create something of more lasting, universal value (David Ormerod, p. 82).

When there are works so rich in aesthetic and humanistic value as Naipaul's are, it is unfortunate that many readers and critics are put off by such peripheral concerns as the author's political affiliations, or the quality of his compassion. This probably cannot be avoided, however, since the writer insists on speaking directly to live issues, and out of a contemporary situation which is almost automatically divisive. Naipaul is neither the first nor is he likely to be the last artist to attempt to keep the vague line between artistic and personal commitments.

By putting his finger on elusive problems, foibles, follies, and vices, re-creating them within recognizable characters, he gives immediacy and comprehendible form to a reality which is otherwise too complex and expansive to grasp. This is no small achievement. Its magnitude is witnessed by the growing seriousness with which his work is being received by critics throughout the English-speaking world.

When we come to *The Mimic Men*, we find an advance in Naipaul's sensibility and political thinking. Although *The Mimic Men* is certainly pessimistic in tone, it possesses a dimension that the previous three books do not. The novel is not only about corruption but also about betrayal, and the recognition of betrayal pre-supposes the existence of a moral consciousness and a scale of human values. In other words, the despair and pessimism that pervades *The Mimic Men* does not lead one to the conclusion that human beings in Isabella are damned or irrelevant. Instead, the novel reveals valuable truths about such a degraded society. It is true that the narrator never displayed any ideals as a practicing politician, but, despite his extreme self-indulgence, he has a moral consciousness, and in his story, he attaches moral significance to what he has seen and experienced and what he himself has done or not done. The story in thus presented to the reader through the sieve of a moral consciousness which recognizes when wrong has been committed. For example, Singh evaluates the fake radicalism he and his fellow-politician Browne made use of:

> What did we talk about? We were, of course, of the left. We were socialist. We stood for the dignity of the working man. We stood for the dignity of distress. We stood for the dignity of our island, the dignity of our indignity. Borrowed phrases! left-wing, right-wing: did it matter? (V.S. Naipaul, p. 198)

This same "left-wing radicalism" leads eventually to race riots and race murders. Telling us his story, Singh blames himself for refusing to get involved but merely arranging for euphemisms to be used to describe the situation:

> Do not give me names. Do not tell me how many people died. Say instead, "Race riots occurred" say, "There was loss of life." (V.S. Naipaul, p. 231)

Singh also writes about the betrayal of an old Negro who had worked for an English firm and had always been passed over when it came to promotions. He was "crazed with distress and passionate for justice"—and thought he would find it through his own leaders. But he does not; he is merely given words, which deceive him for a while into thinking he has been given justice.

And finally, the complete betrayal of 'Independence':

> From London there presently came more offers of technical aid and experts on short-term contracts. We gratefully accepted; so that in the end there were more expatriates than before. Some of our ministers took pains to be seen in public with their English permanent secretaries, who behaved impeccably. It was what these ministers offered their followers: the spectacle of the black man served by the white: the revolution we claimed to have created. (V.S. Naipaul, p. 216)

Although *The Mimic Men* does not offer any solution to the injustices faced by the people as does a novel like Tressels's *The Ragged Trousered Philanthropists*, it does not imply that there is no way out of the morass. The author awakens the consciousness of the readers to the problems, and in doing so he implies the direction of the 'cure' needed. The author has done his share by etching the problems on the moral consciousness of the reader, which he did not do in *The Suffrage of Elvira*.

Corruption, then, is identified in *The Mimic Men* as sheer indifference towards other human beings coupled with a willingness to treat them as inferior beings and to mistreat them for the sake of personal gain, advantage, or position. It reaches its highest point in the form of political corruption, that is, when political leaders use the common people to get them into power by making promises to improve their material condition and then, when in power, merely pursue their interests, their only motivation being naked greed and selfishness. A cynical view of politics, indeed, and a complete contrast to the faith many African writers had in politics at the beginning of the de-colonization phase. Writers and leaders at that point professed the same ideals, and the writer tended to assume that this was the beginning of a new humanist phase in which the newly-freed non-white countries would teach the savage Europeans—who had caused two world wars—a new awareness of the value of human beings. Then came the shattering discovery that given the circumstances, the problems, and the opportunities, their leaders could be no better, no more humanist than the imperialists they had replaced, and sometimes even worse. And with this discovery, over and over again we find disillusionment and despair, an inability to see any break in the vicious circle. Thus, *The Mimic Men*, Achebe's *A Man of the People*, Soyinka's *Kongi's Harvest*, and Rubadiri's *No Bride Price*, all written within a few years of one another, convey this theme. In writing this novel, Naipaul faced the same problem that other "commonwealth" writers faced—what literary technique is one to adopt so as to present the confusing and explosive realities of today in an organised manner? Achebe posed the problem poignantly when he said after the commencement of Biafran/Nigerian hostilities that he had stopped writing and was learning instead to use a gun.

At the end of any number of arguments one may advance, for or against the portrayal of Ralph Singh, the one question that remains is, Naipaul's attitude to the 'politics of living', and the issue of his attitude to the Caribbean, and post-colonial societies. One of the general estimates that emerges from the comments of critics like Victor Ramraj, Peter Nazareth and Landeg White, despite their balanced views, is Singh's painful efforts to belatedly find a sense of commitment, ironically in 'writing', which he had betrayed in the act of living. Derek Walcott, reviewing *The Mimic Men* when it first appeared, put forward a typical anti-Naipaul view germinating from Caribbean writers, that the novel's elegance was indicative of "Naipaul's distrust of his own art, an exercise in self-mockery, a celebration of inertia in a powerful style" (Derek Walcott, p. 9). What Walcott was pointing at was that Naipaul was subtly identifying his own experience with Singh's, and a state of inertia that such a view of things lands one in. In short, a grave pessimism and rejection of Naipaul's handling of Caribbean subjects. What is more, Singh's self-aggrandizing and self-flagellating approach tends to further enhance his posturing, comparing himself to some classical figures, as though he was a victim of belonging to an insensitive, philistine and stupid place, thus indulging in a false mimesis of the West to prove his intellectual 'superiority' and cultural assets acquired through metropolitan upbringing. This is amply illustrated in allusions to Pompeii, Ceaser, Alexander, Aryan conquerors, and Columbus—all hinting at the creations of empires, and imperialist conquerors. At other times he mocks the Caribbean black race and colonial setting, imitating James Anthony Froude, the most widely abused Western commentator and historian, the author of *The English in the West Indies* (1888). Even the style of Singh, cold distant, essayistic, is redolent of Froude while his manners that of the imperial historian. As John Thieme rightly says, "he (Singh) writes essentially from the same outsider's point of view, and presents his society in relation to a long view of Empire...." (V.S. Naipaul, p. 207). This is one aspect that reflects Naipaul's disillusionment with the disorder in half-made societies, and *The Mimic Men* is the only text that informs the idea of personal shipwreck and general dereliction by a monologic, extended commentary that Singh gains 'authority' through.

In Naipaul's fiction, the displacement brought about by the loss of ancestral landscape is always an important theme, but in *The Mimic Men,* the idea of 'shipwreck' carries multiple meanings. Singh's sense of alienation and deracination, the loss of paternal, filiative link connotes one, while his sense of 'taint' derives initially from his view of the Caribbean situation of the unnatural bringing together of peoples who could achieve fulfilment only within the security of their own societies and landscapes. The Empire had, as Singh muses, wiped out all traces of the original Caribs, to further destroy any racial purity by miscegenation. That is perhaps one important way in which Singh sees the whole of the Caribbean in terms of its cultural and historical rootlessness and marginality, which colonialism had affected. Following his abortive attempts to escape his Hindu past, the figure of his elusive, shadowy father and the great religious practices, he meditates detachment from 'the cycle of events', from the four-fold 'ashrama' theory in Hinduism. Singh's sense of waste, then, does not emerge from a calm renunciation; it is a withdrawal generated by a deep sense of despair, a withdrawal from the disorder Singh considers himself a part of. The following statement of Naipaul from "Conrad's Darkness" sums up the author's own fears about the transition from colonial to postcolonial situation in terms of historical periodization, something he found while re-exploring Conrad's world:

> To be a colonial was to know a kind of security; it was to inhabit a fixed world. And I suppose in my fantasy I had seen myself coming to England to some purely literary region, where untrammeled by the accident of history or background, I could make a romantic career for myself as a writer. But in the new world I felt that ground move below me. The new politics, the curious reliance of men on institutions they were yet working to undermine, the simplicity of beliefs and the hideous simplicity of actions, the corruption of causes, half-made societies that seemed doomed to remain half-made: these were the things that began to preoccupy me. (V.S. Naipaul, p. 207)

The statement is famous and significant, apart from other angles, because it appears to echo Ralph's vision of colonial and post-colonial set-up. Interestingly, post-colonial criticism heavily concentrates on the way historical account centres itself in the politics of representation, presided over by authoritarian Western versions of the colonized world. These 'histories' were never written authentically (something that African and West Indian writers have been attempting to correct by drawing upon the real assets of their traditions). Singh's memoir or veiled 'history' however, attempts to project a confessional mode, to give expression to the 'deep disturbance, disorder and restlessness' that lies at the heart of all colonial societies, thus using the textual form to mediate an experiential, objective view of things, including Naipauls' own.

Naipaul's most recycled theme both in his fiction and non-fiction to date has been to rehearse his personal disadvantages as a Caribbean-born writer who escaped that geography at the first opportunity, and his difficult 'journey' from that point to be a writer by moulding a fictional material unfit for any serious writing. In a way, Naipaul has been voicing (however unconvincingly according to his fellow Caribbean writers) a concern with the devaluation of post-colonial experience itself, consigning it to the level of mimicry, something not fit for the canon, or being rendered as 'literature'. Most recently the Caribbean novelist Caryl Phillips has castigated Naipaul for his continuous attempts to "inscribe his self-aggrandizing, and frankly embarrassing, narrative journey into the literary conscience of the West" (Caryl Phillips, p. 9) arguing that it was the same material that has served countless artists, including Aime Cesaire, Alejo Carpentier and Derek Walcott. However, Naipaul has viewed the futility of escaping this debilitating post-colonial condition, because of the disorder and inauthenticity imposed by the centre on the margins of Empire. This aspect that Ralph Singh expresses as a malaise, is the distinction between the authentic experience of the 'real' world and the inauthentic experience of the invalidated periphery. Ralph Singh, however, does not offer many cures to this malady for overcoming it or recovering from it, except his own invention of a creative performance, after many stages of mimicry of fraudulent pretence. This includes language itself, its use that aligns itself with metropolitan/colonial power. As a colonial politician—his central role in the novel—no matter what rhetoric may win him votes, both language and the economic structure of the society he vainly hopes to change, are controlled from outside, a mimicry of the original and the 'true' which exists at the source of power:

> We, here on our island, handling books printed in this world, and using its goods, had been abandoned and forgotten. We pretended to be real, to be learning, to be preparing ourselves for life, we mimic men of the New World. (V.S. Naipaul, p. 175)

Ralph Singh's memoir attempts to graft together the negative components of the borrowed, second-hand legacy inherited by post-colonial societies like the one of Isabella, whether it is the city, the language, politics, tradition or the representation of truth. Importantly, the perception that life, creativity and perception of reality is located at the Centre, and nothingness and disorder is the only possibility for the marginal places, undoubtedly operates as a driving force in Naipaul's work. As stated earlier, Naipaul's attitude to a nexus between imperial-colonial world is fraught with problems. For example, despite his studied awareness, he is paradoxically drawn to the Centre, although conscious of being a part of periphery. Secondly, Naipaul has also experienced as a writer (stated in many of his articles and interviews) that the reality or order of the Centre is also on illusion, "the greater disorder, the final emptiness." In Naipaul's case, as is well known, the authenticity of margins as places, and marginality as a state of experience, hardly provides a positive tension that may yield a rich construction of post-colonial experience. *The Mimic Men* thus remains a novel that remarkably lays bare the ineluctable realities that make-up the discursivity of colonial marginality, but sounding a doubtful note about its release from the given situation. In the words of the authors of *The Empire Writes Back*:

> ...a novel which incorporates the extreme version of the opposition between Centre and margin. The book contrasts the metropolitan centre, which is the location not only of power which comes from the control of language but also of order itself, with the periphery of the colonial world, in which only the illusion of power exists and in which disorder always predominates. (Bill Ashcroft, pp. 88-89)

Works Cited

Ashcroft, Bill, Gareth Griffiths and Helen Tiffin (eds.), *The Empire Writes Back: Theory and Practice in Post-Colonial Literatures* (London: Routledge, 1989).

Fanon, Frantz (Most of these views are a critical summarization from Chapter III, "The Pitfalls of National Consciousness", pp. 119-23).

———, *The Wretched of the Earth* (Harmondsworth: Penguin, 1961).

Lacovia, R.M. "The Medium is the Divide: An Examination of V.S. Naipaul's Early Works", *Black Images*, I, No. 2 (1972).

Lamming, George, *The Pleasures of Exile* (London: Michael Joseph, 1960).

Lee, R.H. "The Novels of V.S. Naipaul", in *Critical Perspectives on V.S. Naipaul,* ed. Robert D. Hamner (Washington: Three Continents Press, 1977).

Lindroth, James R. "The Figure of Performance in *The Mimic Men*", *Modern Fiction Studies*, Vol. 30, No. 3, Autmun, 1984.

Miller, Karl, "V.S. Naipaul and the New Order," in *Critical Perspectives on V.S. Naipaul,* ed. Robert D. Hamner.

Mustafa, Fawzia, *V.S. Naipaul* (Cambridge: Cambridge University Press, 1995).

Naipaul, V.S., "Conrad's Darkness" in *The Return of Eva Peron* (Harmondsworth: Penguin, 1981).

———, *The Mimic Men* (London: Andre Deutsch, 1967).

———, *The Overcrowded Barracoon*, 1972; rpt. (Harmondsworth: Penguin, 1976).

Nazareth, Peter, "*The Mimic Men* as a Study of Corruption", 7, No. 7 (July 1970), pp. 21-22 revised for *Literature and Society in Modern Africa* (Kampala: East African Literature Bureau, 1972).

Ormerod, David, "In a Derelict Land: The Novels of V.S. Naipaul", *Wisconsin Studies in Contemporary Literature*, 9 (Winter 1968).

Phillips, Caryl, "The Enigma of Denial", *Biblio*, January-February 2001.

Ramraj, Victor J., "The All-Embracing Christ like Vision: Tone and Attitude in *The Mimic Men*", in *Commonwealth*, ed. Anna Rutherford (Aarhus: Akademist Boghantel, 1971).

Rohlehr, Gordon, "The Ironic Approach: The Novels of V.S. Naipaul", in *The Islands in Between*, ed. Louis James (London: Oxford University Press, 1968).

Thieme, John, *The Web of Tradition: Uses of Allusion in V.S. Naipaul's Fiction* (Hansib Dangaroo, 1987).

———, *The Web of Tradition: Uses of Allusion in V.S. Naipaul's Fiction*, p. 123.

Walcott, Derek, "Is V.S. Naipaul an Angry Young Man?", *Trinidad Guardian*, 6 August 1967.

Williams, Eric, *From Columbus to Castro: The History of the Caribbean 1492-1969* (New York: Harper and Row, 1970).

Chapter 5

Post-Colonial Displacements and the Perils of Freedom

> Identity—who are we, where we come from, what are we—is difficult to maintain in exile...we are the other, an opposite, a flow in the geometry of resettlement, an exodus. Silence and discretion veil the hurt, slow the body searches, soothe the sting of loss. (Edward Said, pp. 16-17)

Over the last few decades of the twentieth century, a greater stress has been laid on the question of exile, displacement, expatriation and diaspora than could have been imagined. Apart from its economic, ethnic, political, cultural and professionalized connotations, the idea of this shift and change has influenced literary history itself in no uncertain way. The centrality and significance of de-centered experience in the global context in the post-War phase has altered the meanings of what was thought canonical or great, or representative of the experience of the colonized, non-Western world. A result of this upsetting of established literary forms and traditions has been the relative movement to the centre-stage of the erstwhile silent, suppressed or buried histories and ethno-cultural experiences of the ex-colonial world. In a way, the idea of the world in a state of constant movement and crossings of national boundaries, has become trans-continental and inter-ethnic in the complexities that have presided over the structuration of the post-imperial world. Whether one talks of diasporic, exilic or migrant experience, the centrality of dispersed, fragmented and undefined, multi-cultural exposure acquires a unique position. Though it is not of immediate relevance here, the problems in critical theory and creative writing have been geared to the creation of the poetics of alternative, anti-hegemonic and cross-cultural contexts, among others. Naturally, in literature, new idioms and voices have probed the issues of cultural identity, dispossession, colonial impact, and the problems resulting from the above-mentioned post-colonial displacement and the disorders resulting from the imbrication of Western culture in erstwhile colonial settings. What is more, the recent past has brought into prominence the questions of regional, national, ethnic, and personal identity, not only for the average migrant and diasporic, but also that of the scholar and thinker. For example, Edward Said has extensively spoken about the 'paradoxical' nature of his exile as a Palestinian who has intellectually and politically aligned his cultural theories to the cause of 'worldly', material understanding of truth and experience. Having located himself in an in-between or interstitial 'space' between a Palestinian colonial past and an American imperial present, he has empowered himself to speak out, to be the voice of the margianized, the dispossessed. The point to be grasped is that contemporary critical debates on exile, migrancy, expatriation and diasporic identities have emerged from human and intellectual/literary exposures experienced by critics like Said, Homi Bhabha, Abdul Jan Mohammad, Gayatri Spivak and others, who have absorbed the nature of the twentieth-century ideological and cultural conflicts, whatever their source or origination. In another sense, the dream-like view of the lost home or territory acquires an illusionary character for the migrant, for example, the indentured Indian's view of India as 'home' from the Caribbean. Migrancy and subsequent displacement is understood as constructing certain ways of seeing that impact upon both migrants and their descendants. To be blunt, migrancy and the post-colonial displacements/diasporic shifts have effects which last long after the initial act; the journey from 'roots' to 'routes'. As Russell King, John Connell and Paul White argue in the preface to their collection *Writing Across Worlds: Literature and Migration*:

> ...for some groups, migration is not a mere interval between fixed points of departure and arrival, but a mode of being in the world—"migrancy". (Russell King, p. xv)

Before coming to V.S. Naipaul's compelling portrayal of the experience of displacement and dislocation in its different contours in *In a Free State* in this chapter, it is pertinent to stress upon a few aspects about the exclusionary nature of unsettling, away from home and nation. The notion of exile has its antecedents buried in the Eurocentric character. While the dislocated and displaced 'European' exile has been accommodated, and allowed a new home, the position of the 'other' exile has been problematic. The dilemmas and plights faced by diasporic peoples throughout the world have received inadequate attention in the West. Rather than being accommodated, these new exiles (the reasons may be political, cultural or ethnic) are seen (among other things) as a threat to the old order. They are received or construed as unnecessary and superfluous, as appendages to the metropolitan space. Reflecting on his own situation, Homi Bhabha writes:

> I have lived that moment of the scattering of the people than in other times and other places, in the nations of others, becomes a time of gathering. Gatherings of exiles and émigrés and refugees, gathering on the edge of 'foreign' cultures; gathering at the frontiers; gatherings in the ghettos or cafes of city centres; gathering in the half-life, half-light of foreign tongues, or in the uncanny fluency of another's language...gathering the memories of under-development, of other worlds lived retroactively.... Also gathering of the people in the diaspora: indentured, migrant, interned; gathering of incriminatory statistics, educational performance, legal statutes, immigration status. (Homi K. Bhabha (ed.), p. 291)

It should not be surprising that the 'other' exile is not permitted to 'settle', to be part of a permanent community or the multi-cultural spectrum in a national setting. The very construction of the 'other', as eloquently demonstrated by Edward Said in *Orientalism*, is premised upon the difference between the Occident and the Orient. This construction has a distinctly political dimension and is hardly better exemplified than in imperialism. The power imbalance exists, not only in the obvious characteristics of imperialism—brute political, economic and military rationales—but also in terms of culture.

Hence, citing the argument from colonial discourse theory, cultures that have been denigrated and marginalized within the dominant discourse, it would hardly be appropriate to celebrate their exiles. Naipaul's Third World exiles and travellers, as shall be seen, whether from Asia, the Caribbean or elsewhere, are bereft of identity and security, moving through spaces without a centre or home in *In a Free State*. Furthermore, the 'othering' of these travellers and migrants is generally the product of the fracturing and fissuring of societies that have faced the wrath of colonialism and imperialism. However, these figures in *In a Free State*, unlike the more positive or productive experience of exile, are unable to carve out some space from their peripherality and marginalization; they remain unwanted and isolated, victims of so-called free, democratic nations which only make them aware of a punishing destiny. The following statement of Said in *Culture and Imperialism* tellingly lays bare the unsavory truths that lie behind a good deal of twentieth-century modes that have governed civilizations, including Western modernity:

> For surely, it is one of the unhappiest characteristics of the age to have produced more refugees, migrants, displaced persons, and exiles than ever before in history, most of them as an accompaniment to and, ironically enough, as afterthoughts of great post-colonial and imperial conflicts. As the struggle for independence produced new states and new boundaries, it also produced homeless wanderers, nomads, vagrants, unassimilated to the emerging structure of institutional power.... And in so far as these people exist between the old and the new state, their condition articulates the tensions, irresolutions, and contradictions in the overlapping territories shown on the cultural map of imperialism. (Edward Said, pp. 402-03)

What Said in effect means is that the location of culture as fixed, mono-cultural and established experience, has shifted to its un-housed, de-centered and migrant open space, between domains, between homes, and between languages. It is, then, the intellectual and the writer's function to distill and articulate the disfigurements of modernity—the predicaments of humans and communities under this or that imperial or ideological frame—

population transfer, collective dispossession, mass migration or immigration.

It is also important to realize that the possibilities engendered by rethinking or renegotiating identity in terms of cross-cultural fluidity and hybridity have the propensity to alter the ways in which identities are lost and formed, in places culturally and geographically distinct. Avtar Brah captures the idea in her concept of 'diaspora space' (Avtar Brah, p. 209), as one where there is an intersection of borders where subjects and identities become 'juxtaposed, contested, proclaimed or disavowed'. In the acts of transgression, there is, then, little scope for purity or mono-cultural identity (V.S. Naipaul, p. 208). As Brah stresses, it is important to understand that this space is not some kind of post-modern playground of 'anything goes' where all identities are valuable and available as if in a 'multicultural supermarket'. Discourses of power which seek to legitimate certain forms of identity and marginalize others by imposing a logic of binary oppositions remain operable and challenge new forms of identity from emerging (209). This emerges as a relevant point in that *In a Free State* presents people who are afloat, dispersed and in search of balance and adjustment as they come to face opposition and challenges in new geographical locales they travel to.

In a Free State, which foregrounds some of the above-stated compulsive issues intersecting nations, cultures and ethnicities, also marks the well-known shift in Naipaul's own career. Following his success with the non-fictional form, and 'history' in the writing of *The Loss of El Dorado*, he broke through the tyranny of fictional form to create a work based on the continuity of a central trope, very much like in *A Way in the World*. On the other hand, the movement away from a central agency and voice facilitated Naipaul to use exile and displacement itself as a 'text' of experience scattered across geographies, cultures and societies, while his technique articulated the distinctive but intersecting elements of the post-colonial scene. However, marginality and the perils generated by freedom in the post-war world are almost shared alike by Third World and the Euro/Western characters, so that the remnants of imperialism leading to decolonization in the new states work both ways and are fraught with disillusioning possibilities. *In a Free State* was perhaps the first book by a writer of Indo-Caribbean origin to have won the coveted Booker Award, itself a proof that Naipaul's creative vision dealt with the undeniable and disturbing features that mark a world torn by accretions and prejudices of race, colour, origin and place. As such, it could be said with a fair amount of conviction that *In a Free State* anticipated some of the real issues centered in the marginal status of the cosmopolitan, trans-national migrant, and its rather fashionable contemporary theorizing.

In a Free State makes a statement about the relationship between experience, vision and art as a Third World reality. The distance between these aspects of life is regulated by the capacity and circumstances of the concerned individual. The experience of expatriation is seen as a common feature of contemporary life. Now, as never before, the Third World has become aware of its anonymity and unimportance which is as much a consequence of its historical past as of undeniable contemporary political, social and economic pressures. In an increasingly shrinking, industrialized and automated world as more and more individuals and peoples begin to feel unnecessary and obsolete, the struggle for survival acquires greater urgency and obstinacy. Through a work of art the anonymous man achieves an identity, affirmation and individuality.

In a Free State dramatizes human degradation at different levels of experiences, in which the author himself is included. The movement from passivity to a suggestive rebellion at the end underlines the ineluctable element of degradation in human experience. Naipaul's vision is unmistakably dark and bitter, as he chooses to portray people who are helpless, away from home, and constant victims of assault and domination. Everyone has lost something vital; Santosh his caste and nationality; Dayo's brother, his psychic balance; Bobby and Linda their sense of judgement. *In a Free State* is perhaps Naipaul's first work where preoccupation with death, futility of enterprise and failure are considered final. What confounds and alienates the characters is their lack of any vision that would revitalize their quest, if only transiently, as in the case of Mr. Stone, Ralph Singh or Mr. Biswas. Their journeying or freedom is not the result of rebellion or personal victory, on the other hand, it is marked by dependency and vacuum. Their will to fight is futile and meaningless, like their false dreams and fragile sense of freedom. They are small men, having acquiesced in others' brutality and are thus victimized.

Naipaul's fiction after *The Mimic Men* in a way reflects his increasing preoccupation with the post-colonial Third World scene. But the difference in exploring and fictionalizing the experience of expatriation and immigration in his work is marked. Naipaul has disowned and moved away from strictly personal experience; his work beginning with *In a Free State* signals his rejection of any national or cultural location that is directly connected with his personal life or ancestry. His entry into other, and new areas of cross-cultural and transnational entanglements illustrates his search for possible parallels to his own past. The impulse to isolate and deflate the experience of migration and expatriation gains prominence with each novel. Naipaul sees immigration, exile and expatriation as symptomatic of a patternless world, where order, direction and settlement are impossibilities. Economic power, racial revenge and exploitations of all sorts mark the fate of the hopeless immigrant or expatriate exposed to dangers and humiliations at the hands of the post-colonial regimes which bulldoze aliens and outsiders, seeking revenge for their own past oppression and brutalization. Naipaul's expatriates, exiles, immigrants and aliens confront a menacing, racist and a counter, anti-colonial setting seething with violence. There is little respite in Naipaul's later work from pain and anguish of not belonging; homelessness, wandering and journeying assume more insidious overtones, as people with little vision or capacity for resistance find themselves caught in situations of unrest, anger and racial confrontation.

Naipaul's detached observation of these 'theatrics' in modern nation states sharpens his ironic stance in satirizing the futile attempts at controlling disorder through borrowed power and resources. The lack of sympathy or compassion is more glaring, for the reason that Naipaul now looks at the whole traffic of people moving from one to the other place as conditioned by drift and anonymity as a way of life. The 'little' men and the mimic men of Naipaul are replaced by invisible people who have lost their bearings and consequently, the metaphor of homelessness acquires a wider, inter-continental meaning. They are not defined by any national boundary or history; like orphans and destitutes in the New World scenario, their fate seems to illustrate the ultimate disappearance of certainties and authenticities of the old order. The bleakness of Naipaulian vision is accompanied by his political views on the futility of achieving a real freedom in the face of the resurfacing of neo-imperial corporate capitalism supported and valorized by the urban-elite and as much by the political set-up. Through his intransigent and uncompromising stance, Naipaul sees the negative ironies in operation in contemporary civilizational structures, from a 'free' state wherein the ideological frames of control have worked since the Second World War. In a similar vein, the decolonizing periods have produced a disturbance and disorder for which the unstable and politically dependent structures in the Third World are responsible. As J.J. Healy puts it:

> What he has tried to do with an overreaching intelligence in his journalism and restrained, tensed imagination in his fiction, is to see clearly the darkened, purgatorial disfigurations of contemporary history. (J.J. Healy, p. 49)

Along with, the journalistic peregrinations of Naipaul into countries and areas apparently distinct from each other—India, Africa, Latin America, the Islamic world—have yielded results and insights which unmask the ideologies and the psychological make-up of the colonized. In the later works, the truth unravels the shallowness of human attitudes and relationships, which becomes a kind of subtext of violence, politics and sexuality that force themselves increasingly in our times. The means of access to new trouble spots of the world, in a distinctly altered way through journalistic and anthropological approach has also changed Naipaul's way to write these places and societies close to ways in which a Greene or a Durrell could approach Africa, Egypt or Vietnam. Naipaul unmasks through a frame of reference the negatives of colony, blackness, the non-rational in relation to the Western, colonizing and dominating strategies. However, Greene and Durrell represent the white attitudes through a

British, known literary tradition with their roots entrenched firmly in religion and morality. Naipaul, on the other hand, enters this world, precisely without a 'backing' of tradition and a sense of belonging. "He has", as Healy says, "a fugitive post-Enlightenment sensibility with a keen eye for dark ages, dark places" (J.J. Healy, p. 59).

In a Free State is a statement on the perils of being 'free'—a freedom that involves the loss of selfhood—conceived in an exclusively different form. It contains a string of long and short stories, two journalistic pieces, and a novella having a unity in thematic terms. A sustained, fixed eye on the increasing threat to identity and personality in various countries and societies here marks Naipaul's treatment of the harassed and economically marginalized/underprivileged characters. Naipaul's prose operates through a painful focus on a character to highlight the underlying irony and pathos, as in the case of Santosh, the hero of "One out of Many." Interestingly, all stories and sketches are about people far from their home country, a theme Naipaul continues to exploit in *Guerrillas* and in *A Bend in the River*. In totality, the book suggests a certain novelty in the post-war international scene. For the first time, racial confrontation is shown as menacing in the leading novella. Irony and pathos are conjoined to bring about the vision of placelessness, which is a global phenomenon in *In a Free State*. The book is full of transients, tourists, exiles, colonialists and emissaries in the newly-freed Africa, England and America. The metaphor of lost identity and drift is captured through a fear psychosis, with all the figures yearning, sick for a home that is not home. Indeed, the narrative combines to give the book a sense of fictional continuity with the themes of colonial retreat by the whites, or the sense of menace and lostness of the Indians and the West Indians in the white world. The perspective of anti-climax is here further heightened by the massacre of individual dreams and positive hopes of emigration. Anarchy, which was a subject limited to the West Indies or India is now universalized.

From 'the wretched of the earth' to the 'insecure of the earth'—this marks the complex variations of the experience of movement or displacement in *In a Free State*. The panorama ranges from the most deprived and dispossessed—the 'Third World's third world'—people like Santosh, Dayos' brother, Arab urchins, Egyptian soldiers returning defeated from Sinai, the refugees, the tramp—to the materially sound and secure people like Bobby and Linda, the Lebanese businessman, the American and European tourists and affluent young Egyptians studying abroad. The shaping statement of the narratives articulates the unbridgeable gap between the rich and the poor, the margins and the centre—they shall never 'meet'—though separated only by the distance of a deck of a steamer. As the narration proceeds amidst a heightening pitch of violence and anguish, the important, aggressive world recedes and the subjective reality of the unimportant emerges as the significant fact of each story. For example, London, Washington and the African state symbolically become less than meaningful when a Santosh is faced with the powerful reality of his body and his mortality, Dayo's brother with the futility of his possessive love for his brother, and Bobby with the insecurity of the compound. In general, as *In a Free State* presents, the world is indifferent, if not hostile, to the subjective reality of the sensitive, reflective Third World man who in his own way seeks to possess it. The narrator also presents an emphatic image of the protagonist of each episode, literally and literarily in a 'free state', detached from contingency as a result of a negative encounter with reality. By contrast, Naipaul's fiction shows that the greatest traps to freedom and self-expression are oppressive, rigid social systems, and the possibility of one's growth and self-awareness lies in one's freedom from contingent reality and its contours.

The most frequently discussed aspect of *In a Free State* is its treatment of the twin themes of freedom and alienation which is mediated by Naipaul's ironic stance. Naipaul demystifies the myth surrounding the misperceptions that one must be elsewhere to be 'free'. In the older sense, the work establishes situations which were earlier understood as East-West encounters or 'culture clashes'—though inevitably governed by one's act of choice. Post-colonial upheaval and rootlessness are compounded realities in which deracination, economic compulsions and the simple acts of will also play part; it is the post-colonial generation's existential crisis. The feeling of being unnecessary and marginal is part of this 'baggage' of fate however pure the intentions behind such a movement or displacement may be. A critic has summed it up insightfully:

> Naipaul is careful to show that past of its origin is the result of misplaced and sometimes misled desire, his acuity in explaining the metropolitan-centered development of colonial identity-formations still cannot wrest itself from historical determinism. (Fawzia Mustafa, p. 115)

In a Free State is clearly great prose written out of obsessive insight into a natural void of uncombined elements and 'politically' liberated states. The pieces in the novel are not occasional, but form an entity in structural terms, meaning thereby that they are related to the personal vision of Naipaul delineated in *A House for Mr Biswas*. In *In a Free State* too the characters are both participants and observers of the recurrent feelings of humiliation and alienation. Like Ralph Singh, Bobby too feels that he is playing a part, or is involved in a drama. Here, as well as in *The Mimic Men*, it is not merely the photographic image of reality that is significant, but the vision of the protagonists also becomes meaningful. In *In a Free State*, while the individualized experience is intense, the concentration on certain basic aspects that make characters share a general experience of exile and lost identity is significant. Naipaul makes them identical with mankind elsewhere. The barbarism and the violence of post-imperialist civilizations, the degration of personal freedom, whether of expatriates or workers are portrayed in a mirror of despair and cynicism in *In a Free State*. Set in a variety of countries and places, *In a Free State* is perhaps Naipaul's most serious and controlled criticism of the human situation in the modern 'free' states, a world which smacks of irony, considering the humiliation his characters experience. "Hate oppression; fear the oppressed" is what Ralph Singh advised in *The Mimic Men*. It is more the fear of the oppressed and the anchorless in an alien situation which breeds a despairing view of life. Strong and discriminatory as Naipaul's journalistic sensibility is, *In a Free State* liberates him from the restrictions of a single man's fictional portrayal. The stories, and the novella after the main title, stress without disguise the violence and barbarism that still afflict the so-called, advanced, 'civilized' world.

Naipaul's fiction underlines in the literary and the real sense, the loss of tradition and landscape; while the values of the Western literary tradition in which Naipaul is himself situated are recoverable, the lack of tradition in terms of a deeper existential loss is irrecoverable and irreplaceable. It amounts to a total amnesia of one's heritage and place. Camus expresses man's experience of absurdity in similar terms in *The Myth of Sisyphus*:

> But in a universe that is suddenly deprived of illusion and of light man feels a stranger. He is an irremediable exile, because he is deprived of memories of a lost homeland as much as he lacks the hope of a promised land to come. This divorce between man and his life, the actor and his setting, truly constitutes the feeling of absurdity. (Albert Camus quoted by Shashi Kamra, p. 220)

Naipaul's protagonist is not only a stranger but an orphan, unrelated, in a world of relationships, of which he is keenly aware. All the negative aspects of experience and their constructive resolution seems to be the privilege of societies secure within a tradition. Insecure societies can only hope to imitate and thus remain second and third rate cultures. And those who are products of these societies, as in *In a Free State*, are most likely to encounter the dangers of race, class, politics and dictatorship. Not equipped with the inner liberation of the self, these exiles experience the absurd, dispossessed state of being, unable to exercise resistance against those who oppress them.

Rebellion, flight, danger, homelessness, dependency—these are linked concepts in Naipaul's work. *In a Free State* contains people who, as a result of their voluntary or involuntary migration and self-exiled state have become lost souls. As Paul Theroux has remarked: "They are all casualties of freedom" (Paul Theroux, p. 96). Their lives have been, like Singh's, altered by escape to a new landscape, but unlike Singh, they cannot assess the difference. They have come too far from where there is no going back. It is not one man but whole groups of people who are seen as lost. The contrast between the whole idea of place and placelessness, the problem of the rooted and eternally uprooted is brought into painful focus. The modern phenomenon of drift on the one hand, and the psychological clutching at one's past and place, is one of its peculiar paradoxes. Through his own geographical and personal distancing from places, Naipaul has probed the sense of barriers—physical, social, historical—and the sense of negation and emptiness that such a barrier-sense induces. In turn, it has to do with another kind of association within this alienating frame of reflection, of these negative components with colony, blackness, cultural removal, the quality of experience that is non-Western. When one has moved away from anchorage to aloneness—an expatriate's destiny—away from the family, state, abandoned by its historical frame, one finds the world, like Santosh in "One out of Many" a typological purgatory. This is the writer's or the man's shape of destiny; to etch out meanings and values through this dangling condition of cultivated and endured freedom.

In *In a Free State*, Naipaul explores the ironies of the exile's predicament. The experience of exile which is voluntary and free to start out with, soon becomes deeply disillusioning to the exiled individuals and it is then they realize that they have nothing to fall back on, and are trapped in the situation they themselves have chosen. The three fictional pieces in the volume, are enclosed by two extracts from Naipaul's journals where, as traveller, the author witnesses two acts of debasement and feels the helplessness of his own anger. "The Tramp at Piraeus" presents an incident of simple persecution, where the tramp on the refugee ship is hounded for his crazy and foolish ways. In "The Circus at Luxor", Naipaul retaliates, at an incident in Egypt, where beggar boys scrounging for food from Italian tourists, are stage-managed by the whip of the camel driver, who puts up the show for the tourists' photographs. In this world, Naipaul feels, distinctions are no longer in terms of white and black, colonizer and colonized. His sensibility shrinks from those subtle and sporadic acts of violence, which, springing from non-identifiable camp or cause, take man by surprise.

The ambience of the neo-colonial displacement is established in the Prologue, in which an elderly English tramp aboard a steamer travelling from the Piraeus to Alexandria is persecuted by his cabin-mates for some offence. Interestingly, the setting of the Prologue in respect of Egypt is not without significance; Egypt stands at the confluence of many empires, and as Naipaul hints, is 'free' after many humiliations. The people on board the steamer are all casualties of freedom of one kind or another. The tramp himself boasts that he is a 'citizen of the world', a prototype of the romantic wanderer of an earlier generation. The 'Prologue', like the 'Epilogue' constitutes the documentary bracket that allows Naipaul to present his fictional rendering of postcolonial chaos in the frame of travelling people. Both the Prologue and the Epilogue foreshadow the study of aggression that is undertaken in varying degrees within the volume's stories. In the first, Naipaul remains a strict observer without decisively intervening in the action to rescue the humiliated Tramp. By the time of the 'Epilogue', it is as though things have reached an impasse, an impossible level of racial abuse and human degradation, so that intervention becomes necessary to stop the naked play of aggression leading to despair. The Chinese, who are members of a large circus group in Milan, are close to Naipaul himself; they being 'wanderers in industrial Europe' (p. 249) and he an isolated Asiatic. However, deciding to drop his mask of detachment to stop the Germans and Italians throwing crumbs at the children, he also realizes the futility of the act; the children would soon be back, 'raking the sand' to search for food.

The central experience of all three pieces is that of homelessness, realized with either a sense of clarity or confusion. Santosh, the domestic servant in 'One Out of Many' who has journeyed to Washington in the trail of his employer, knows he can never be part of its "television life." Cut off from his roots in Bombay where he "was once part of the flow, never thinking of [himself] as a presence," Santosh is terrified by the burden of freedom, responsibility and identity which exile imposes on him. Out of terror, he marries a "hubshi" and resigns himself to the deadening prison of the other country, whose tempo, goals and norms are totally alien to his communal self: "Washington is not Bombay" as his employer, a government official, had warned him before Santosh pleaded to be taken there. With a wife and children back home in the village to whom he can never return, Santosh, in Washington, is either in hiding or seeking escape, until his marriage makes him a legal citizen. Nevertheless he has not learnt, like the restaurant owner Priya, "to cope with Washington." It is "the exile's habit of constantly comparing two worlds which links the narratives in the volume, rather than the journey" (Landeg White, p. 195), which is only a preamble to a disturbed centre of experience.

Santosh represents an alien's predicament in a society he can hardly comprehend in terms of its sheer pace and complexity. He finds on the television screen something that upsets the daily reality. Once he runs away from his dominance to cease being a part of his master's luggage, he makes himself a law-breaker in America. Existentially speaking, Santosh's act is an act of choice and free will, of the right to personal destiny, but it is a desperate way to carve out his identity, lost in the process of migration. After working as a chef in a restaurant and finally marrying a "hubshi" woman, he becomes an American citizen and is free. But he cheers himself only by saying, "to be empty is to be calm" (55).

Apparently, the story appears to be comic, but Santosh's blundering and his scrapes are closer to the predicament of trapped victims. They are more pathetic than merely comic. At the end, he too is a 'casualty of freedom,' waiting for the final emptiness. He says: "I hadn't escaped; I had never been free. I had been abandoned. I was like nothing; I had made myself nothing. And I couldn't turn back" (p. 53). Freedom here suggests emptiness, an estrangement from everything except death. This is perhaps the only instance where a Naipaul story ends in a total atmosphere of gloom and death: "It was only after it happened that I realized how badly I needed such a victory, how far, gaining my freedom, I had begun to accept death not as the end but as the goal" (51). The end of the story leaves the reader with the impression of the unenviable destiny of the protagonist, despite the suspicion that the author may be involving the role of the United States for the lure of wealth and luxury that it produces in people of Third World post-colonial societies. Santosh's marriage to the 'Hubshi' woman ironically sentences him to a life of exile from his Hindu roots. Baffled at being labeled a 'Soul Brother' during a period of race riots and reflecting on the anguished burden of his new found 'freedom', he muses:

> I was once a part of the flow, never thinking of myself as a presence. Then I looked in the mirror and decided to be free. All that my freedom has brought me is the knowledge that I have a face and have a body, that I must feed this body and clothe this body for a certain number of years. Then it will be over. (57-58)

Santosh, having accidentally jumped out of the world of the unconscious, awakens to the desolate knowledge of life. His quest for identity and freedom is based on his chained existence of living under authority and suppressed emotions. It is the logical extension of the earlier historical dislocation that took place a century back when adventurers landed in India from another continent, first for trade, then to establish their political domination. Santosh's quest is nothing profound, but a part of the larger historico-geographical movement elsewhere. Santosh might well appear to be an extension of Mr. Biswas, though on a much smaller scale. He too yearns for a permanent place, whereas so far he has had only pavements or his master's cupboard to live in. He is freed from his constricted and slavish life by marrying a black woman. However, Santosh's individualism and grit, if any, are presented at a puerile level, compared with the struggle of Biswas against a system. As the title of the story indicates, Santosh is just one out of many left to struggle and shape a destiny in yet another alien landscape.

"Tell Me Who to Kill" is symbolically a journey into the 'heart of darkness', breathing anger, repulsion and hatred. Compared with the placid, resigned tone of "One Out of Many", we have here a mind revolting against indifference and betrayal. To judge it in the migrant's context, it may well be a common experience Naipaul is portraying; of a man being proud and protective towards his brother Dayo, whom he has sent to England, away from the native Caribbean squalor and disorder, only to discover that he is a liar, a mere idler and thus unworthy of attention. The narrator refers to his journey (another voyage leading to Hindu acculturation) to England as one across black waters, and even though this obscures the fact that his ancestors had already severed the link with Mother India by coming to the New World as indentured labourers, the sense of having betrayed their ancestral roots, remains. The protagonist's hysteria becomes a perpetual torment, which is again any emigrant's anxiety, till the final severance comes when Dayo weds an English girl. What the story views, despite the protagonist—the narrator's somewhat too severe cynicism and self-destructive mind—is the opposition between the uses of freedom. It is yet a new variety added to the disgrace and rage of a displaced person. The ideal being pursued is the typical Caribbean one; of Dayo to attain a professional position by raising himself in a highly developed society.

The narrator's fantasy of a gentleman's life for his brother Dayo, whom he wishes to release from the "shame of their poverty-stricken West Indian background ends in a great sadness of disillusionment. As he learns in slow, laboured stages, life in England does nothing to remake his brother or himself. Marriage to a white girl effects Dayo's compromise with England, but the narrator has lost his own self and Dayo's, without knowing whom to blame, and whom to kill for it. Trying to save Dayo from a mediocre fate back home, the narrator finds he has done worse by leaving home and loosing it. Possessing the faculty to "see things so much better than the rest of [his] family" and possessing "the ambition and the shame for all of them" the narrator had envied "people going away to further their studies and coming back as big men" (65). He "used to have a vision of a big city...the pavement covered with flat leaves of a perfect shape in pretty colours..." but in the city much later, the irony of his alienated condition is that he has "nobody to write and send a leaf or a flower to." About his own life there, he feels that he "throw that away", the phrase communicating his disorientation and futility of being. He cannot belong and his homelessness hurts. "The mystery land is theirs, the stranger is you. None of the houses in the rain there belong to you" (79).

For the exile, the envy is directed towards those who are secure in the possession of their houses: "They (the foreign tourists the narrator watches) have countries to go back to, they have houses." The narrator's fantasy of the life of opportunity abroad ends in the reality of "...I feel that I too have nowhere to go, and that the life in London is over." His Hindu sensibility surfaces in response to the blankness of Dayo's wedding ceremony: "no turban, no procession, no drums, no ceremony of welcome, no green arches, no lights in the wedding-tent, no wedding songs" (99) and speaks out of a Hindu philosophical negation when he tells himself: "I came with nothing, I have nothing. I will leave nothing." "They spoil my life" (106). The atmosphere of the occasion makes him nauseated, leaves him feeling that it is more like a funeral than a wedding. Dayo, who is the indirect cause of the narrator's woe and despair, is however, not the central problem that so afflicts the expatriate-turned marginal man. Significantly, he comes to see himself as a 'dead man', indicating his having had a breakdown. Naipaul refers to having a sensation of the 'exploding head' in *The Enigma of Arrival*, in the tormenting process of his own adjustment as a man from another continent, another culture. A recent critical opinion characterizes the narrator's 'dementia' as "designed to illustrate the pathological side of migratory process where a sense of self is lost rather than gained" (Fawzia Mustafa, p. 116). The obsessive paternalistic (sometimes even bordering on homosexuality) concern with his brother's life develops into insanity which we see unfold itself. The sense of massive disjunction that has effected his desire for revenge instead of responsibility, the need for killing somebody, is unmistakable. Migration entails loss, but it can also be overcome by assimilation and understanding the 'power' that lies at the heart of the strong metropolitan culture and values. In this case, as the story conveys, the choice and the migratory process (in retrospect) convey all the familiar features of the impoverished Caribbean society that led to mass journeys to the colonizer's country. But *en route*, the dangers of this mirage of another Western dream, turn out to be not only abortive, but terminally destructive in the personal and filial sense. The narrator accuses the whites at his brother's wedding party, but he cannot be certain they are "the enemy." Naipaul again shows the folly of being weak, dependent and confused in exile.

In the main novella, *In a Free State*, Naipaul deals with two whites expatriated in Africa, at the mercy of political change, knowing security only within their own compound. Out of their country, Bobby and Linda are thrown together in a long car ride from the capital back to their town. Bobby, an administrative officer in the Central Government, had been participating in a seminar there. The whites, supporting the President against the king, both tribal rivals, trigger off hostilities and the king is hunted down. But through this thin plot, Naipaul explores the white expatriate life in its attitudes to Africans, and to each other. Bobby, a homosexual on the hunt for African partners, and Linda with a reputation of a "man-eater", are shown by Naipaul to be hard and secretive without, and with no dignity within. His sympathies for the Indian and West-Indian expatriates on the other hand, are expressed through a depiction of the true mental agony of Santosh and Dayo's brother—both genuinely free of posturing, and "victims of a life chosen without prior understanding" (Landeg White, p. 193).

Naipaul returns to the theme of menace and violence on a much larger scale in the title novella. Here the whites, having no link whatsoever with the African landscape and turbulence of the racial retribution, confront the absurdity and brutality of the situation as they drive towards an African town from the capital. Here again, Naipaul stresses the non-relationship between man and landscape. Bobby and Linda are small people, having in their experience an air of artificiality. This is compounded by the complete severance of the African politics and way of life from their own past. Naipaul reduces them to the role of mere spectators, and later, victims of the wrath of those who now rule the state after independence. Their isolation and extraneous role do not provide any sensitive response. Their humiliation obviously underlines the dubious state of the white ex-colonizer in the now changed set-up. Naipaul's subtle penetrations into the English couples' psychic make-up appear to anticipate the characters of Peter Roche and Jane in *Guerrillas*—people without any consistent vision or view of life. Bobby and Linda might have as well been going through a Western film watching the wild African bush as they drive through. Bobby, an English homosexual, who works for the new government as an officer, picks up a young Zulu on his last night in the capital while on a visit. After having been lured towards him, the Zulu spits in his face. Africa has entranced Bobby, like Jane who is in search of adventure and variety in *Guerrillas*. For Bobby, it means open spaces and an apparent promise of safe adventure, being a member of the privileged whites. But Africa is going to leave him even more disillusioned, lost and alone than ever before. He becomes another casualty of the illusionary idea of freedom. After he is beaten up by African soldiers, he, along with Linda, reaches the government compound. Bobby is left alone, only to think and come to terms with his disgrace and humiliation. As in the rest of the book, Naipaul reveals the depth or the 'otherness' of Africa against the so-called sensible, educated middle-class people's imagination of its ethos. In the process, there is a massacre of obstinate illusions. It is the men and women damaged by fantasy who invariably have miscalculated conclusions about places and people. Bobby and Linda too are damaged by this trait of misreading Africa through their personal, theatrical and self-confident views. This is particularly so of Linda, who has at best an immature, oddly romantic and silly ideas about things in life. Bobby and Linda are aware that they do not belong there, but lacking sensitivity and mature views, fail to see the danger around. Bobby too has ceased to be a whole person; his self is divided between his wish to merely exist in a country which he knows holds out no promise for him.

The novella describes in detail Bobby's sense of security and freedom of action. The incident in the bar at the New Shropshire with the Zulu elaborates the gestures of a man at ease in his environment. He is not disturbed at all when the Zulu boy spits at him:

> Africa was for Bobby the empty spaces, the safe adventures of long fatiguing drives on open roads, the other Africans, boys built like men'you want lift? You big boy, you no go school? ...when I born again I want your colour. You no frighten. You want five shillings. (p. 109)
>
> That evening he had broken all rules; the evening had shown how right his rules were. He felt no bitterness, no

> hurt. He didn't blame the Zulu, he didn't blame Linda. Before Africa, the incident of the evening might have driven him out adventuring for hours more in dangerous places,...but now he knew that the mood would pass; the morning would come. Even with Linda as his passenger, the drive remained. (110)

Throughout the journey, till the very end, Bobby and Linda are travel companions, sensitive to sights and sounds, indulging freely in light conversation, aware of each feeling as it passes through their minds. Bobby ignores or suppresses all impressions of impending danger. As they move into the future, the new unknown Africa, his sense of insecurity deepens till they are almost in a panic to reach the safety of the compound. Hardly two pages are ascribed to the description of this safety which is part of the trap into which Bobby falls and from which it will be hard for him to release himself. Bobby's unconscious assumption of the role of the colonial master is not very relevant in his context: he has shifted into a world as fragile and exposed at that outside the compound:

> Bobby thought: I will have to leave. But the compound was safe; the soldiers guarded the gate. Bobby thought: I will have to sack Luke. (238)

Similarly, Santosh's and Dayo's brother's sense of release is enlarged upon in the contextual setting rather than their traps till a final 'free' state is the trap of the alienated subjective life.

Finality for the narrator is the ultimate trap. He depicts each protagonist in a final state from which the narrator releases him through story-telling. Self-awareness adds the dimension of dignity to their personalities. We appreciate these failed men who can live with the knowledge of failure like the Egyptian soldiers on their way home from Sinai, "lost, trying to walk back home, casting long shadows on the sand" (246). The narrator of the epilogue sees himself as one such. Release, then, for the narrator is in the art of narration and in having an idea. The idea, separating from existence, becoming an abstraction, ends up as an absurdity. For the artist, seeing the world as paradox, the greatest trap is the temptation to inaction and the highest free state is to re-examine an idea and to act, to write another book.

The question raised by an overview of Naipaul's fiction, in which the fictive parameters are guided by considerations of entrapment and release, is: what is the relationship between being trapped, being in a free state and the idea of freedom? Philosophically and psychologically, this can be restated as having a fresh look at the relationship that exists between existence, absurdity and self-awareness on the one hand and abstraction, freedom and non-existence on the other. Abstractions, urging a man in unknown directions, have 'existed', if at all, in the past. For abstraction engages the concepts of oneness, wholeness, purity and innocence, which, as permanent features of life today are beyond definition. They are the artist's vision of the past which suggests 'nothing' for the future. Absurdity, both as existential anguish in the face of the void and the rational awareness of irony (the outer limits of subjectivity and objectivity) is the great turning point or dividing line where the trapped protagonist unites in his self-awareness, however briefly and lightly, the frontiers of freedom/abstraction with existence.

The awareness of absurdity is a virtue and man's saving grace in Naipaul's fiction, promising the only freedom available today for his Third World characters: that of growing individuation, whose parameters are limitless, outwards towards the world and inwards by reflecting on it. Thus, entrapped and free states become conditions of awareness, ranging from the literal to the literary, and are not unalterables known and examined independently of the protagonist's existence. We see the absurdity that brings about despair most vividly in Salim's condition in *A Bend in the River*. Turning to *In a Free State*, the naked tribal Africans running at the edge of the road, viewed by Bobby in his moving car, are not only mirage-like, but, if yet existent, render modern Africa an absurdity. The tramp, wandering meaninglessly round the globle, lives on the margin between existence and non-existence, a character with whom the narrator can readily empathize—aware of the world, wanting but unable to be a part of it.

Naipaul's little man is seen as one who makes great efforts, in spite of his almost insurmountable handicaps, to realign himself to an ill-defined present, ending up as a failure either in his own estimation or in that of the narrator. Naipaul's vision is focussed on a particular Third World reality—the homeless man in search of an identity which dignifies. That he fails is also a particular truth of his situation today. He uses the tools of analysis to see for man's possibilities in an impossible world. That none of his protagonists ever commits suicide, is sufficient evidence of Naipaul's semblance of faith in humanity. What everyone's private heaven or hell is, is not his concern, for no one can know another's existential anguish. But the fact that they face it distinguishes the individual from a faceless society.

Naipaul's later work in a way records some unavoidable developments in post-war scene of the Third World. With the virtual exhaustion of grand systems and total theories, Soviet and Chinese collective economies, the anti-imperialist nationalism, we have entered a period of vast uncertainty. The contemporary world, suspended between post-colonial developments and liberal capitalist attractions, betrays one definition or inscription. Most Third World areas are frighteningly dependent—intellectually, politically, ethnically and of course, economically. No one is purely one person or one thing. The dubious results of the imperialist consolidation of mixture of cultures and identities on a global scale reflect a dissolved, amorphous life in unlikely landscapes and settings. Naipaul's 'lost centre' has extended its erasures further, and a search for a point or milestone of stable, unmoving centre is now impossible, as his writings bear testimony.

By choosing to explore an expatriate mentality in *In a Free State*, Naipaul focuses on a source material most available to a literary endeavour which has schooled itself in the already articulated utterance of developing colonialist perceptions. From the observations of a Froude to the more studied examinations of a Kipling or a Conrad, the habits of an imperial gaze are filtered through the narrower visions of a post-settler perspective that still carries the traces of paranoia about Africa's 'evolution'. The closed and cliched conversation between Bobby and Linda as they drive from the capital to their compound in the Southern Collectorate, and which makes up the bulk of the novella, is Naipaul's first sustained, protracted fictional dialogue, the course of which allows his characters to voice almost every received assumption ever developed within the lexicon of British colonial Africa. The anchor that the 'idea' of South Africa provides Linda, for example, is an acutely replicated moment of an internal colonial response which, in the African context, has always allowed the oddest apologia to white settlers looking for a legislated heaven and escape. The realization of his own insecurity and irrelevance by Bobby in fact arises from his vaguely romantic and adventurist notions of Africa and its landscape. Bobby calls the landscape 'Bergman Country', while Linda compares an impressive view to a scene in John Ford Western. But, as John Thieme rightly remarks, "these film allusions help the metropolitan reader unfamiliar with East Africa to visualize the landscape of the 'free state', and also that the Bergman reference evokes the angst-ridden mental landscape...which finds a parallel in Naipaul's story" (John Thieme, p. 158). Both Bobby and Linda fail to learn anything from this trial-ridden journey leading to a disillusioning end. Bobby's earlier fantasy of a night-journey during one of his illnesses serves as an ironic counterpoint to the car journey which they are actually taking. Off and on in the bush clearing, they see shadowy African figures in the landscape, much like Marlow's fleeting glimpses in *Heart of Darkness*. What is significant is that continuing with Conrad's fine portrayal of the impact of African environment on the Europeans, the Africans here are little more than ciphers who function as a part of the allegorical landscape in a fictive journey re-taken up by Europeans:

> "That's the sort of thing that makes me feel far from home". Linda said, "I feel that sort of forest life has been going on forever. You've been reading too much Conrad. I hate that book, don't you?" (169-70)

Naipaul fully compromises Bobby's more idealistic and apparently humanistic stand by casting him as a homosexual first and an administrator second, and then by rewarding his individual commitment with the arbitrary and ineluctable violence of a military checkpoint, where soldiers brutally beat him for no apparent reason.

Despite the novella's emphasis upon Bobby and Linda, the story's, sharpest impact remains the menace conveyed by the 'tribal' politics being played out within the newly independent African state. Never named, the country is obviously a composite of Uganda and Kenya, which is to become, with Rawanda, Burundi, and Zaire, the even more seamless starting point and setting of Naipaul's more sophisticated 'African' work, *A Bend in the River*. But where Naipaul creates distinct nations through which his protagonist travels in *A Bend in the River*, his unnamed nation in *In a Free State*, is deliberately charted as an amorphous political space. Naipaul's attempt is to create a political atmosphere charged with all the turmoil and volatility associated with the transfer of power at the advent of decolonization. In doing so, however, he condenses the events of several different histories with the result that his new African nation is unnecessarily over determined. Naipaul's ideological point is that the triumph of nationalism in the Third World not only suppresses the very real tensions unresolved in the post-colonial state, but also eliminates a possibility of resistance against the traces of Western influence. Edward Said comments in this overall context in *Culture and Imperialism*:

> .... His attack on the post-colonial world for its religious fanaticism (in *Among the Believers*), degenerate politics (in *Guerrillas*), and fundamental inferiority (in his books on India), is part of a disenchantment with the Third World that overtook many people during in 1970s and 1980s.... Questions of power and authority once directed at the classical Empires of Britain and France are now thrown at despotic successor regimes, and against the idea that African and Asian countries should remain in thrall and dependency. (Edward Said, pp. 322-23)

This is the kind of situation that the novella reveals as the post-colonial politics of 'liberation' and the new 'insurgency' threaten to slide back into yet another extension of the older forms of imperialism. While this tactic may draw upon a rich harvest of post-independence conflicts, its conflation within a single nation is a dubious basis for Naipaul's thesis about Africa's and African's preparedness for 'independence.' Thus, Bobby and Linda's drive through the Great Rift Valley, periodically dotted with blackface advertisements, runs parallel with the President's helicopter searching for the hiding king. Their stops, at checkpoints and for refreshments at formerly white—only safari lodges and an isolated home of an Asian family, are episodes that conspire to present a picture of a fragmented and torn social order. Nowhere does the story suggest a deeper awareness of the political complexities and economic handicaps created by Africa's colonization.

Works Cited

Albert Camus quoted by Shashi Kamra, *The Novels of V.S. Naipaul,* New Delhi: Prestige, 1990.

Bhabha, Homi K. (ed.), *Nation and Narration,* London: Routledge, 1990.

Brah, Avtar, *Cartographies of Diaspora: Contesting Identities,* London: Routledge, 1997.

Fawzia Mustafa, *V.S. Naipaul,* Cambridge: Cambridge University Press, 1995.

Healy, J.J., "Friction, Voice and the Rough Ground of Feeling: Naipaul After Twenty-Five Years", *The University of Toronto Quarterly*, Fall, 1985.

King, Russell, John Connell, and Paul White (eds.), *Writing Across Worlds: Literature and Migration,* London: Routledge, 1995.

Naipaul, V.S., *In a Free State* (Andre Deutsch, 1971; rpt. Harmondsworth: Penguin Books, 1982). All subsequent references are from this edition and are given in parenthesis.

Said, Edward, *After the Last Sky: Palestinian Lives,* New York: Pantheon, 1986.

———, *Culture and Imperialism*, 1993; rpt. (London: Vintage, 1994).

Theroux, Paul, *V.S. Naipaul: An Introduction to His Work,* London: Andre Deutsch, 1972.

Thieme, John, *The Web of Tradition: Uses of Allusion in V.S. Naipaul's Fiction,* Hansib Dangaroo, 1987.

White, Landeg, *V.S. Naipaul: A Critical Introduction,* London: Macmillan, 1975.

Chapter 6

Into Third World Politics of Marginality

As stated earlier, imperialism and its ineluctable machineries have generated national, cultural and geographical dislocations that have radically altered the meanings of monolithic or static national and political myths. The fragmentation of the once fixed locatable identity in terms of religion, culture, ecology or race has posed problems of articulating one, single identity. The 'floating' individual destiny in the twentieth-century post-war atmosphere, the break-up of empires, the post-colonial political realities, and the violence in sub-continents, conjure up the dissolution of a world controlled by a single idea of progress. The earlier, overriding idea of pure, national identity can only be achieved through the negation of the complex interweavings of history. Contemporary Third World presents disturbing and volatile acts of racial/communal/national tensions. The Sinhalese-Tamil conflict, the Serbian war, the Iraq-Kuwait conflict and its spill-overs, the brutalities in South Africa, the contemporary feud in Zaire, the Indo-Pak wrangling over Kashmir, the crack-up of Russian unity and the simmering continued violence in Ireland, and now, the American-Afghan conflict are facets of nations sliding into new disorders. This seems unending, while the developing world is fast getting absorbed in the all-pervasive liberal-capitalist economy of the West.

One aspect of the rampant inter-community or racial tensions in nation states is the dispersal of the peasant or the pre-capitalist classes during colonial era into often abruptly urbanized and restless ones tied to the economic and political power of the metropolitan West.

Naipaul's fiction after *The Mimic Men* in a way reflects his increasing preoccupation with the post-imperial Third World scene. His entry into other, troubled areas of consciousness and new spaces of cross-cultural and transnational entanglements illustrates his search for parallels to his own past. None of the works under consideration in this chapter, *Guerrillas* and *A Bend in the River*, configure a purely national, ethnic or intimately personal concern with human life. On the other hand, the impulse to isolate and deflate the experience of migration and expatriation gains prominence with each novel. Naipaul sees immigration, exile and expatriation as symptomatic of a patternless world, where order, direction and settlement are beyond hope. Economic power, racial revenge and exploitations of all sorts mark the fate of the hopeless immigrant or expatriate exposed to dangers and humiliations at the hands of the new post-colonial powers which bulldoze aliens and outsiders, seeking revenge for their own past oppression and brutalization. Naipaul's expatriates, exiles, immigrants and aliens confront a menacing, racist and a counter, post-colonial setting seething with violence. There is little respite in Naipaul's later work from pain and anguish of not belonging; indeed, the accidents of fate, chance and history throw up situations which more often than not, place individuals who get trapped in national and ethnic imbroglio.

Naipaul's distant, detached observation of these 'theatrics' in modern nation states sharpens his ironic stance in satirizing the futile attempts at controlling disorder through borrowed power and resources. The lack of sympathy or compassion is more glaring, for the reason that Naipaul now looks at the whole traffic of people moving from one to the other place as conditioned by drift and anonymity as a way of life. The 'little' men and the mimic men of Naipaul are replaced by invisible people who have lost their bearings and consequently, the metaphor of homelessness and marginality acquires a wider, inter-national meaning. They are not defined by any national boundary or history; like orphans and destitutes in the New World scenario, their fate seems to illustrate the ultimate disappearance of certainties and authenticities of the old order. The bleakness of Naipaulian vision is accompanied by his political views on the futility of achieving a real freedom in the face of the resurfacing of neo-imperial, corporate capitalism supported and valorized by the urban-elite and as much by the political set-up. Through his incorrigible and uncompromising stance, Naipaul sees the negative ironies in operation in contemporary civilizational structures, from a 'free' state wherein the ideological frames of control have worked since the Second World War. In a similar vein, the decolonizing periods have produced a disturbance and disorder for which the unstable and politically dependent structures in the Third World are responsible. As J.J. Healy puts it:

> What he has tried to with an overreaching intelligence in his journalism and restrained, tensed imagination in his fiction, is to see clearly the darkened, purgatorial disfigurations of contemporary history. (J.J. Healy, p. 49)

Along with, the journalistic peregrinations of Naipaul into countries and areas apparently distinct from each other—India, Africa, Latin America, the Islamic world—have yielded results and insights which unmask the ideologies and the psychological make-up of the colonized. Naipaul's later work records some unavoidable developments in post-war scene of the Third World. With the virtual exhaustion of grand systems and total theories, Soviet and Chinese collective economies, the anti-imperialist nationalism, we have entered a period of vast uncertainty. The contemporary world, suspended between post-colonial developments and liberal capitalist attractions, betrays one definition or inscription. Most Third World areas are frighteningly interdependent—intellectually, politically, ethnically and of course, economically. The dubious results of the imperialist consolidation of mixture of cultures and identities on a global scale reflect a dissolved, hybrid life in dissimilar landscapes and settings. Naipaul's 'lost centre' has extended its erasures further, beyond India and the Caribbean, for a point or milestone of stable, unmoving centre now betrays a possibility.

Naipaul's fiction, partly journalistic and documented, is equipped with a special sense of contemporary post-colonial realities. *Guerrillas* and *A Bend in the River* are in related ways illuminated by his travel and mediation between human, racial and political compulsions that make up an immigrant, dispersed world. Naipaul's evocation of landscape and geography, expressly connected with the motif of journeying in both works, is never without its sinister, bleak and menacing overtones. The swamp, debris, pollution, decay, darkness, natural wilderness serve to unnerve the average outsider, and are always full of unpleasant, rude jolts and shocks. The negatives of experience are focussed through an unresponsive, oppressive landscape that can send no signals of identification or belonging to an exhausted, dependent expatriate sensibility. Linda, Bobby, Peter Roche, Jane and Salim are never at home with the mysterious turns of land, the river or the bush. While Naipaul's travel writings about India, the Islamic world and South America illustrate the political struggles, sectarian violence and huge historical traditions ushered into the present-day climate of change, his fictions based on travel have another, more complex function to perform. Many of his personal/travel accounts are meant to convey a story, a fiction finely transmuted into narrative art. Both *Guerrillas* and *A Bend in the River* illustrate this predilection. As he points out in *Among the Believers,* the novel never lies; it deepens the observed contents of people, places and things:

> People can hide behind direct statements; fiction, by its seeming indirections, can make hidden impulses clear. (V.S. Naipaul, p. 17)

Peter Hughes (Peter Hughes, p. 59) calls this turning of travel writing into fiction as Naipaul's 'paired narratives', which convey his complex vision of reality, that according to the author, 'reaches closer to the truth'. A writer like Naipaul, excluded from what Conrad calls 'organized social life', must be true, if hurtful too, to his particular experience because this is all he has. "Every one has to fight his own little war, everyone is a guerrilla", says Jimmy Ahmed in *Guerrillas*. In Naipaul's Third World of power politics where survival is a great consolation, everyone—Asians, Africans, Europeans, Indians—are 'on the run', no point of rest or home is now granted or guaranteed.

In Naipaul's later fiction, locales and societies characterize a disjunctive, mixed scenario, of people having travelled from all kinds of places and cultures, for reasons of their own. Naipaul's entry into the 'Dark Continent' exactly seventy years after Conrad, has interested literary critics, for Africa presents a changed perspective in Naipaul during the post-imperial period of nationalism. Likewise, the role and the persona of the expatriate is saturated with real-life confrontations that Naipul renders without the romance, and the mystery that earlier writers did evoke while writing of Africa. Naipaul said in "Conrad's Darkness":

> But we read at different times for different things. We take to novels our own ideas of what the novel should be; and those ideas are made of our needs, our education, our background or perhaps our ideas of our background. (V.S. Naipaul, p. 205)

The expatriate that Naipaul portrays is hardly important; unlike a Kurtz on 'civilizing mission' and Marlow as his altergo, Naipaul's newcomers into Africa and other alien cultures are apolitical, ordinary, at the low economic rung, even students and seekers. The post-imperial Third World's continuous attraction for the West and its productions, the knotted relations of the ex-colonial nations with the former colonial powers, the rights of overseas 'commonwealth' settlers in African states and Britain serve as an interesting backdrop of the placements of the immigrant/expatriate individual. However, Naipaul's own immense difficulties as an uprooted East Indian and the subsequent move from Caribbean are translated into this international metaphor he delves into in *In a Free State* and *A Bend in the River* in particular. John Updike, commenting on *A Bend in the River* asserted: "It proves once more that he is incomparably well-equipped to bring us news of one of the contemporary world's great subjects—the mingling of its peoples." Two things acquire significance, following Naipaul's cold and detached observations about the New World in and after *The Mimic Men*. It was doubted then whether Naipaul could take his observations to a more distilled and detached degree. *In a Free State* belied those predilections, including the one that doubted

Naipauls' ability to produce more fictions, for he arrives, in the words of Alastair Niven at an "un-Forsterian position of total disconnection." In a way, Naipaul's special relation to the Third World notwithstanding, the lack of this 'connectedness' can only be understood in terms of an existential urgency. On the other hand, others have seen this stance as inconsistent and audacious, considering Naipaul's deliberate sense of un-belonging to areas that are his subject-matter. The question that arises is: What is the basis for the proprietary nature of his claim to 'authority' about the greater Third World?

The 1970s unfolded some instances of Naipauls' comment over the intricacies of post-colonial casualty. *The Overcrowded Barraccoon* for one, established this steady development of idiom and opinion, in that it provided an update of Naipaul's reading of places and issues that had figured in his earlier writings. As *The Overcrowded Barraccoon* ends with the section 'Columbus and Crusoe', it not only replicates the materials used in *The Middle Passage* and *The Loss of El Dorado* but are also projected to rehearse Naipaul's agenda for what his studies of empires had alerted him to: the necessary and inevitable failure of modernity in former European colonies. Naipaul's analysis also allows him to give his own perspective on 'discovery' that correctly places the brutality and accompanying "banality" of conquest within the generality of all forms and exercises of imperialism. And when the romance of imperial adventure, the utopia turns into disappointment, then the debasing cycle of imperial fantasias is re-deployed, thus allowing a repetitive replay, well into the twentieth century, of an unequal exchange between the colonizer and the colonized, between the civilized and the 'primitive' (a subject that Edward Said theoretically pioneered within the post-colonial discourse theory in *Orientalism*, and later substantiated in *Culture and Imperialism*). This allows Naipaul to conclude his observations by conflating Columbus' discoveries and all subsequent imperial, colonial and post-colonial metropole—peripheral relations. As Fawzia Mustafa rightly comments:

> Naipaul's analysis carries with it a sense of an intractable, fixed posture of historical petrifaction between colonizer and colonized. (Fawzia Mustafa, p. 124)

Transitioning into the present, the above determinants are reimposed to perceive the damage, or its possibility in *Guerrillas* and *A Bend in the River*, each of which charts moments of profound collapse in already fragile societies. The singular point made is an *a priori* futility at the core of both novels' political setting, just as his other works of the same period, *The Return of Eva Peron* and *Among the Believers* are reiterations of Naipaul's considered views or theses of colonial and post-colonial pathologies of almost any hue. This phase, then, concretizes his engagement with the troubled modernity of the greater Third World, to fictionalize cleverly and discursively the several 'divides'—political, economic, ethnic, cultural, religious—that mark the migrant/exile's predicament.

Guerrillas and *A Bend in the River* are heavily inscribed by the expatriate/exile's journey motif. Both these novels feed themselves on material originally treated in journalistic articles by Naipaul and included in *The Return of Eva Peron*. The theme of the Third World politics, the leaders that promise a nationalistic utopia and the émigré experience, loosely constitute the context of displacement that is underlined in the stories of the two novels. Though Michael X or Abdul Malik—turned Jimmy Ahmed, and the President have little in common otherwise, their lives and roles illustrate how fantasies and personal deficiencies background their promise of charismatic leadership. But in these novels, as also in *The Return of Era Peron*, one comes to a knowledge of the leadership cult that unleashes a trail of violence and reprisals against one's past humiliations. Ultimately, neither the leader nor the led can hope to nourish a future hope of stability or peace; all that is left is a growing sense of futility and terror which lead to the common expatriate/exile's flight from this disorder. Both the novels unmask the facade of mimicry and nationalistic jingoism that characterize the ironies of Third World societies, left to relive the present through past echoes. Within this ambit, the author focuses on the racial character of politics in the two novels in separate ways. While 'Michael X' or Jimmy Ahmed brings to the fore the West Indian inter-racial antagonisms and divides, the other story in a way returns to the 'Indian' theme as it now resurfaces through Salim in the complex politico-racial scenario in modern-day Zaire. The descriptions of landscape and environment are again acutely suggestive of violence, fear and bleakness. In fact, *Guerrillas* and *A Bend in the River* are both marked by Naipaul's sense of attenuation and waste, the debris of previous acts of violence and oppression that seem to retribute and control the fates of the twentieth-century men.

The external world of both novels—*Guerrillas* and *A Bend in the River*—is as chaotic, disordered, violent and almost deranged, as their mental landscapes are. This ferment, containing all the promise of creation, remains unresolved in these novels where it is dramatized as a destructive element. It is no longer possible for Salim to feel as Ralph Singh does:

> The city made by man but passed out of his control: breakdown, the negative reaction, activity the positive: opposite but equal aspects of an accommodation to a sense of place which, like memory, when grown acute, becomes a source of pain. (V.S. Naipaul, p. 52)

Jane sinks in it. Roche and Salim survive through retreat. Each novel lays bare the emotional and passionate reality of despair and hysterical fear which underlies the contemporary human situation, ignored, dismissed or suppressed by the general euphoria and optimism generated by incalculable wealth and power. Naipaul reveals the vulnerability of a world which wastes its potential—the sense of a community gone wrong; the protagonist realizes himself as a victim of his environment:

> Once it had been a respectable lower-class area—But the community once contained in this area of greenery and red roofs and narrow lanes had exploded. Families still lived in certain houses; but many of the houses had become camping places, where young men looked for occasional shelter and an occasional meal, young men who at an early age had found themselves in the streets, without families, knowing only the older women of some houses as 'aunts'. It was a community now without rules; and the area was now apparently without municipal regulation. Empty house lots had been turned into steel-band yards or open-air motor repair shop;—The walls were scrawled, and sometimes carefully marked, with old election slogans,

> racial slogans, and made-up African names:—Humour, of a sort, was intended; and it seemed at variance with the words of threat and danger. (V.S. Naipaul, p. 104)

"You mustn't think it's bad just for you. It's bad for everybody. That's the terrible thing. It's bad for Prosper, bad for the man they gave your shop to, bad for everybody. Nobody's going anywhere—Nothing has any meaning. That is why every one is frantic—the bush runs itself. But there is no place to go to. I've been on tour in the villages. It's a nightmare. All these airfields the man has built, the foreign companies have built—nowhere is safe." (V.S. Naipaul, p. 291)

The terms in which these novels are structured, producing resonances which deepen the despair and gloom of the existential reality, vibrate obversely off-stage. The melodrama of petty heroics (historical as well as autobiographical), self-pity and physical violence (murders, torture, sadism) became an absurd tragedy as the narrator presents on the fringes of his protagonist's memories of the awareness of an ordered past. Most of the real action of *Guerrillas* consists in characters talking nostalgically of the past, and Salim's whole exercise consists in recalling a happier time when he was vital. The past they sought to escape from, to reject or alter is now a life—line in the destructive present, when the glamour of existence has materialized into the paralysis of fear. The charm of distant places, of new and better worlds, dissipates as they realize that all places are the same place; they experience the same resistance to ideational living everywhere as well as discover the corrupt core of their own beings. Having wasted time they became grabbers and opportunists of the moment. In Nazruddin's words:

> You must always know when to pull out.
>
> (V.S. Naipaul, p. 30)

For moving in one direction only, literally and literarily, we see them exhausted, having soon reached the limits of their imaginative existence. The sense of being out of step with the times come to Peter, Jane, Jim, Harry and other characters in *Guerrillas*. They all repeat at some point in their lives: 'It is too late'. The sense of time slipping is the impetus to action in *A Bend in the River*:

> They're going to kill everybody who can read and write, everybody who ever put on a jacket and tie.... They're going to kill all the masters and all the servants.... They're going to kill and kill. They say it is only way, to go back to the beginning before it's too late. (V.S. Naipaul, p. 293)

We see lonely people searching for emotional richness ending up more alienated, insulated and ridden by fear if not hatred. In *Guerrillas,* the narrator's sympathies are with all the characters. Whilst depicting their actions he simultaneously probes their psyches so that though they are critical of one another. We see them as essentially victims of their situations: their greatnesses are measured against their failures, so that even the worst of them, the murderous gang leader, Jimmy, is a pathetic figure:

> She grew heavy; his strength became useless; and as he felt her fail a desolation began to grow on him. And then there was nothing except desolation.... Then he was lost, lost since the beginning of time. But time had no beginning and he was disembodied. He was nothing more than this sense of loss that grew deeper and deeper as he awakened to it. (V.S. Naipaul, p. 243)

Salim in *A Bend in the River* is the well-defined protagonist of the novel. He weighs and assesses his various worlds. Yet Salim's voice, as that of the first person autobiographical narrator, is finally sympathetic and reductive. He is one of them. The adventurous son of a business and slave-owning family of considerable importance and antiquity on the east coast, he finally admits to Metty, his slave-servant, that he is scarcely able to take care of himself, leave alone be responsible for him. His humiliations resolve themselves into a philosophical understanding of men:

> The world is what it is; men who are nothing, who allow themselves to become nothing, have no place in it. (V.S. Naipaul, p. 9)

Naipaul shows that in democratic world which stresses respect for the individual, survival is possible only in power groups. The individual not supported by power is always hunted. The elements of choice and freedom, which gave dignity to existentialist thought, in today's political set-up, are no more the inherent right of the individualist but of the man in power. The Big Man in *A Bend in the River* plays fast and loose with men and machines, ideas and history. And Jimmy, the *hakwai Chinese* born in the back room of a Chinese Grocery, knows:

> They've got to support me, massa. Sablich's and everybody else. They've got to make me bigger. Because, if I fail... hmm. I'm the only man that stands between them and revolution, and they know it now, massa. That's why I'm the only man they're afraid of.... I'm the friend of every capitalist in the country. Everybody is my friend. (V.S. Naipaul, p. 27)

In *Guerrillas* and *A Bend in the River*, Naipaul, through the omniscient, impersonal narrator, creates the personal, individualistic, self-aware, self-centred world of subjective reality. The characters, aware of an external world from which they are detached and free-floating, form a community of the fearful and the lost. They communicate with others only insofar as they understand the 'other' in terms of themselves, forming a single gigantic world personality. The distinction between the role of the protagonist and the other characters in the novels serves the artistic purpose of verisimilitude and authenticity. Thematically, he merges the quality of the life of the island and the town in the two novels, respectively. The subjective realities of the nameless island and the unnamed town, as free-floating and dislocated as their inhabitants, are perceived to be as static, alienated and egotistical as the literal world of ritual and tradition or that confined by materialistic goals as embodied by the East coast life of Africa and the Ridge community of the island, respectively. Naipaul defines the motivation behind these realities as 'self-cherishing' or 'self-regard': The understanding of the self and the other in terms of power, possession and superiority rather than equality. The objective world of political and societal reality, as a thing in itself, does not exist in these novels. It is real and meaningful only insofar as it impinges on the experiential awareness of the character and forms the stuff of his subjective existence. Objective reality, mingled with the past and present, with aspiration and fantasy, is distorted and made bizarre. If choice is the core of true existence there does not seem much to choose between. At least the material world (money and automatic living) provides a foothold for survival for people who have exhausted their resources and know their limits. Transcontinental and international travel ends in repeated journeys between the ridge, the town and the Grange in *Guerrillas*. For Salim, the decisive car rides are between his shop and flat and the residences of the various people with whom, out of his needs, he establishes ties, particularly with Yvette at the Domain. Heightened subjectivity, expanding the consciousness, has narrowed the scope of existence. Freedom is in conflict with security and the novels end on a low note suggestively:

> Life in our town was arbitrary enough. Yvette seeing me as settled, with everything waiting for me somewhere, had seen her own life as fluid. She felt she wasn't prepared as the rest of us; she had to look out for herself. That was how we all felt, though: we saw our own lives as fluid, we saw the other man or person as soldier. But in the town, where all was arbitrary and the law was what it was, all our lives were fluid. We, none of us, had certainties of any kind. Without always knowing what we were doing we were constantly adjusting to the arbitrariness by which we were surrounded. In the end we couldn't say where we stood.
>
> We stood for ourselves. We all had to survive. But because we felt our lives to be fluid we all felt isolated, and we no longer felt accountable to anyone or anything. That was what had happened to Mahesh. It isn't that there's no right and wrong here. There's no right! That was what had happened to me. It was the opposite of the life of our family and community on the coast. That life was full of rules. Too many rules; it was a pre-packed kind of life. Here I had stripped myself of all the rules. During the rebellion—such a long time ago—I had also discovered that I had stripped myself of the support the rules gave. To think of it like that was to feel myself floating and lost.

> And I preferred not to think about it...it was too much like the panic you could at anytime make yourself feel if you thought hard enough about the physical position of the town in the continent, and your own place in that town. (V.S. Naipaul, pp. 206-07)

Few writers of fiction have documented marginality as well as V.S. Naipaul. His originality lies in his denial of any originality to his characters, his insistence on derivation as the essence of culture born of colonialism. Behind his settings and characters is the curse of Caliban for the conquerors of his island—"The red plague rid you for learning me your language." Among his works, *Guerrillas* occupies a special place in his contribution to colonial literature for its striking portrayal of derivative culture. Naipaul returns to an imaginary Caribbean island, presumably Trinidad, for the setting of his work, which is loosely based on the life of Michael de Freitas, a West Indian Black Muslim celebrity also known as Michael X and Michael Abdul Malik, who spent a number of years in London, was charged under England's Race Relations Act for incitive language, and was eventually hanged in Trinidad for the murder of two people, one of them a white Englishwoman. Malik, like the character of Jimmy Ahmed who is patterned on him, was sponsored and encouraged as a revolutionary leader by London liberals but also ridiculed by some of his own compatriots as a playboy and hustler (D.A.N. Jones, p. 1013). In *Guerrillas,* Jimmy Ahmed, just returned from London, where he has been accused of sexual assault and forthwith abandoned by many of his white supporters, is the leader of what purports to be an agricultural commune populated by a handful of slum youths. Part Chinese and part black, Ahmed lives at a remove from the commune's huts in a house that mimics English middle-class suburbia.

The novel concerns itself with the interaction among three characters: Ahmed and two recent English arrivals on the island, Peter Roche and Jane. Tortured for his anti-apartheid work in South Africa, Peter has written a book about that experience and is at present a public relations and welfare worker for a firm that attempts to make up for its tainted past as slave traders by financing Ahmed's commune. Jane has followed Roche to the island as part of her search for commitment and action through affairs with men; she believes him to be an engaged doer. Her disillusionment with Roche leads her to Ahmed, and, after sexual encounters with him that are more political than personal, she is offered by Ahmed to his male lover, Bryant, in a ritual murder. This takes place against a backdrop of gang rioting and frenzied reggae music. Jimmy is abandoned by both the white firm that finances him and by the black movement he supposedly represents, just as American military helicopters take over the island to insure American bauxite investments.

Naipaul broadens the scope of his theme, marginality, first by having Jimmy's 'master' present as a force on the island, thereby emphasizing the native's delusions of power and independence, and second, by giving Jimmy a powerless, pathetic alter ego. Each of these fictional characters underscores Jimmy's inauthenticity and pretensions, while also casting him more clearly in the role of the victim, as both victimizer and victimized appear as actual characters. Roche is the person Jimmy secretly wishes to be, and Bryant the person Jimmy feels he has not yet escaped being. In another critical change in characterization, Naipaul eliminates the presence of a wife and child for Jimmy and makes Jane Jimmy's lover, rather than the lover of his 'partner' on the commune, as was the case with Gale Benson and Hakim Jamal, the Boston "Black Power Man." This revision from journalism to fiction foregrounds the theme of marginality, for both Jane and Jimmy are types of the 'other' in a white male-dominated society, and each is the other's slave, depending on whether the context is race or gender. The fictional Michael X, Jimmy of *Guerrillas*, is a more sympathetic character than is Michael X of "The Trinidad Killings" because Naipaul places him in a social and psychological context that focuses on his victimization. With Michael X, Naipaul portrays a man who could make money out of race; with Jimmy, Naipaul portrays a man who can't construct a coherent self.

Naipaul's attitudes to these rootless white expatriates is that they exist in insecurity, and envy one another the prospect of return to England. Their relationships are marked by mistrust and Naipaul lays bare their shallowness, and the shifting nature of their political and emotional commitments. Without loyalties to England, the expatriates seek escape to England.

Images of sexual sadism in their patterns of triumph and humiliation, connect with a backbone of colonial supremacy and suppression, which is a reality Naipaul can never ignore. Jane is the unfeeling, racially superior white mistress. She flaunts her status, insults Jimmy, provokes him by taking sex and giving no love, and is infinitely patronizing. Jimmy, the black native in the neo-colonial world replies with his own brand of crude sexual insult by spitting in Jane's mouth, forcing painful anal intercourse on her, and finally, having her slashed to death by his homosexual underling Bryant.

As in *Guerrillas*, Africa as a textual/sexual site is played out as well. Following *Guerrillas*, Naipaul seems impelled to depict the betrayal of post-colonial history in stylized scenes of sexual humiliation between men and women, or men and men, of different races. Just as Jimmy seeks vicarious pleasure and a sexual 'triumph' over the white Jane in *Guerrillas*, Salim's affair with Raymond's wife Yvette, is that it ascribes on the language that so defines the colonizer and the colonized. Salim has known only brothel sex (like Willy Chandran in *Half a Life*), and fantasis of conquest and degradation where the woman is the willing participant in her own degradation. The sexual politics in Salim's affair with Yvette assumes an undertone of imperial fantasy. In the words of Fawzia Mustafa:

> Yvette becomes an image of the conquerability of Africa, while the Indian Salim assumes all the anxieties and glee of the conquering European...thus rehearsing the colonial wonder with the hidden-erotic-historical experience that Africa represents. (Fawzia Mustafa, p. 152)

Violence brims out of this novel, as in no other of Naipaul's, and the white expatriate is most vulnerable. An outsider by race, having taken up residence in a world to which he cannot belong, and a misfit in his own country by belief or temperament, the expatriate is full of the weariness born when neither place nor relationships offer home.

Roche has had his ideals and is now experiencing the "melancholy" of knowing them to be misplaced. In a game, he plays at Harry's, Roche confesses that his one wish which is "to have the most enormous sexual powers." But for the white expatriates—Harry, Jane and Roche—the god of sex (as far Ralph in *The Mimic Men*) has failed. Country, persons, ideals, even self, have failed to provide roots. Roche, taking stock in the course of his 'Encounter' radio interview with Meredith realizes this with a melancholy born of homelessness:

> The sense of the end of the day, a feeling of futility, of being physically lost in an immense world.
>
> Melancholy, at the same time for the others, more rooted than himself.... (V.S. Naipaul, p. 215)

The image of the house now surfaces in Roche's thoughts, standing for a 'fragility', rather than the solidity visualised by Biswas. The very notion of house as home (the home, or a home) is now questioned by Naipaul. Roche in Stephen's (leader of a city gang) house had felt:

> It was easy to have a sense of the house as a hollow flimsy structure. (V.S. Naipaul, p. 107)

The instability of the expatriate, one now finds, cannot allow to stand even the vision of completeness and permanence. It is only childhood which offers permanence to the expatriate and Roche observes that 'childhood' figures importantly in expatriate talk, whenever they get together as a group: "It was odd here how people spoke about their childhood's, as of a period only just discovered and understood" (V.S. Naipaul, p. 143). As adults wearing masks which are subtle, changing and treacherous, the expatriates wish to hold on to the simple certainties of childhood.

Guerrillas presents a bunch of white expatriates in former colonies (Naipaul now traces the reverse process to Ralph Singh's exile), individual in their appetites and failures, linked nonetheless by an unfulfilled need for home. Shallow, restless, driven to the nomadic life, as the case may be, they remain unaccepted in their country of exile, and in turn, refuse to accept its life and ways. They live constantly under threat and a need to escape, though the destination they must return to offers no succour.

In a sense, Naipaul has remained true to one aspect of his experience: the careful nurture of his 'outsider's' status always translates into his fiction as characters who, for one reason or another, do not 'belong'. Like *Guerrillas*, *A Bend in the River's* principal players have arrived at the scene of the action from elsewhere. They are either Asian (the generic term adopted for Indian subcontinental immigrants in East and Central Africa), European settlers and expatriates, members of distant groups (for Naipaul, 'tribes'), or people of a mixed ancestry that denies them full status as any kind of 'authentic' group member. Thus, even while this displacement has always been one of Naipaul's 'themes', it also serves as a plot or device that allows him to narrativize the events from the 'outside', looking 'in'. Not only does this device lend itself to an often full exploration of existential questions, it also seems to give Naipaul's fiction the license of experience in the guise of history. In other words, the political action of *A Bend in the River*, against which the characters are pitted, is only presented as a series of brutal but tangential developments witnessed but not participated in by the protagonist, Salim. Thus, the pitiless first-person voice actually functions with the veneer of a guarded neutrality normally associated with a third-person narrative. The events depicted impinge upon Salim's existence rather than emerge as an integral form of action consequent upon the character's participation. The political events of a post-colonial 'Africa', therefore, appear to operate with the sinister force of a ghostly, disembodied spectre of power imaged solely as a Conradian 'immensity'.

The sources for *A Bend in the River*, then, include Conrad's vision of Africa in the days of imperialism, as well as Naipaul's own analysis of post-colonial Zaire. The racial and political tensions in the town at the bend in the river, a sense of encroaching disorder, and the "congruent corruptions of colonizer and colonized" are focused through the experiences of Salim, the novel's central character and narrator. But Naipaul's use of *Heart of Darkness* and "A New King for the Congo" as source material for the novel goes well beyond expression of these shared historical and political themes.

The tone and the tenor which express the experience underneath the need to survive, to somehow go on, are quite distinct from Naipaul's earlier work. For one thing, Naipaul this time penetrates deep into the making of modern Africa and its national socio-political structures, but not by playing upon the familiar themes of exile and its fruits. *A Bend in the River* has an immediate, contemporary quality that finely blends with the past imponderables affecting human locations in the present. The Zaire that Naipaul centres upon is not some imaginary 'hell' that fixes into its fire the characters in *Guerrillas*.

A Bend in the River, though it hides a terrible sense of flux and ennui, nevertheless expands to probe the complex varieties of life through a rich array of characters, each representing a different geographical and cultural form of his or her connection with place. The controlling metaphor of this pattern is the link between the old and the new, the traditional and the modern, Eastern and Western, tribal vs. the rational approach, fixity vs. movement, and so forth. And Naipaul picks up mixed, fragmented and incomplete bits of lives to weave them into a subtle fictional architectonics. This articulation through artistic refinement creates a 'point of view' that in turn illuminates a set of experiences necessitated in the post-colonial and the post-imperial world. Salim, Indar, Raymond, Yvette, Shobha and Mahesh carry with them the exigencies of global, hemispherical dislocations, while Zabeth, Ferdinand and Father Huismans are the insiders, trying to adjust to the disturbing realities, living between the old and the new regimes. The centrality of Salim in his urge to adjust, to live out one's residence in a place, is obviously done through a modern picaresque technique. The journey-patterns of the expatriate take on variegated hues and complexions, so that the Eastern, Oriental and European tend to assimilate into a leading motif of unstatic points of arrival in the late twentieth century, heavily inscribed in ethnic and diasporic movements. The political compulsions to flaunt power and 'control' through the President's armed forces are ironically matched by a maneuvered aim to eulogize that power through public consent. Those who become the victims of this revival of native, black authority and oppression do not have a stake this or that way. Naipaul's Africa is a long way from an imagined, hidden mystery that stalks the European mind; it is, on the other hand, a land where Africans fight another kind of battle, the battle to assert native bush culture in the face of cosmopolitan and capitalist pressures. Likewise, the manipulations and 'ordering' of peripheries (minorities in the case of *A Bend in the River*) and even the natives themselves, expose the 'pathology of power' in the post-imperial nation states where real tensions cannot be suppressed by technological advances or market consumerism triggered by liberal capitalism.

Salim's portrayal as an exiled, displaced Asian Muslim in a city at a bend in the river, it would appear, has been carefully handled. Right from the beginning Salim's brooding, meditative and passive tone of recollection and confession sets the mood of the story, the centrally structured idea of displacement and anonymity. His clear verdict of the destiny awaiting people like him, a verdict that sounds universal, places him as a modern-day Ulysses—like figure, having almost forgotten the necessity of relating his present with past roots. As one goes through the documentary piece 'A New King for Congo: Mobutu and the Nihilism of Africa' one gets the impression that Salim's character is partially modelled on Simon, the manager of the nationalized company. Simon's reticence, vulnerability, the sense of danger and inner resentment offer a clue to Naipaul's creation of the alienated Salim, who unlike Simon, is a rank outsider in the turbulent rage and 'nihilism' of modern Africa that threatens to tear apart all external elements in its social structures. Simon is only a small example of the human sense of menace and fear; Salim is enlarged to convey and accommodate a much larger idea of the marginal man's experience. 'Everyone is here for money', echoes the Zairean lust for acquisition in the documentary piece by Naipaul, and nearly everyone in the novel—Salim, Shobha, Mahesh, Indar, Metty, Ferdinand—find themselves busy in making the best of the Western investments in peripheral places like the one where they live. And Naipaul evokes through Salim's narrative the buried, erased history of the Congo and its underlying mystery—African kingdoms, Arab trading empire, Belgian colony, and now under Mobutu, the kingdom of Zaire—a period that foregrounds another violent erasure. In fact, the history of this erasure has infiltrated the mind and reflexes of the expatriate characters. The historically bruised and violated 'land of Kurtz' has expanded inwards (and now the skin is not white, but black and maddened by a contact, ironically not with wilderness and primitivism, but with civilization) to embody this erasure in characters, who by their words and acts insist on the need to 'trample on the past'. The only alternative left for people like Salim (and Indar) is to dwell on a destroyed past. Unlike Mr. Biswas who compulsively feeds on the past of his race, ancestry and parents to reassess the present, in a *A Bend in the River* the present is created by the destruction of memory. Naipaul's limiting Salim to a common trading class expatriate's role offers immense scope to place it against those equipped with power, wealth and knowledge. 'Washed up' (much like Ralph Singh's 'shipwreck' refrain) and weak in the seething African war of races, people like Salim had long ago ceased to be masters of their fate. They had lived between one tide of history that had brought them to Africa, while the new tide (Mobutu's kingdom) was waiting to wash them up again. Naipaul may be using his persona to expose the mentality of the Asian entrepreneur in Africa, yet, in focusing almost exclusively on the question of survival, it is rarely suggested that Salim is narrowly materialistic. His small store and the attached shabby flat, kitchen and the white-painted bedroom illustrate his wish to merely pull on, survive. His relationship with Metty (another terrified, on-the-run figure) which never reaches a stage of assurance or understanding, ends up with Metty's desperate drive to free himself from servitude and poverty. Salim's problematic and uneasy attempts to educate and 'control' Ferdinand—who will rise to become one of the 'new men' of Africa—also explain the former's inability to measure up to the changing tide of relations that are fast being guided by the President's directives to celebrate the native strength and cultural authenticity. Ultimately, the native and expatriate meet at the end of the story; Ferdinand, now an officer, pays back Salim in terms of a last chance for the latter to escape from jail, and from the country. Much before this 'ending', the town at the bend of the river has already been rocked by unrest, looting and killing, the sense of 'a great chaos coming'. Salim's small hidden wealth of gold and ivory is captured, so that he has to face his own symbolic 'heart of darkness'. Father Huismans, the principal at the lycee, where Ferdinand is sent, and who appears to have a robust faith in the rise of modern Africa which he loves, has been killed mercilessly in the bush. His spiked head comes as a grim warning of the atavistic violence waiting in the peripheries against the hoax of modernity in the town and the Domain. Salim's belated act to quit, his knowledge of something fatal ready to hit him, comes not because of his expatriate status or race, but precisely because people like him are not required.

Edward said, while praising Naipaul as a 'remarkably gifted travel writer and novelist' in *Culture and Imperialism* sees in his stance an indictment of the post-colonial states which have landed themselves in a greater mess, apparently unable to control the real and unresolved tensions. Under Mobutu's 'invented tribal traditions', much like Qaddafi's Green book, the violence and killings leave little to be retained even at the survival level. Those who serve in the literal physical sense—like Salim—decide that the situation is hopeless and another emigration is required. Said says that Naipaul, "...successfully dramatizes an ideological position in the West from which it is possible to indict the post-colonial states for having succeeded unconditionally in gaining independence. His attack on the post-colonial world for its religious fanaticism (in *Among the Believers*), degenerate politics (in *Guerrillas*), and fundamental inferiority (in the first two books on India) is a part of a disenchantment with the Third World that overtook many people during the 1970s and 1980s..." (Edward Said, p. 320).

Naipaul's travel literature, always transparent in its contrasts and contradictions between society, culture, history, religion and their relationship to modernization in the post-imperial phase, brings out the worst possible illusion and gaffe the people are caught up in. Mobutu's promise of liberation and 'authenticity' is amusingly based on his belief that "the industrial west is collapsing and decadent, that Zaire must rid itself from the plagues of the consumer society". Quoting from *Elima* in "A New King for Congo", Naipaul recalls the writer's representations of 'Mubutuism' that by the year 2000, the Western Europe will be in its post-industrial decadence, Arab oil will be exhausted, Russia, Eastern Europe and India will form one bloc, and then Zaire should have its day, attracting investment from developed countries, importing 'factories whole'. This delusion of getting rid of consumer society ironically promises another, and worst variety of it, which is doubtlessly based on the enormous success of Western capitalist economy. How confused and impractical this vision is, from the authenticity of bush life and the primitive African personality Mobutu seeks to reinstate, to the dream of advanced industrial economy, is more than obvious. Naipaul says:

> So the borrowed ideas—about colonialism and alienation, the consumer society and the decline of the West—the dream of ancestral past restored is allied to the dream of a future of magical power. The confusion is not new, and is not peculiar to Zaire.
>
> .... It is lunacy, despair.... For many, authenticity and Negroness...are only words that stand for the despair and powerlessness of the man of Africa faced with the discouraging immensity of his under development. (V.S. Naipaul, p. 111)

Naipaul's assessment and observation of the big hoax presided over by Mobutu over three decades was prophetic and unambiguous, as contemporary events show. The armed struggle launched by Laurent Kabila against the despotic, corrupt and intolerable rule of Mobutu Sese Seko, is proof enough of Mobutu's ruining the economy and assets and dehumanizing the average man in Zaire. For, the Central Intelligence Agency (CIA) planted Mobutu as its man when he seized power in 1965. A recent American view is startlingly relevant to Third World nations: what responsibility should the Americans feel when their government, for policy reasons, imposes on another country a regime that reduces it to misery. As Mobutu fed people on rhetoric and the bravado of native rebellions, he filled his pockets with dollars, while Zaire was left to decay. The Third World theatrics, directed by the CIA are not limited to Zaire alone—Asia, Middle-East, South America present equally outrageous examples. Naipaul, however, made no direct reference to the American involvement in *A Bend in the River*, except the mingling of intellectuals and technocrats at 'the Domain'. *A Bend in the River* is an important work because it foretells the fate of borrowed economies such as in Zaire, and indirectly points towards the long line (now almost ended) of dictators spawned by the Cold War. In this gallery of rogues, Mobutu held an honoured place as a protege with Dyvaliers of Haiti, Marcos of Philippines, Syngman of South Korea, Lon Nol of South Vietnam, the Shah of Iran, Ayub and Yahya Khan of Pakistan, Anastasio Somoza of Nicargua and others who continued the tradition of the despotic monarchs equating the country and its wealth, with themselves. The irony of the tyrannical rule of these autocrats was that it had the full support of one of the world's most powerful democracies—the U.S. Mobutu, was perhaps the most odious of all such characters who enjoyed American patronage.

Naipaul's final viewpoint in *A Bend in the River* is far from a liberation or a possibility of human freedom, as violence and fire rage in the city at the bend in the river. Yet, the defeat of Mobutu signals the end of the Dark period, now that tyrants with borrowed power have been sidelined. The expectation is that governments will extend more freedom to their people. Naipaul's despair, matched by Salim's exit, is an indicator that nations without a concern for a collective experience of races and communities will collapse under the weight of their own ill-formed logic, the compulsions of city vs. bush in Africa notwithstanding. The legacy of men like Mobutu in a moribund non-country (the killings, the battles and the huge refugee exodus that accompanied the contemporary power feud) that only great skill and fortune can revive. The reason for this is the changed politics and power equations with the end of the Cold War, something that colonial powers like France, often described as the 'policeman' of Frocophone Africa, have belatedly realized. Countries like Zaire (as also others which Naipaul selects as his targets of attack being 'unproductive', inhuman or grossly fanatical) will have to face both their people and the collective coalition of African states, past the time when African conflicts were often hatched and resolved in Western capitals.

The contemporary Zaire dramatizes both the imprisonment in the long Mobutu rule, and the resultant misery writ large on their faces. Interestingly, what Naipaul wrote about the daily life of the Zairean town is still close to truth, and is understandable in the humorous term 'the Congolere miracle.' It relates to the myriad means that families used to make ends meet: petty trading, doing odd jobs, growing food, bartering, general hustling. In the society that Naipaul portrayed in *A Bend in the River*, life somehow crawled, went on despite everything, which holds true today in the post-Mobutu deliverance. Yet, the general character must remain more or less identical, for regimes can bring political change that may not be complimented by economic or moral transitions. As Naipaul had detailed brilliantly, restlessness and anguish go along with the general banal ways of life.

Works Cited

Healy, J.J., "Friction, Voice and the Rough Ground of Feeling: Naipaul after Twenty-five Years", *The University of Toronto Quarterly*, Fall, 1985.

Hughes, Peter, *V.S. Naipaul* (Contemporary Writers) (London and New York: 1988).

Jones, D.A.N., in a Review of *Guerrillas, Times Literary Supplement*, 12 September 1975.

Mustafa, Fawzia, *V.S. Naipaul* (Cambridge: Cambridge University Press, 1995).

Niven, Alastair, "V.S. Naipaul's Free Statement", in Hena Maes Jelinek (ed.), *Commonwealth Literature and the Modern World* (Brussels: Didier, 1975), p. 9.

Said, Edward, *Culture and Imperialism*, 1993, rpt. (London: Vintage, 1994).

V.S. Naipaul, *A Bend in the River* (Delhi: Clarion Books, 1980).

———, *Guerrillas* (Harmondsworth: Penguin, 1977).

———, *The Return of Eva Peron* 1980; rpt. (Harmondsworth: Penguin, 1981).

———, *The Mimic Men* (London: Andre Deutsch, 1967).

"The New Naipaul" in *India Today Plus*, First Quarter, 1997, p. 54.

Chapter 7

Summing Up

Evaluating Naipaul's exceptional contribution to the novel as a genre, and his situation as a post-colonial writer acquires a special significance, after his being awarded the coveted Nobel Prize for Literature. If anything, Naipaul's unremitting and inflexible stance about the second rate, underdeveloped and half-made societies—Trinidad, India, the Islamic world and others, has been positively marked by the Nobel Committee's citation as the prominence given to "suppressed-histories". This itself implies that the undeniable, if belated, recognition of Naipaul's long odyssey into the historical and colonized dark spots of the world affirm his extraordinary literary and intellectual point of view towards the glaring inequalities in the contemporary, political, cultural and racial set-up. In this sense, it hardly requires any re-assertion to understand Naipaul's intervention as a way of repudiating the human experience arising out of degrading colonial experience which he sees as a legacy of oppression and marginality.

Today, in both the post-modernist and the post-colonial sense, suppressed cultures, histories, communities and subalternism have been sought to be given the much required attention as a way of contesting all forms of domination, whether it is meta-history, grand narrative, cultural and political hegemony or the question of representation. In most theoretical debates, it is the marginalized, ex-colonial world that has been provided significance so that the issue of any kind of discrimination or denial tends to get focused through varied forms of political or literary expressions. In a way, after much jargonized and fashionable theorizing of the above one concludes that Naipaul along with other well-known Third World contemporaries had signaled these real and uncomfortable realities much earlier, whatever may have been their literary or personal stance for this expression. To come back to the original argument, Naipaul's uncompromising view of the lingering colonial legacies is today even move relevant, looking at the new racial, ideological conflicts that have erupted in the twenty-first century—signalling the continuity of neo-colonial and other forms of domination in the now globalized world. Hence, Naipaul's view of marginality, centre-periphery, opposition, the condition of exile, all get related to the idea of way stations along the rusty wreckage of history. Naipaul has himself risen and expanded much beyond his own shadow as a literary outsider and as such he leaves behind as his own enviable legacy through those who have trodden the routes of his own enviable legacy through those who have trodden the routes of his fictional geography irrespective of continents, cultures and histories. He has essentialized the idea of place, exile and adjustment into a larger than life metaphor that now extends any barrier of this or that national context. His exile, traveler or the marginalized man has become, like himself, a symbol and a signifier of a state of experience who traverses the numerous forms of contemporary mutations.

Naipaul continues to write and his work may yet take new directions. However, on the evidence of his fictional output of more than four decades, it is possible to arrives at certain tentative conclusions in a given context. Although the tone of his writing has changed considerably, from the broad comedy of *The Mystic Masseur* and *The Suffrage of Elvira* to the descriptive manner of *Guerrillas* and *A Bend in the River,* his fiction thus far seems to be all of a piece. He himself says:

> All my work is really one. I'm really writing one big book. (V.S. Naipaul, p. 367)

If at first this comment appears a little puzzling, in view of the difference in tone between his early and more recent work and the diversity of the milieus and character-types that he has treated, close scrutiny makes it clear and there has been little real change, except in the extent of the self-awareness displayed both by characters and the author. In both cases, there is a movement from the passive acquiescence of the colonial mentality—often compounded by the psychological consequences of *Karma*—to a 'free' or a neutral world. On the surface level this is explored through the treatment of the break-up of traditional communities; on a more archetypal level it finds expression in terms of the myth of the Fall. Naipaul doubts whether a pristine state has ever existed and when, at the end of *In a Free State,* he reflects on the 'complete vision' enjoyed by the 'ancient artist', it is to conclude that people's such wholeness has never been more than a mental construct:

> ...it was hard, travelling back to Cairo, looking with my stranger's eye at the fields and the people who worked in them, the dusty towns, the agitated peasant crowds at railway stations, it was hard to believe that there had been such innocence. Perhaps that vision of the land, in which the Nile was only water, a blue-green chevron, had always been a fabrication, a cause for yearning, something for the tomb. (V.S. Naipaul, p. 225-26)

Naipaul is undecided as to whether the severing of the link between man and his landscape is a product of a post-lapsarian situation or something which is ingrained in the human condition itself. Either way it is, as he sees it, the crux of the twentieth-century experience, and deracination and dislocation is his ubiquitous subject.

On the stylistic level, it has its equivalent in structures which are the formal correlative of this experience of alienation. His quest for a tradition seems to resolve itself through the realization that it is 'his' lack of one which gives his work its distinctive force, and he is able to find a precursor in Conrad, for one.

Naipaul is, of course, a writer who, because of his scathing portrayal of Third World societies, particularly in his non-fiction, has attracted more than his fair share of critical praise—usually, though not always from metropolitan commentators—and censure—usually, though not always, form non-metropolitan ones. For the former he is a man with crystal-clear lucidity of vision who unflinchingly exposes the shortcomings of 'developing' societies, which are in reality regressing back into savagery and unreason. For the latter he is a man who has repudiated his origins and yet trades on them to allow him to propound a view of Third World society which would be deemed racist if it issued from the pen of a white writer. He thus ministers to the tastes of the metropolitan market by reflecting its prejudices so well.

It seems reasonable to agree with the latter view to the extent by suggesting that Naipaul has been lucky in finding a sympathetic readership in the 'developed' world. This is not to say that his work has been overvalued or that it has been perceptively read, simply that it has been taken over for certain of his readers' own purposes with some aspects being given undue prominence. Witness for instance, the attention paid in the United States to the alleged exposure of black radicalism in the character of Jimmy Ahmed in *Guerrillas*. Naipaul's primary concern in the novel would seem to be with a much broader spectrum of compromise, betrayal and lost idealism than is embodied in the character of Jimmy. Indeed, Jimmy is arguably treated more sympathetically than Jane or Roche, and in the least it is clear that other readings are possible. But books do read 'into' people and such a reaction greatly enhanced Naipaul's American reputation.

Naipaul claims he lacks a tradition, but inevitably he creates his 'own'. He spins a web of tradition which brings together many of the strands of his multi-cultural background. In Caribbean terms, this might suggest that he subscribes to a 'mulatto' view of culture, one which insists on drawing on all the ancestral strains which have gone into the making of that society. Upto a point this is implicit in his fictional practice, but unlike such writers and poets as Wilson Harris, George Lamming and Derek Walcott, whose works embody the creative potential latent in their heterogeneous world, Naipaul explicitly rejects most of his background. Yet to take him at his own estimate is, in the last resort, delimiting, for, like all writers, his sensibility is inevitably shaped by the cultural influences of his formative years. Thus, for all his satire of Hinduism, his thinking is crucially determined by his reaction to Hindu psychological attitudes and, for all his dismissal of the Caribbean, he is, in his perennial concern with cultural and racial cross-pollination, quintessentially West

Indian. His sensibility of his own, however creatively 'reductive' it may be seen as.

Naipaul's early satiric portrayal of the Trinidadian waywardness and buffoonery in *Miguel Street, The Mystic Masseur* and *The Suffrage of Elvira* presents him as a detached, unconcerned spectator of the drama of illiterate, powerless hordes of trapped people. Naipaul is "a colonial in crisis", a man whose psychic centre is that of Europe, whose violent turmoil of having been born in an unknown, ghetto-like corner of the world (and not in a metropolis) that characterizes his psychic trauma, deep inferiority which results, as stated earlier, in a stasis, rather than a positive comprehension or analysis of socio-historical forces that a positive comprehension or analysis of socio-historical forces that have shaped the Third World nations. Ironically, though his father Seepersad Naipaul was never a happy man, he could yet adjust (and much before Naipaul's expressed horror of it) in the creolized socialization in the Trinidadian society. The other, and the much circulated view is Naipaul's hope to escape the provincial and staid pre-occupations in the Hindu/Brahmin culture. His final 'escape' was ironically sponsored by the colonial Trinidad he has never emotionally embraced. Having seen the wretchedness and humiliations of his father in a family where he was an appendage, Naipaul's dreams (human and literary) lay outside Trinidad. In Naipaul's case, the craze, the dream to realize his Western cringe can thus be located in factors which he as a child and adolescent grew into for a variety of reasons, as he has detailed them in the early chapters in *A Way in the World*. The shaping of his aesthetic and personal responses is obviously tagged to his conception of the mixed, chaotic and disorderly Caribbean set-up. This also explains in an understandable way, his but more specifically to seek out his own placing as one with a Hindu/Brahminical past, a fact he comes back to in the recent *Half a Life*.

Naipaul has often written about his dislike of life in a big city; the impersonality, the isolation, the lack of communal life. The writer's life, as *The Enigma of Arrival* illustrates, is one of continuous wrestlings with one's marginal location and its relations with the past. *The Enigma of Arrival* is a text that indirectly underlines some of the most remarkable features of diasporic writing, especially the way Naipaul, through a subtle technique and style attempts, what he calls "a synthesis of the worlds and cultures that made me." The idea of availability of all cultures of the world for consumption by the individual consciousness has been growing in tandem with the history of colonialism, and has gained more prominence in the contemporary era. Pound, Eliot and Hesse signaled a real shift, from the age of old colonialism to the age of modern imperialism proper, though in a much more sanguine way. What is remarkably new in the contemporary metropolitan philosophies and literary ideologies since the 1960s along with restructurings in communication systems and information networks is that everything seems to be available *a la* the metropolitan supermarket that houses everything under one roof. Aijaz Ahmad says in this context:

> ...the idea of belonging is itself being abandoned as antiquated false consciousness. The terrors of High Modernism at the prospect of inner fragmentation and social disconnection have now been striped, in Derridian strands of postmodernism, of their tragic edge, pushing that experience of loss, instead, in a celebratory direction; the idea of belonging is itself seen now as a bad faith, a mere 'myth of origins'. The truth of being, to the extent that truth is at all possible, resides now in occupying a multiplicity of subject positions and an excess of belonging; not only does the writer have all cultures available to his or her as resource, for consumption but he or she actually belongs in all of them by virtue of belonging properly in none. (Aijaz Ahmed, pp. 129-30)

In a similar vein, Edward Said has explained this free choice from which to pick up any and all subject positions as "beyond all structure and all system" in *The World, the Text and the Critic* (Edward Said, 30). In connection with writers like Naipaul and their expatriation/migration, another distinction is of some significance. There is a 'conditional' difference between an exiled and a self-exiled writer. Rushdie's case, after he was sentenced to death by Khomeini, is a point. The existential suffering of the exile, and the absent readership can become deeply intertwined with his writing (as has happened in Rushdie's case) and his imagination. The self-exile has no such irrevocable bond; he is free to make a choice of that bonding to whichever stretch or limit he may will. His migrancy and expatriation does not necessary bring him into a material confrontation with a place or ideological system. On the other hand, *Midnight's Children,* with all its Rebelaisian fantasy and Shandian complexities of form is basically an attack on India, as *Shame* is on Pakistan: both countries being Rushdie's background of birth of growth. As Rushdie has said in his now famous words: "the writer has floated upwards from history, from memory, from time" (Salman Rushdie, 17). Naipaul sees himself having 'floated' from a conglomeration and an accident of history, of fate, or out of huge imperialistic phenomena of the confrontation of cultures. Not insignificantly, Naipaul now writing for a country or a people, for the reason that "writing is a state of being".

But it could be said that the imaginative apprehension of totality is always constructed on the basis of those bits and slices of concrete experiences which constitute any individual's life, migrant or not. The migrant, as Rushdie says in his essay on Gunter Grass, is a metaphor for 'the human condition', that in the ontological sense we are 'all migrants' in the sense that 'we all cross frontiers'. Self-exile and 'vagrancy' (as Raymond Williams terms it), have become common among artists in every successive phase of modern history, and experience itself has been chosen with greater frequency, the migrant intellect 'rooting itself in itself frequently:

> Above all, we lack power, and we do not understand that we lack power.... Our transitional or makeshift societies do not cushion us.... For those who lose, and nearly everyone in the end loses, there is only one course: flight. Flight to the greater disorder, the final emptiness: London and the home countries. (V.S. Naipaul, p. 67)

The above excerpt from *The Mimic Men* conveys nothing new or alarming about what is already quite well-known—Naipaul's caustic and unchanging meditations on the fate of men and societies. It is interesting to note that in these twenty years or so the meanings and the critical correlatives of these views have altered remarkably. The novels themselves, which deal with this early preoccupation with the Caribbean society's lack or order and authenticity—*Miguel Street, The Mystic Masseur, A House for Mr Biswas* and *The Mimic Men*—stand testimony to the writer's original stance which produced them. The three stages in these works; colonial mimicry and illiteracy, the existential trauma, and finally, the colonized politics in the phase of de-colonization constitute a longish journey in Naipaul's own career from 1957 to 1967. These works constitute a sub-corpus of pure Caribbean fictional setting that includes Naipaul's own close and intensified observation of its multi-racial and multi-lingual manifestation. Naipaul, after this, has never returned to this kind of localized fictionalizing, starting from *In a Free State,* for his growing interest in the politics and the travails of immigration; the Third World politico-racial imbroglio replicated in other nations and societies, and his later, and present obsession with his own complex placement as a writer. Another point is that Naipaul's so-called detachment or 'dissociation' (as J.J. Healy contends) from the Caribbean scene is less than convincing. Naipaul was never really an 'insider' to minutely or emotionally respond to the heterogeneity or the variety of Caribbean social experience the way Lamming, Harris, Sam Selvon, Vic Reid or John Hearne did. Nowhere except in *A House for Mr Biswas* does Naipaul plunge deep into a reciprocity or empathy towards the individual or collective human experience, howsoever fragmented. And even in *A House for Mr Biswas* the leading motif, informed by the house, stems from his familial, East Indian background, especially the dissatisfied life of his father in the conglomerated chaos of extended Indian families. Nearly all these works, in one way or the other, owe something to documentation and travel, especially Naipaul's return visit to Trinidad and other islands in 1960 that culminated in the writing of *The Middle Passage.* Hardly any work of Naipaul's can be read or understood without this corresponding travel or journalistic counterpoint, a factor which is even more glaringly obvious now as Naipaul appears to have tilted his writing interests into a non-fictional *oeuvre.*

Naipaul, with the packaging of sardonic humour and sharp wit, was able to look at the mixed, transient and unlikely world of Trinidad with a degree of compassion in *Miguel Street* and *The Mystic Masseur.* There was already enough material for fantasy and caricature for him to invent; his struggle to write himself into the remembered world of the Caribbean required, more than anything else, the exile's total recall. The playing off of history, calypso and fiction, are all part of the comic fantasy of the stories in *Miguel Street.* Through them Naipaul realizes the echoes that one could hear through the carnivalesque setting of calypso culture. Since calypso is central to the writing of *Miguel Street*, 'love, love, love alone', 'The Maternal Instinct', 'Man-Man', 'Titus Hoyt', 'Bogart' are variants on ways one lives in the wretchedness of limited, powerless life, a wry expression of paralysis. But calypso is also a form of escape, fantasy and the overcoming of the futility of all endeavour.

The characters of *Miguel Street* typify the vacancy and waste in the years when the middle-class was vying for importance in the newly emerging social circumstances. The peripheral figures in this work are those without education and power, whose predicament and wilderness is shaped by the colonial situation and its psychological consequences. With a language barrier and illiteracy, they are cut off from the creole-speaking majority, without a hope of promotion into the ranks of the elite. The seediness of life contrasted with metropolitan fantasy is itself a clue to their colonial mimicry in the absence of any other outlet. The imposture and fraud, the skill of surviving, which are central to *The Mystic Masseur* and *The Suffrage of Elvira,* nevertheless have their germ in *Miguel Street,* these being the inevitable outgrowths of a stunted and bruised colonized society. The political gimmickry and fraud perpetrated by the politicians on the people in *The Suffrage of Elvira* is an offshoot of the same syndrome mentioned above. The trickery and opportunism represented by Harbans or a Baksh in this novel essentially foregrounds its limited aim to expose through comedy and irony the 'democratic institutions' which were taking root in Trinidad in the 1940s and 1950s. However, the statement of Dr. Eric Williams, the Prime Minister of Trinidad and Tobago, underlines the very concept of mimicry that Naipaul conceptualizes:

> Political form and social institutions, were imitated rather than created, borrowed rather than relevant, reflecting the forms in the particular metropolitan country from which they were derived. (Eric Williams, p. 501)

The chaos resulting from blind imitation of the West is anticipated in its relation to Naipaul's bitter and harsh attacks on other Third World societies in *Guerrillas* and *A Bend in the River.* The inflated rhetoric of the contestants likewise, echoes their total lack of concern for any morals or conscience, and the flirtations with democracy. However, in Naipaul's overtones, for the innocent farce of politics in *The Suffrage of Elvira* will turn into racial antagonism, leading to murder and outrage in the post-imperial world.

In a well-known article, "Culture or Mimicry?", Derek Walcott expands the literary/poetic ramifications of mimicry, particularly in the context of its Caribbean abuses. The essay begins as a response to Naipaul and others who have lamented post-colonial mimicry of the West, in the face of destitution and marginality. Walcott cites the example of *An Area of Darkness* where Naipaul calls Indian mimicry of the English as a 'double' mimicry; for this mimicry was originally of the colonizing culture's values. However, the English mimicry is not of England, but of 'a fairy land of Anglo-India', of clubs and *sahibs*, as if an entire society has fallen for a casual confidence trickster.

But while Naipaul reels from the vertigo of this doublenss, seeing it as a two-fold debasement, Walcott catches in it a breath of the commonplace. Walcott sees in this mimicry as another, extended absurdity; he questions whether the Indian context underscored an absurdity that existed in England itself, its clubs mimicking another distant culture? Walcott thus traces as an alternative in "Culture or Mimicry?" its widening spiral. In the Caribbean context Walcott works through dexterous manipulations, light and shade, inside and outside while handling the fluctuating role of America as "economically benign yet politically malevolent". To cut the argument short, 'becoming' American means containing multitudes. "The shadow of the British empire has passed through...and over", and the American one looms at present, the Caribbean is (as Walcott's own ancestry testifies) good at absorbing things, hinting at its experience of different empires:

> .... Perhaps powerlessness leaves the Third World, the ex-colonial world, no alternative but to imitate those systems offered to or forced on it by the major powers. Most Third World politicians are trapped in the concept of a world proposed by those who rule it. (Derek Walcott, p. 5)

The point that is intended to be made here is that while Naipaul sees mimicry as a pre-condition of colonial debasement rising out of any possibility of originality, Walcott views mimicry as something normative, productive. The above quotation does bear out Naipaul that mimicry of power defrauds people, but while Naipaul believes that postcolonial culture goes awry because of this, Walcott argues that "the content of its mimicry (and as a product of marginalized state) is at times ill-chosen, yet leaves open the possibility of assimilation, of metamorphosis; that degradations have endured to the point of irrelevancy" (Derek Walcott, p. 6). To quote him finally, Walcott's generative language shows that mimicry has become in the Caribbean archipelago a way; it is aligned with the capacity to live:

> Mr. Naipaul's epitaph on all West Indian endeavour has not aborted the passion with which the West Indian culture continues to procreate mimicry, because life, if we can call it that in the archipelago, defiantly continues. (Derek Walcott, p. 6)

The political fraud and metropolitan mimicry in *Miguel Street* and *The Suffrage of Elvira* is a simpler theme, compared with the life and times of the master confidence trickster Ganesh Ram Sumair in *The Mystic Masseur.* Yet, Naipaul traces another facet of the destitution and derivativeness of Trinidad society to survive, for, Ganesh, the successful mystic turned politician is an illustration of the scandalous ways to ascend the ladder in the colonized outposts. Ganesh, a rank outsider to politics and an East-Indian post-indenture survivor, much like Biswas, symbolizes the Indians' art of aggrandizing the colonial powers, at whatever price. The result is unbelievable: from Ganesh Ram Sumair to G. Ramsay Muir; from Fuente Grove to London, the journey of mimicry is also a journey from the peasant anonymity to metropolitan 'recognition'. Ganesh is as much part of the unrelieved squalor of Trinidad's cultural attenuation as the figures in *Miguel Street*. But then, Ganesh is a fraud, a trickster by design and desire; he must escape and overcome the constrictions and the claustrophobia of the East-Indian agricultural fixity in the graph of Trinidad's racial plurality. Ganesh is hardly a match for the sophisticated, cultured and westernized Ralph Singh who can see through the delusion, the waste, the ennui that forecloses the life of the colonial politician. Ganesh, the confidence man, the imperial insider, is flaunted, as a fit material for being a 'hero', in effect a demonstration by Naipaul that 'you get the politicians you deserve' in axiomatic terms. From 'hero' to the anti-hero, this constitutes the mimic man's journey in Naipaulian sense from *The Mystic Masseur* to *The Mimic Men*.

A House for Mr Biswas presents an experience of colonization on a different plane in both tone and intention, theme and breath, compared with the early work of Naipaul. *A House for Mr Biswas* is the state of one's being colonized by system, society, institution, power, authority and economic forces. Secondly, the hero of this novel, Mr. Biswas, is not an accomplice or a passive participant in his own colonization. In contrast to Ganesh, Harbans and Ralph Singh, who accept or see through their entrapment and inscription of being colonized or mimic men, Mr. Biswas finds himself caught in the above-mentioned figures, Biswas's sensitivity to his existential and human desires, his longings to be a happy man, to own a small home, separate him from Ganesh or Ralph Singh who have entered into a pact with their marginalized state. Biswas may be colonized in the physical, economic, and 'political' sense but his emotional urge for freedom, his sensitivity to humiliation and slavery are signs of a temperament that bristles with rebellion and subversion. The discontentment and inner violence that characterize a 'little man's' disgruntled quest for order and independence is a far city from the parody and self-exhibitionism of Ralph Singh, or the cheap lumpen rhetoric of the comparatively uneducated Ganesh.

Naipaul's fiction after *The Mimic Men* in a way reflects his increasing preoccupation with the post-imperial Third World scene. Naipaul has disowned and moved away from strictly personal experience; his work beginning with *In a Free State* signals his rejection of any national or cultural location that is directly connected with his personal life or ancestry. His entry into other, troubled and new areas of cross-cultural and transnational entanglements illustrates his search for parallels to his own past. None of his works like *In a Free State, Guerrillas* and *A Bend in the River* configure a purely national, ethnic or intimately personal concern with human life. On the other hand, the impulse to isolate and deflate the experience of migration and expatriation gains prominence with each novel. Economic power, racial revenge and exploitations of all sorts mark the fate of the hopeless immigrant or expatriate exposed to dangers and humiliations at the hands of the new post-colonial powers which bulldoze aliens and outsiders, seeking revenge for their own past oppression and brutalization. Naipaul's expatriates, exiles, immigrants and aliens conform a menacing, racist and a counter, anti-colonial setting seething with violence. There is little respite in Naipaul's later work journeying assume more destructive overtones, as people with little vision or capacity for resistance find themselves caught in situations of unrest, anger and racial confrontation. The dubious result of the imperialist consolidation of mixture of cultures and identities on a global scale reflect a dissolved, amorphous life in unlikely landscapes and setting. Naipaul's 'lost centre' has extended its erasures further, and a search for a point or milestone of stable, unmoving centre is now impossible, as his writings bear testimony.

Indeed, if anything, after the award of Nobel Prize, Naipaul's achievement as a 'creator' in fiction of 'suppressed histories'—a postmodernist cliche by now—has acquired and angle the reader can view him from. Naipaul has earned the title of nourishing a 'bizarre imagination', a reputation of extremes for having picked up his subjects spawning those real 'areas' and societies through or in which he has grown and gained knowledge about the ways of the world. As if this were not enough, his receiving the Nobel is not without controversy either; the post-September 2001 situation following terrorist attacks on America that seem to have challenged notions such as 'End of History', and to have sparked off a new battle of civilizations and ways of life—Western and Islamic. However, it would be naïve for obvious reasons to say that the award of Nobel has come only for the controversy surrounding Naipaul's portrayal of the Islamic world in his works. Naipaul has been a spokesman, a caustic observer of the Third World scenario elsewhere—India, Argentina, Africa the West Indies, etc.—and his fictional and non-fictional agenda has paralleled the function Naipaul has made use of in case of Islamic world. At the same time, as critical commentaries have alternatively celebrated or castigated Naipaul's crucial positioning as a writer, his observations and inflections have made significant change in one's outlook, in reinforcing the idea how histories, societies, ideologies and experience should be looked at the end of the twentieth century. This is so in admitting that the news from the newly freed societies conveyed through his major works has been deeply and unremittingly grim, whether it is this or that side of corruption, brutality or hostility: "half-made societies that seemed doomed to remain half-made", a point that has been finally driven home in *Half a Life* (2001). It is interesting to note that Naipaul's 'complicit' stance favouring England, its tradition, and the West, and the Caribbean/African antipathy against Naipaul's defective imagination to overlook the Afro-Caribbean heritage, was perhaps one of the reasons that Naipaul was passed over in 1992 for the Nobel. The reason—reservations about Naipaul's 'suitability to represent' the Caribbean. It is strangely the same Naipaul with his distempered view of the Third World, his 'lack' of empathy, passion or compassion for human and societal limitations, who has bounced back, since there has been little or no change in him intellectually or temperamentally as a writer the world has known for his penchant for telling unsavoury truths, a novelist of disorder and breakdown. And what has hurt people, this or that side of the fence, apart from Third World's presumption and pathetic mimicry, is the burden of Naipaul's fiction that the world is basically unequal and right thinking cannot alter what are facts of life. Prejudices and inequalities, Naipaul believes, are an accretion of observation and cannot be destroyed by simple contradiction. Nearly the whole burden of Naipaul's writing after *In a Free State* demonstrates a reaching out to absorb the consequences of the changed shapes of societies, nations and communities and the altered visage of human personality disfigured by the effects of powerlessness and anonymity. If Mubutuism has been a curse for the Zairean man and his country, the reminders of the corrupting and dehumanizing forms of neo-colonialism have been no less destructive in a host of other places. And as though to add to the above travelling influences into contemporary life, Naipaul constantly strives to dramatize his own ancestry and background as an offshoot of similar manifestations.

Naipaul's return to the fictional form, with *Half a life,* despite his several comments and disapprovals about the adequacy of fictional form for literary expression, will perhaps continue to serve his creative *oeuvre* in the twenty-first century. Both *The Enigma of Arrival* and *A Way in the World,* despite being classified as 'novels' only partially reflect the concerns of fiction in the formalistic sense; the former being more or less the writer's literary-biographical odyssey in coming to terms with his cultural and intellectual deprivation in England, while the latter coalesces the historical strands of West Indian experience by putting together under a kind of sieve the collective meaning of older and modern encounters, respectively in pre- and post-colonial situations. None of these works, however, are attempts to rescue the reader's impression that the stories told therein are deliberately sought to put on a mask of fiction to serve a purpose. It did appear, almost finally a few years back that Naipaul was standing at the brink of the novel's funereal journey, a journey he had himself embarked on brilliantly with *A House for Mr Biswas,* carrying on the nineteenth-century tradition of the English Novel. However, what was being privileged over the 'dying' art form was perhaps more a result of Naipaul's own compulsions, twists and turns to see and know the world through observation and reportage, and less at the imminent 'death' of the fictional form. The narrator of unanchored destinies, historical traps and civilizational conceits was appearing to the world to have become larger than his fictional text, a disillusioned spectator and a chronicler of mutant beings trying to tell another story about stories told earlier by him. The 'enigma of arrival' marked a mysterious entry into another chiraco world, marked by uncertainties and accidents.

Half a Life marks another 'enigma' of return; this time, a desperate search for stability, a place in a post-colonial climate, stretching across India, England, Africa and Portugal. In short, a revisit to the familiar Naipaulian sites, amid landscapes of imagination together with his intellectual burden of rediscovering the meaning of one's location and its unalterable relation with past. The novel this time, as it unwinds itself becomes an accelerated instrument of departures and renewals, filial and affiliated memories and ties, unfolding, at times in cinematic terms flashes of past recollection of scenes, at time in cinematic terms flashes of past recollection of scenes, sites, words, acts that serve to further negotiate the hero's attempts to move away to uncharted locales. Surprisingly though, in a short novel like *Half a Life,* Naipaul has been able to pack and compress so much: the Indian setting of the Empire, the figure of Willie Chandran's enigmatic father who takes on several roles, the quick journey to England and Willie's experiences as a struggler of sorts, the attempts at literary vocation, the sexual adventure, the decisive shift to the Portuguese-African colony with Ana for eighteen long years, the turbulent period of revolution, disorder and unsettling, and finally, Willie's final departure from the estate for having Ana's life 'for too long', for an unknown destination. If this is the pattern of the unmarked route that Willie's life takes, it brings him headlong into confrontation with other lives, lives half-lived and half-wasted, a version of mixed, amorphous quality of cultural collisions that signal the uncertainties of post-war world of movement and drift. That reminds one of *A Bend in the River* where the world portrayed is as merciless as it is irrelevant with people like Salim having little chance to sustain or balance their tormented lives and a turbulent past.

Half a Life is a contemporary work among others which extends the fictional landscape to areas which never found a mention, hardly qualified for a definition of experience in world literature other than what was thought readable or significant. What is more, Willie Somerset Chandran is a hero quite on the lines of Biswas, Ralph Singh, Salim and others in that he resolves to turn away from the sordid, marginal, uneventful, philistine and claustrophobic life to initially attain a personal meaning of things; in this case migration, flight, escape are the very conditions to move over into zones of cross-cultural worlds, European and others.

What *Half a Life* sets out to project is what we have known the protagonist do directly or indirectly in Naipaul's fictional corpus; a known post-colonial's discovery of England and other locales when the Empire has ceased. Ralph Singh discovering the changing shades of English weather, Biswas imaginatively reliving a tradition through the English book, and above all, the narrator of *The Enigma of Arrival* setting out for his daily walks to rediscover a link with England's prehistory, an inversion in the colonial outsider's entry into a world that was ever a part of his psychic make-up. The other manifestation that informs the deliberate sequences of movements into succeeding stages of growth and mutation are the unfinished narratives, or textually speaking, the acts of 'translation'. The 'half' in the novel's title refers to, among other things, 'the half-and-half. People in the book—Willie himself, his father, his backward mother whom his father marries as an act of Gandhian sacrifice, Percy Cato, a Jamaican of mixed parentage, Marcus, Ana, and his sister Sarojini, who too like Willie escapes and meets him much later in Berlin. It is also a comment on the nature of quintessential incompleteness of everything, the hybridized quality of reality itself, around which Willie initiates himself into all that is incomplete in him—the art of seduction on which he repeatedly fails, his desperate attempts to attain manhood through prostitution sex in the sub-life of London, his creative urge to patch-up unrelated experiences in his 'stories', and finally, his learning the art of story-telling. It seems that Naipaul may have put part of his own struggles in the 1950s to be an aspiring writer into Willie's constrained attempts to attain a measure of balance by trying to overcome his hatred for all that was ancestral and nagging. Like the average Naipaul protagonist who lives with the idea of defeat and drift, Willie clings to this or that substitute for sustenance, that too, temporary, in material, human and sexual terms—Percy Cato, Roger, Ana, Graca and others. For that reason the narrative does not connect with what it seeks to, rather dis-connections move farther to take the centre stage, so that at the end all that the reader has in his mind is a web of inauthentic experience charted by those and witnessed by others like Willie who have nothing or little to do with those sites, histories and revolutions, like the one that brings disorder and chaos to the Portuguese-African colony. And Willie muses at this point, towards the end of the narrative:

> Of course, with my background, I had thought a lot about Africans in a political way.... I began to have an idea that there was something in the African heart that was shut away from the rest of us, and beyond politics. (V.S. Naipaul, p. 118)

Perhaps, the unifying vision of the novel is provided (though negatively) by the sexual choices Willie makes and most of them are driven by the urge to replace, shift or simply to move away from one passionate state to another, one body to the next—in short, his failed career as a student, writer and then a migrant makes a typical Naipaulian statement about every journey as one of the well-known Rushdie remark in *Imaginary Homelands* about scattered concepts of belonging and broken mirrors of identity:

> Having been borne across the world, we are translated men. It is normally supposed that something always gets lost in translation; I cling, obstinately to the notion that something can also be gained. (Salman Rushdie, p. 17)

In the case of Willie, as for Naipaul and his gallery of restless movers, there are 'translations' but there is perhaps little to be acquired in the collective burden and baggage of such an experience. Like Salim in *A Bend in the River* a shift, a move must signal another fretful departure, another town with its shimmering lights from the departing ship, every life must confront a life of denial and future mystery. So like Willie, already forty-one, is the spitting cobra in Graca's brother's verandah—African but the energy is stagnant. Naipaul's vision, as *Half a Life* exemplifies yet again, precludes a station, a halt, a milestone, essentially because the dubious credentials of Naipaul's protagonists are products of a past, ancestry, culture, history and religious cast that cannot be superannuated and transgressed because they carry those collective residues anywhere and everywhere. These things ultimately link *Half a Life* to Naipaul's world unmistakably: the figure of the father, the life of the writer, and finally, an enquiry into the origins of colonial landscape itself. And the metaphor of the 'half' but expanded and divided world that shapes the story emerges as a sign, as a marker of the convulsions of the post-colonial world with its loss, residues of oppression as discursive knowledges one gathers, by extension, through engagement with the act of literary reproduction.

Works Cited

Ahmed, Aijaz, *In Theory: Classes, Nations,* Literatures (Bombay: Oxford, 1993).

Naipaul, V.S., *Mimic Men* (London: Andre Dentsch, 1967).

———, *Half a Life* (London: Picador, 2001).

———, *In a Free State* (Harmondsworth: Penguin, 1973).

Naipaul interviewed by Ronald Bryden, *The Listener,* 22 March 1973.

Rushdie, Salman, *Imaginary Homelands: Essays and Criticism 1981-1991* (London: Granta, 1991).

Walcott, Derek, "The Caribbean: Culture or Mimicry?", *Journal of Inter American Studies and World Affairs,* 16 (1974).

Williams, Eric, *From Columbus to Castro: The History of the Caribbean 1492-1969* (New York: Harper and Row, 1970).

Selected Bibliography

A. Primary Sources

Naipaul, V.S. *The Mystic Masseur.* London: Andre Deutsch, 1957.

———. *The Suffrage of Elvira.* London: Andre Deutsch, 1958.

———. *Miguel Street.* London: Andre Deutsch, 1959.

———. *A House for Mr Biswas.* 1962; rpt. Harmondsworth: Penguin, 1969.

———. *The Middle Passage.* 1962; rpt. Harmondsworth: Penguin, 1969.

———. *Mr. Stone and the Knight's Companion,* 1963; Harmondsworth: Penguin, 1973.

———. *An Area of Darkness.* 1964; Harmondsworth: Penguin, 1970.

———. *The Mimic Men.* London: Andre Deutsch, 1967.

———. *A Flag on the Island.* 1967; Harmondsworth: Penguin, 1969.

———. *The Loss of El Dorado.* London: Andre Deutsch, 1969.

———. *In a Free State.* 1971; Harmondsworth: Penguin, 1973.

———. *The Overcrowded Barracoon.* 1972; Harmondsworth: Penguin, 1976.

———. *Guerrillas.* London: Andre Deutsch, 1975.

———. *India: A Wounded Civilization.* Bombay: Vikas Publishing House, 1977.

———. *A Bend in the River*. 1979, Delhi: Clarion Books, 1980.

———. *The Return of Eva Peron with the Killings in Trinidad*. 1980; Harmondsworth: Penguin, 1981.

———. *Among the Believers: An Islamic Journey*. London: Andre Deutsch, 1981.

———. *Finding the Centre*. 1984; Harmondsworth: Penguin, 1985.

———. *The Enigma of Arrival*. Harmondsworth: Penguin, 1987.

———. *A Turn in the South*. New York: Knopf, 1989.

———. *India: A Million Mutinies Now*. London: Minerva, Mandarin Paperbacks, 1990.

———. *A Way in the World*. London: Heinemann, 1994.

———. *Beyond Belief: Islamic Excursions Among the Converted Peoples*. New York: Random House, 1998.

———. *Letters Between a Father and Son*. London: Little Brown, 1999.

———. *Half a Life*. London: Picador, 2001.

B. Secondary Sources

Achebe, Chinua. *Morning Yet on Creation Day*. Gardencity, New York: Doubleday, 1975.

Ahmad, Aijaz. *In Theory: Classes, Nations, Literatures*. Bombay: Oxford, 1993.

———. *Lineages of the Present: Political Essays*. Delhi, 1996.

Albertazzi, Silvia. *Translating India: Travel and Cross-Cultrual Transference in Post-Colonial Fiction in English*. Bologna: Editrice Bologna, 1993.

Amrithānayagam, Guy. *Writers in East-West Encounters: New Cultural Bearings*. London: Macmillan, 1982.

Amur, G.S. and Desai, S.K. eds. *Colonial Consciousness in Commonwealth Literature*. Bombay: Somaya Publications, 1984.

Anderson, Benedict. *Imagined Communities: Reflections on the Origin and Spread of Nationalism*. London and New York: Verso, 1983.

Ashcroft, Bill, Griffiths, Gareth and Tiffin, Helen. eds. *The Empire Writes Back: Theory and Practice in Post-Colonial Literatures.* London and New York, 1989.

Ashcroft, Bill, Griffiths, Gareth and Tiffin, Helen. eds. *The Post-Colonial Studies Reader.* London and New York: Routledge, 1995.

Atwood, Margaret. *Survival: A Thematic Guide to Canadian Literature.* Toronto: Anansi, 1972.

Balibar, Etienne and Wallestein, Immanuel. *Race, Nation, Class: Ambiguous Identities.* London: Verso, 1991.

Bakhtin, M. *The Dialogic Imagination.* Austin: University of Texas Press, 1981.

Baugh, Edward. Ed. *Critics on Caribbean Literature.* London: George Allen and Unwin, 1978.

Bhabha, Homi K. ed. *Nation and Narration.* London: Routledge, 1990.

———. *The Location of Culture.* London and New York Routledge; 1994.

Boechmer, Elleke, *Colonial and Post Colonial Literature: Migrant Metaphors.* Oxford: Oxford University Press, 1995.

Boxhill, Anthony. *V.S. Naipaul's Fiction: In Quest of the Enemy,* Fredricton: New Brunswick: York Press, 1983.

Bratlinger, P. *The Rule of Darkness: British Literature and Imperialism 1830-1914.* Ithaca: Cornell University Press, 1988.

Brennan, Timothy. *Salman Rushdie and the Third World.* London: Macmillan, 1989.

Camus, Albert. *The Stranger.* New York: Knopf, 1946.

Cesaire, Aime *Discourse on Colonialism.* New York: Monthly Review Press, 1972.

Chaudhary, Nirad C. *Autobiography of an Unknown Indian.* 1951; Bombay: Jaico Books, 1971.

'Commonwealth': *Essays and Studies* (on V.S. Naipaul), Vol. 6, No. 1, Autumn 1983.

Cooke, M.G. ed. *Modern Black Novelists: Twentieth Century Views*. New Jersey: Prentice Hall, 1971.

Coulthard, G.R. *Race and Colour in Caribbean Literature*. London: Oxford University Press, 1962.

Cudjoe, Selwyn. *Resistance and Caribbean Literature*. Athens: Ohio University Press, 1980.

———. *V.S. Naipaul: A Materialist Reading*. Amherst: University of Massachusetts Press, 1988.

Dabydeen, David. *The Black Presence in English Literature*. Manchester: Manchester University Press, 1985.

Deleuze, Gilles and Guattari, Felix. *Anti-Oedipus: Capitalism and Schizopherenia*. New York: Viking, 1977.

Dhawan, R.K. ed. *Commonwealth Fiction*, 3 Vols. New Delhi: Classical Publishing Company, 1988.

Dhawan, R.K. et al. eds. *Recent Commonwealth Literature*, 2 Vols. New Delhi: Prestige Books, 1989.

Docherty, Thomas. *Postmodernism: A Reader*. Harvester: Hemel Hampstead, 1992.

Donald, James and Rattansi, Ali. eds. *Race, Cultures in English*. Paris: Longman France, 1993.

Eagleton, Terry. *Exiles and Emigres*. London: Chatto and Windus, 1970.

Eagleton, Terry, Jameson, Fredric and Said, Edward. *Nationalism, Colonialism and Literature*. Minneapolis: University of Minnesota Press, 1990.

Fanon, Frantz. *Black Skins, White Masks*. 1952; London: Pluto Press, 1980.

———. *Studies in a Dying Colonialism*. 1959; Harmondsworth: Penguin, 1970.

———. *The Wretched of the Earth*. 1961; Harmondsworth: Penguin, 1971.

Feder, Lillian. *Naipaul's Truth: The Making of a Writer*. New Delhi: Indialog Publications Pvt. Ltd., 2001.

Foucault, Michel. *Madness and Civilization.* trans. R. Howard. New York: Pantheon, 1965.

———. *The Order of Things.* Trans. A. Sheridan. New York: Random House, 1970.

———. *Discipline and Punish.* Trans. A. Sheridan. New York: Pantheon, 1977.

Fryer, Peter. *Black People in the British Empire.* London: Pluto Press, 1987.

Gates, Henry Louis Jr. Ed. *Black Jardan Roll: The World the Slave Made.* London and New York: Metheun, 1984.

Genovese, Eugene. *Roll Jardan Roll: The World the Slaves Made.* London and New York: Metheun, 1984.

Genovese, Eugne. *Roll Jardan Roll: The World the Slaves Made.* London: Andre Deutsch, 1975.

Gilkes, Micheal. *The West Indian Novel.* Boston: Twayne, 1981.

Goonatilake, Susantha. *Crippled Minds: An Exploration into Colonial Culture.* Bombay: Vikas, 1982.

Gordimer, Nadine. "Living in the Interregnum". *The Essential Gesture: Writing, Politics, and Places.* Ed. Stephen Clingman, 1988; rpt. New York: Penguin, 1989.

Gowda, H.H. *The Colonial and Neo-Colonial Encounters in Commonwealth Literature.* Mysore: Mysore University Press, 1973.

Griffiths, Gareth. *A Double Exile: African and West Indian Writing Between Two Cultures.* London: Marian Boyars, 1988.

Guha, Ranajit. Ed. *Subaltern Studies, 1 & II—Writings on South Asian History and Society.* Delhi: Oxford University Press, 1982 and 1983.

Gutting, Gary. *The Cambridge Companion to Foucault.* Cambridge: Cambridge University Press, 1994.

Haley, Alex. *Roots.* London: Picador, 1976.

Hammer, Robert D. *V.S. Naipaul.* New York: Twayne, 1973.

———. Ed. *Critical Perspectives on V.S. Naipaul.* Washington: Three Continents Press, 1977.

Harris, Wilson. *The Tradition, the Writer and Society.* Port of Spain: New Beacon, 1967.

———. *The Womb of Space: The Cross-Cultural Imagination.* Westport C.T.: Greenwood Press, 1983.

Hobsbawm, E.J. *The Age of Empire.* London: Weidenfield and Nicholson, 1987.

———. *Nations and Nationalisms since 1780: Programme, Myth, Reality.* Cambridge: Cambridge University Press, 1990.

Howe, Irving. *Politics and the Novel.* Paris: Menton, 1967.

Hughes, Peter. *V.S. Naipaul (Contemporary Writers).* London and New York, 1988.

Hulme, Peter. Ed. *Post-Colonial Theory and Colonial Discourse.* Manchester: Manchester University Press, 1993.

———. *Colonial Encounters: Europe and the Native Caribbean 1492-1797.* London: Metheun, 1986.

Huntington, Samuel. *The Clash of Civilization and the Remarking of World Order.* New York: Simon and Schuster, 1996.

Hutcheon, Linda. *A Poetics of Postmodernism: History, Theory, Fiction.* London and New York, 1988.

Jain, Jasbir. *Problems of Post-Colonial Literatures and Other Essays.* Jaipur: Printwell, 1991.

James, C.L.R. *Spheres of Existence.* London: Allison and Busby, 1980.

Jameson, Fredric. *The Political Unconscious: Narrative as a Socially Symbolic Act.* London: Metheun, 1981.

James, Louis. Ed. *The Islands in Between: Essays on West Indian Literature.* London: Oxford University Press, 1968.

Janmohammed, Abdul R. *Manichean Aesthetics: The Politics of Literature in Colonial Africa.* Amherst: University of Massachusetts Press, 1983.

Jelinek, Hena Maes, Peterson, Kirst Holst and Rutherford, Anna. Eds. *A Shaping of Connections: Commonwealth Literary Studies, Then and Now.* Dangaroo Press, 1989.

Joshi, Chandra B. *V.S. Naipaul: The Voice of Exile*. New Delhi: Sterling Publishers Pvt. Ltd., 1994.

Jussawala, Adil. Ed. *New Writing in India*. Harmondsworth: Penguin, 1974.

Kamra, Shashi. *The Novels of V.S. Naipaul*. New Delhi: Prestige Books Pvt. Ltd., 1990.

Khilnani, Sunil. *The Idea of India*. New York: Farrar, Strans, Giroux, 1998.

Kiernan, V.G. *Marxism and Imperialism*. New York: St. Martins Press, 1974.

King, Bruce. Ed. *Literatures of the World in English*. London: Routledge, 1974.

———. Ed. *West Indian Literature*. London: Macmillan, 1979.

———. *The New English Literatures: Cultural Nationalism in a Changing World*. New York: St. Martins Press, Ltd., 1980.

———. *V.S. Naipaul*. London: The Macmillan Press, Ltd., 1993.

———. Ed. *New National and Post-Colonial Literatures*. Oxford: The Clarendon Press, 1996.

Kirpal, Vinay. *The Third World Novel of Expatriation*. New Delhi: Sterling, 1989.

Kovel, Joel. *White Racism: A Psychohistory*. New York: Pantheon Books, 1970.

Kundera, Milan. *The Art of the Novel*. 1988; Delhi: Rupa, 1995.

Kureishi, Hanif. *My Beautiful Launderette and the Rainbow Sign*. London: Faber and Faber, 1986.

Lamming, George. *In the Castle of My Skin. 1953;* London: Longman Drumbeat, 1979.

———. *The Pleasures of Exile*. London: Michael Joseph, 1960.

———. *Natives of My Person*. 1972; London: Picador, 1974.

Levine, Laurence. *Black Culture and Black Consciousness*. New York: Oxford University Press, 1977.

Lichtheime, George. *Imperialism*. Harmondsworth: Penguin, 1974.

Loomba, Aniah. *Colonialism/Postcolonialism*. London and New York: Routledge, 1998.

Lyotard, Jean-Francois. *The Post-Modern Condition: A Report on Knowledge*. Manchester: University of Manchester Press, 1979.

Macherey, Pierre. *A Theory of Literary Production*. London: Routledge, 1978.

Mackenzie, John. *Propaganda and Empire*. Manchester: Manchester University Press, 1984.

Mackey, Sandra. *The Iranians: Persia, Islam, and the Soul of a Nation:* New York: Dutton, 1996.

Mahood, M.M. *The Colonial Encounter:* London: Rex Collings, 1977.

Malik, Michael Abdul. *From Michael de Freitas to Michael X*. London: Andre Deutsch, 1968.

Mannoni, O. *Prospero and Caliban: The Psychology of Colonization*. New York: Praeger, 1964.

Mason, Nondita. *The Fiction of V.S. Naipaul*. Calcutta: The World Press Pvt., 1986.

Massa, Daniel. *Individual and Community in Commonwealth Literature*. MSIDA: University of Malta Press, 1979.

Mc Leod, A.L. ed. *Subjects Worthy Fame: Essays on Commonwealth Literature*. New Delhi: Sterling, 1989.

Mc Leod, John. *Beginning Postcolonialism*. Manchester and New York: University of Manchester Press, 2000.

Mc Sweeny, Kerry. *Four Contemporary Novelists: Angus Wilson, Brian Moore, John Fowles, V.S. Naipaul. Montreal,* Quebec: McGill University Press, 1983.

Memmi, Albert. *The Colonizer and the Colonized*. New York: Orion Press, 1965.

Meyers, Jeffrey. *Fiction and the Colonial Experience*. IPSWICH: The Boydell Press, 1973.

Mills, Sara. *Discourses of Difference*. London: Routledge, 1991.

Modern Fiction Studies, Vol. 30, No. 3, Autumn 1984. (V.S. Naipaul Special Number).

Moi, Toril. *Sexual/Textual Politics: Feminist Literary Theory.* London: Metheun, 1987.

Morris, Robert K. *Paradoxes of Order: Some Perspectives on the Fiction of V.S. Naipaul.* Columbia: University of Missouri Press, 1975.

Mustafa, Fawzia. *V.S. Naipaul.* New York: Cambridge University Press, 1995.

Naipaul, Seepersad. *The Adventures of Gurudeva and Other Stories.* London: Andre Deutsch, 1976.

Nanda Kumar, Prema. *V.S. Naipaul: The Glory and the Good.* New Delhi: Asia Publishing House, 1965.

Nandy, Ashis. *The Intimate Enemy: Loss and Recovery of Self under Colonialism.* Oxford University Press, 1983.

Narasimhaiah, C.D. Ed. *Commonwealth Literature: A Handbook of Select Reading Lists.* Delhi: Oxford University Press, 1976.

———. Ed. *Awakened Conscience: Studies in Commonwealth Literature.* New Delhi: Sterling, 1978.

———. Ed. *Commonwealth Literature: Problems of Response.* Madras: Macmillan, 1981.

Narayan, R.K. *Gods, Demons, and Others.* 1964; reprint. New York: Bantam, 1986.

Newman, Judie. *The Ballistic Bard: Post-Colonial Fiction.* London: Arnold, 1995.

New, W.H. *Among Worlds.* Erin, Ontario: Press Porcepir, 1975.

Ngugi Wa Thiong'O. *Homecoming: Essays on African and Caribbean Literature, Culture and Politics.* London: Heinemann, 1972.

———. *Writers in Politics.* London: Heinemann, 1981.

———. *Decolonizing the Mind: The Politics of Language in African Literature.* London: James Curry, 1986.

Nightingale, Peggy. *Journey Through Darkness: The Writing of V.S. Naipaul.* St. Lucia: University of Queensland Press, 1987.

Nixon, Rob. *London Calling: V.S. Naipaul, Postcolonial Mandarin*. New York: Oxford University Press, 1992.

Pratt, Mary Louis. *Imperial Eyes: Travel Writing and Transculturation*. London: Routledge, 1992.

Press, John. Ed. *Commonwealth Literature*. London: Heinemann, 1965.

Rai, Sudha. *V.S. Naipaul: A Study in Expatriate Sensibility*. New Delhi: Arnold Heinemann, 1982.

———. *Homeless by Choice: Naipaul Rushdie, Jhabwala*. Jaipur: Printwell, 1992.

Rajan, P.K. et al. Eds. *Commonwealth Literature: Themes and Techniques*. Delhi: Ajanta Books International, 1993.

Ramchand, Kenneth. *The West Indian Novel and its Background*. London: Faber and Faber, 1970.

———. *An Introduction to the Study of West Indian Literature*. London: Faber and Faber, 1976.

Rattansi, Ali and Westwood, Sallie. eds. *Racism, Modernity and Identity on the Western Front*. Cambridge: Polity Press, 1994.

Reid, V.S. *New Day*. London: Heinemann, 1949.

Rich, Paul B. *Race and Empire in British Politics*. Cambridge: Cambridge University Press, 1986.

Ross, Robert. *Racism and Colonialism*. The Hague: Martinus Nighoff for Leiden University Press, 1982.

Roth, Philip. *The Facts: A Novelist's Autobiography*. 1988; rpt. New York: Penguin, 1989.

Rushdie, Salman. *Imaginary Homelands: Essays and Criticism 1981-1991*. London: Granta, 1991.

Said, Edward. *Orientalism*. 1978; Harmondsworth: Penguin, 1995.

———. *The World, the Text and the Critic*. London: Faber and Faber, 1984.

———. *Culture and Imperialism*. 1993; London: Faber and Faber, 1994.

Sakaana, Amon Saba. *The Colonial Legacy in Caribbean Literature*. London: Karnak House, 1987.

Schrire, Carmel. *Digging Through Darkness: Chronicles of an Archaeologist*. Charlottesville & London: University of Virginia Press, 1995.

Sharma, Govind Narain. Ed. *Literature and Commitment: A Commonwealth Perspective*. Toronto: Canadian Association of Commonwealth Literature and Language Studies, 1988.

Sherry, Norman. *Conrad's Eastern World*. Cambridge: Cambridge University Press, 1971.

———. *Joseph Conrad: A Commemoration*. London: Macmillan, 1976.

Singh, Manjit Inder. *V.S. Naipaul*. New Delhi: Rawat Publications, 1998.

———. *The Poetics of Alienation and Identity: V.S. Naipaul and George Lamming*. Delhi: Ajanta Books International, 1998.

———. *The Cratical Space: Studies in Literature, Theory, Nationalism and Diaspora*. Jaspar; National Publishing House, 2004.

Soyinka, Wole: *Myth, Literature and the African World*. Cambridge: Cambridge University Press, 1976.

———. *The Open Sore of a Continent: A Personal Narrative of the Nigerian Crisis*. New York: Oxford University Press, 1996.

Spenglar, Oswald. *The Decline of the West*. New York: Random House, 1962.

Spivak, Gayatri. *In Other Words: Essays in Cultural Politics*. London Metheun, 1987.

———. *The Post-Colonial Critic: Interviews, Strategies, Dialogues*. London and New York: Routledge, 1990.

Srivastava, Avdhesh K. Ed. *Alien Voice: Perspectives on Commonwealth Literature*. Lucknow: Print House, 1981.

Steiner, George, *Extraterritorial*. Harmondsworth: Penguin, 1971.

Suleri, Sara. *The Rhetoric of English India.* Chicago : University of Chicago Press, 1992.

Swinden, Patrick. *Unofficial Selves: Character in the Novel from Dickens to the Present Day.* New York: Barnes and Noble, 1973.

Theroux, Paul. *V.S. Naipaul: An Introduction to His Work.* New York: Africana Publishing Co., 1972.

———. *Sir Vidia's Shadow.* Harmondsworth: Penguins, 1998.

Thieme, John. *The Web of Tradition: Uses of Allusion in V.S. Naipaul's Fiction.* Hansib Dangaroo Press, 1987.

Thornton, A.P. *The Imperial Idea and its Enemies: A Study of British Power.* Basingstoke: Macmillan, 1985.

Thorpe, Michael. *V.S. Naipaul.* London: British Council Longman, 1976.

Tiffin, Chris and Lawson Allan. Eds. *De-Scribing Empire: Post-Colonialism in Textuality.* London: Routledge, 1994.

Tinker, Hugh. *A New System of Slavery.* London: Oxford University Press, 1974.

Tomllinson, John. *Cultural Imperialism.* London: Pinter, 1991.

Trollope, Anthony. *The West Indies and the Spanish Main.* London: Chapman and Hall, 1959.

Viswanathan, Gauri. *Masks of Conquest: Literary Study and British Rule in India.* London: Faber & Faber, 1990.

Walvin, James. *Black Ivory: A History of British Slavery.* London: Harper Collins, 1992.

Walsh, William. *V.S. Naipaul.* London: Oliver and Boyd, 1973.

———. Ed. *A Manifold Voice: Studies in Commonwealth Literature.* London: Chatto and Windus, 1970.

———. Ed. *Readings in Commonwealth Literature.* Oxford: The Clarendon Press, 1973.

Ward, J.R. *British West Indian Slavery, 1750-1834: The Process of Amelioration.* Oxford: The Clarendon Press, 1988.

Williams, Eric. *Capitalism and Slavery.* London: Andre Deutsch, 1964.

———. *From Columbus to Castro: The History of the Caribbean, 1492-1967*. New York: Harper and Row, 1970.

White, Landeg. *V.S. Naipaul: A Critical Introduction*. London: Macmillan, 1975.

Williams, Patrick and Chrisman, Laura. eds. *Colonial Discourse and Post-Colonial Theory: A Reader.* Hertfordshire: Harvester Wheatsheaf, 1994.

Williams, Raymond. *Culture and Society. 1780-1950*. London: Chatto and Windus, 1958.

Wurgaft, Lewis. *The Imperial Imagination*. Middletown: Wesleyan University Press, 1983.

Young, J.C. *Colonial Desire: Hybridity in Theory, Culture and Race*. London: Routledge, 1995.

C. Articles and Reviews

Ahmad, Aijaz. "Post-Colonial Theory and the 'Post-Condition'". Talk delivered at the Punjabi University, Patiala in May 1997, pp. 1-40.

Anjrosino, M.B. "V.S. Naipaul and the Colonial Image". *Caribbean Quarterly*, 21, III (1975), pp. 1-11.

Ashcroft, W.D. "Intersecting Marginalities: Post-Colonialism and Feminism". *Kunapipi,* Vol. XI, No. 2, 1989, pp. 23-35.

Boxhill, Anthony. "The Physical and Historical Environment in V.S. Naipaul's. *The Mystic Masseur* and *The Suffrage of Elvira*". *Journal of Canadian Fiction,* 3 (IV) (1975), pp. 52-55.

Brydon, Diana. "Commonwealth or Common Poverty? The New Literature in English and the New Discourses of Marginality." *Kunapipi,* XII, 1989, pp. 1-16.

Campbell, Elaine. "A Refinement of Rage: V.S. Naipaul's *A Bend in the River*". *World Literature Written in English,* 18 (1979), pp. 394-406.

Chrisman, Laura. "The Imperial Unconscious?: Representations of Imperial Discourse." *Critical Quarterly,* Vol. 32, No. 3, Autumn 1990, pp. 38-58.

Cooke, John. "A Vision of the Land: V.S. Naipaul's later Novels." *Caribbean Quarterly,* 25 iv (1979), pp. 31-47.

Cotter, Michael. "Identity and Compulsion: George Lamming's *Natives of My Person*". *New Literature Review,* No. 1, 1977, pp. 29-35.

Dash, Michael. "In Search of the Lost Body: Redefining the Subject in Caribbean Literature". *Kunapipi,* XI, 1, 1989, pp. 17-26.

Derrick, A.C. "Naipaul's Technique as a Novelist." *Journal of Commonwealth Literature.* 7 July 1969, pp. 32-39.

Gilroy, Paul. "It aint where you're from, its where you're at: The Dialectics of Diasporic Identification." *Third Text,* 13 Winter 1990, pp. 3-16.

Glynn, Patrick. "The Swelling Democratic Tide." *Times Literary Supplement,* April 11, 1997, pp. 10-11.

Goodheart, Eugene. "Naipaul and the Voices of Negation." *Salmagundi,* 54 (1981), pp. 44-58.

Gugelberger, George M. "Decolonizing the Canon: Considerations of Third World Literature." *New Literary History,* 22, 1991, pp. 505-24.

Gussow, Mel. "The Enigma of V.S. Naipaul's Search for Himself in Writing." *New York Times,* April 25, 1987, p. 16.

Healy, J.J. "Friction, Voice and the Rough Ground of Feeling: Naipaul after Twenty-five Years." *University of Toronto Quarterly.* Fall 1985, pp. 45-63.

Hemenway, Robert. "Sex and Politics in V.S. Naipaul." *Studies in the Novel,* 14(ii) (1982), pp. 189-202.

Hussein, Aamer, "Delivering the Truth, An Interview with V.S. Naipaul." *Times Literary Supplement,* September 2, 1994, p. 3.

Hutcheon, Linda. "Circling the Downspout of Empire: Post-colonialism and Postmodernism." *Ariel,* 20 (4), pp. 149-75.

Jain, Jasbir. "The Motif of Homecoming in Naipaul's Journeys." *Jodhpur Studies in English,* Vol. 6, 1995, pp. 24-35.

James, Louis. "The Trickster God: Imagination and Reality in African and Caribbean Literatures". *IACLALS Bulletin,* 4th Series, No. 2, 1975, pp. 1-8.

Maes Jelinek, Hena. "The Myth of E1 Dorado in the Caribbean Novel." *Journal of Commonwealth Literature*, 6, No. 1, June 1971, pp. 113-28.

Mathews, John P. "Lifeboats for the Titanic: Patterns of Identity in Commonwealth Literature". *ACLALS Bulletin,* 5th Series, 2, 1979.

Michener, Charles. "The Dark Visions of V.S. Naipaul." *Newsweek*. November 16, 1981, p. 109.

Mishra, Pankaj. "A New, Nuclear, India?" *The New York Review of Books,* June 25, 1998, pp. 63-64.

Mishra, Vijay. "Mythic Fabulation: Naipaul's India." *New Literature Review,* 4 (1978), pp. 59-65.

Mitchell, W.J.T. "Postcolonial Culture, Postimperial Criticism." *Transition,* 55, 1992.

Mukherjee, Meenakshi. "Inside the Outsider". In *Awakened Conscience: Studies in Commonwealth Literature*. Ed. C.D. Narasimhaiah. New Delhi: Sterling, 1978.

Nachman, Larry David. "The Worlds of V.S. Naipaul". *Salmagundi,* 54 (1981), pp. 59-76.

Naipaul, V.S. "On Being a Writer." *The New York Review of Books*. April 23, 1987, p. 7.

———. "Our Universal Civilization". *The New York Review of Books*. January 31, 1991, pp. 22-25.

Nazreth, Peter, "Out of Darkness: Conrad and Other Third World Writers." *Conradiana*. 14(iii) (1982), pp. 173-87.

Neill, Michael, "Guerrillas and Gangs: Frantz Fanon and V.S. Naipaul." *Ariel,* 13(iv) (1982), pp. 21-62.

Nunez-Harrell, Elizabeth. "Lamming and Naipaul: Some Criteria for Evaluating the Third World Novel." *Contemporary Literature,* 19(i) (1978), pp. 26-47.

Ormerod, David. "In a Derelict Land: The Novels of V.S. Naipaul." *Wisconsin Studies in Contemporary Literature,* 9, No. 1 (Winter 1968), pp. 74-90.

Parrinder, Patrick. "V.S. Naipaul and the Uses of Literacy." *Critical Quarterly,* 21(ii) (1979), pp. 5-13.

Phillips, Cary. "Living and Writing in the Caribbean: An Experiment." *Kunapipi,* Vol. XI, No. 2, 1989, pp. 23-35.

———. "The Enigma of Denial: V.S. Naipaul's Negotiation of his Homeland". *Biblio.* Vol. VI. Nos. 1 and 2. January-February 2001, pp. 6-10.

Rohlehr, Gordon. "The Ironic Approach to the Novels of V.S. Naipaul". *The Islands in Between: Essays in West Indian Literature.* Ed. Louis, James. New York: Oxford University Press, 1968.

Salgado, Gamini. "V.S. Naipaul and the Politics of Fiction" in Boris Ford. Ed. *New Pelican Guide to English Literature,* Vol. 8, Harmondsworth: Penguin, 1983, pp. 314-27.

Schiff, Stephen. "The Ultimate Exile." *The New Yorker,* May 23, 1994, p. 70.

Shankar, Israel. "V.S. Naipaul: Man Without a Society". *New York Times Book Review.* 17 October 1971, p. 22-24.

Singh, Manjit Inder. "V.S. Naipaul and George Lamming: Two Approaches to the Problem of Caribbean Identity." *Rajasthan University Studies in English,* Vol. XII, 1979, pp. 49-60.

———. "Beyond E1 Dorado: Caribbean Aesthetics, Literary Theory and Commonwealth Literature." *Punjab Journal of English Studies,* Guru Nanak Dev University, Amritsar, Vol. VI, 1991, pp. 59-70.

Slemon, Stephen. "Monuments of Empire: Allegory/Counter Discourse/Post-colonial Writing". *Kunapipi,* 9, 3, 1987, pp. 1-16.

Spivak, Gayatri. "Can the Subaltern Speak?" in Nelson, C. and Grossberg, L. eds. *Marxism and the Interpretation of Culture.* Basingstoke: Macmillan Educational, 1988, pp. 271-313.

Staples, Brent. "Con Men and Conquerors". *Review of A Way in the World. New York Times Book Review.* May 22, 1994, p. 1.

Tiffin, Helen. "Post-Colonialism, Post-modernism and the Rehabilitation of Post-colonial History". *Journal of Commonwealth Literature,* 23, I, 1988, pp. 169-81.

Trotter, David. "Colonial Subjects." *Critical Quarterly,* Vol. 32, No. 3, Autumn, 1990, pp. 3-20.

West, Cornel. "The Dilemma of the Black Intellectual." *Critical Quarterly,* Vol. 29, No. 4, Winter 1987, pp. 40-52.

Walcott, Derek. "The Garden Path: *The Enigma of Arrival by* V.S. Naipaul." *The New Republic.* April 13, 1987, p. 27.

Woodcock, George. "V.S. Naipaul and the Politics of Fiction". *Queen's Quarterly.* 87 (1980), pp. 679-92.